The
Merseyside & Cheshire
Bus Handbook

Body codes used in the Bus Handbook series:

Type:
A	Articulated vehicle
B	Bus, either single-deck or double-deck
BC	Suburban - high-back seated bus
C	Coach
M	Minibus with design capacity of 16 seats or less
N	Low-floor bus (*Niederflur*), either single-deck or double-deck
O	Open-top bus (CO = convertible - PO = partial open-top)

Seating capacity is then shown. For double-decks the upper deck quantity is followed by the lower deck.

Door position:-
C	Centre entrance/exit
D	Dual doorway.
F	Front entrance/exit
R	Rear entrance/exit (no distinction between doored and open)
T	Three or more access points

Equipment:-
L	Lift for wheelchair	TV	Training vehicle.
M	Mail compartment	RV	Used as tow bus or engineers vehicle.
T	Toilet	w	Vehicle is withdrawn from service.

e.g. - B32/28F is a double-deck bus with thirty-two seats upstairs, twenty-eight down and a front entrance/exit.
N43D is a low-floor bus with two doorways.

Re-registrations:-
Where a vehicle has gained new index marks the details are listed at the end of each fleet showing the current mark, followed in sequence by those previously carried starting with the original mark.

Regional books in the series:
The Scottish Bus Handbook
The Ireland & Islands Bus Handbook
The North East Bus Handbook
The Yorkshire Bus Handbook
The Lancashire, Cumbria and Manchester Bus Handbook
The Merseyside and Cheshire Bus Handbook
The East Midlands Bus Handbook
The West Midlands Bus Handbook
The Welsh Bus Handbook
The Chilterns and West Anglia Bus Handbook
The East Anglia Bus Handbook
The South East Bus Handbook
The South West Bus Handbook
The South Central Bus Handbook

Annual books are produced for the major groups:
The Stagecoach Bus Handbook
The FirstBus Bus Handbook
The Arriva Bus Handbook
The National Express Handbook
Editions for earlier years are available. Please contact the publisher.

Associated series:
The Hong Kong Bus Handbook
The Leyland Lynx Handbook
The Model Bus Handbook
The Postbus Handbook
The Overall Advertisment Bus Handbook - Volume 1
The Toy & Model Bus Handbook - Volume 1 - Early Diecasts
The Fire Brigade Handbook (fleet list of each local authority fire brigade)
The Fire Brigade Handbook - Special Appliances Volume 1
The Fire Brigade Handbook - Special Appliances Volume 2
The Police Range Rover Handbook

Contents

The Cheshire & Merseyside Bus Handbook

This second edition of the Bus Handbook covering Merseyside, Cheshire and north Staffordshire is part of a series that details the fleets of bus and express coach operators from across Britain. A list of current editions is shown on page 2. The operators included in this edition cover those who provide tendered and commercial services in the former counties and the unitary boroughs. Also included are a number of those operators who provide significant coaching activities.

Quality photographs for inclusion in the series are welcome, for which a fee is payable. The publishers unfortunately cannot accept responsibility for any loss and request you show your name on each picture or slide.

To keep the fleet information up to date we recommend the Ian Allan publication, Buses, published monthly, or for more detailed information, the PSV Circle monthly news sheets.

The writer and publisher would be glad to hear from readers should any information be available which corrects or enhances that given in this publication.

Series Editor: Bill Potter
Principal Editors for *The West Midlands Bus Handbook:* **Bill Potter and David Donati**

Acknowledgments:
We are grateful to Cliff Beeton, Mark Jameson, the PSV Circle and the operating companies for their assistance in the compilation of this book.

The cover photograph is by Tony Wilson while the rear cover pictures are by Paul Wigan and Cliff Beeton. The fronticepiece is by Cliff Beeton.

Earlier editions of the area covered by the Merseyside & Cheshire Bus Handbook:
1st Edition - 1996 1-897990-14-6 (Merseyside & Cheshire Bus Handbook)

ISBN 1 897990 46 4 (2nd Edition)
Published by *British Bus Publishing Ltd*
The Vyne, 16 St Margaret's Drive, Wellington, Telford, TF1 3PH

Telephone: 01952 255669 - Facsimile 01952 222397 - www.britishbuspublishing.co.uk
© British Bus Publishing Ltd, November 2000

A1A TRAVEL

A1A Ltd, 363 Cleveland Street, Birkenhead, Wirral, CH41 4JW

1	T111JBA	Mercedes-Benz Vario O814	Plaxton Beaver 2	B32F	1999	
2	AIA9000	Volvo B10M-61	Plaxton Paramount 3500 III	C51FT	1988	P&O Lloyd, Bagillt, 2000
3	M13BUS	Mercedes-Benz 609D	Buscraft	B17F	1995	
8	B128VJX	Mercedes-Benz 307D	Reeve Burgess	M12	1984	Rees, Brynford, 1999
9	D892NDS	Mercedes-Benz L608D	PMT Hanbridge	BC21F	1986	Dicksons of Erskine, 1998
12	H62WNN	Mercedes-Benz 709D	Scott	BC29F	1990	Skills, Nottingham, 1996
13	E134VOK	Freight Rover Sherpa	Carlyle Citybus 2	B20F	1988	Merry Hill Minibus, 1996
22	F212AKG	Freight Rover Sherpa	Carlyle Citybus 2	B20F	1988	Shamrock, Pontypridd, 1993
41	S41FWY	Optare Solo M850	Optare	N29F	1999	
42	S42FWY	Optare Solo M850	Optare	N29F	1999	
45	R845FWW	Optare Excel L960	Optare	N28F	1998	
46	R846FWW	Optare Excel L960	Optare	N28F	1998	
50	P450SWX	Optare MetroRider MR15	Optare	B29F	1997	
51	P451SWX	Optare MetroRider MR15	Optare	B29F	1997	
53	R970MGB	Dennis Dart SLF	Plaxton Pointer 2	N39F	1998	
54	R954JYS	Dennis Dart SLF	Plaxton Pointer 2	N39F	1998	
95	WDZ6951	Mercedes-Benz L608D	Alexander AM	B20F	1986	Stagecoach Western, 1999
96	WDZ6962	Mercedes-Benz L608D	Alexander AM	B20F	1986	Stagecoach Western, 1999

Previous Registrations:

		H62WNN	H62WNN, AIA9000
AIA5505	-	WDZ6951	D136NUS
AIA9000	E241BMA, A4BOB, E358ERR, 5375PO, E135BCC	WDZ6962	D130NUS

Livery: White, pale blue and red

Pictured while heading for Penny Lane is 46, R846FWW in the A1A fleet. It is one of a pair of Optare Excel buses which introduced low floor buses into this Birkenhead-based fleet. *Phillip Stephenson*

A2B TRAVEL

W G Evans, 5 Prenton Way, North Cheshire Ind Est, Prenton, Wirral, CH43 3DU

SND437X	Leyland Atlantean AN68A/1R	Northern Counties	B43/32F	1981	GMS Buses, Stockport, 1996
SND440X	Leyland Atlantean AN68A/1R	Northern Counties	B43/32F	1981	GMS Buses, Stockport, 1996
A2BDO	ACE Puma	Van Hool Alizée H	C33F	1985	Bennetts, Warrington, 1998
B179WYV	Leyland Cub CU435	Wadham Stringer Vanguard	B32F	1984	LB Hackney, 1995
B154XUU	Leyland Cub CU435	Wadham Stringer Vanguard	B32F	1985	LB Southwark, 1995
E56MMT	Mercedes-Benz L307D	Reeve Burgess	M12	1987	Time Transport, Thornton Heath, 1992
E835EUT	Mercedes-Benz L307D	Yeates	M12	1987	Angel, Tottenham, 1994
F477PAE	Mercedes-Benz 407D	Made-to-Measure	M16	1988	John Hunter, Woodchurch, 1999
A2BTO	Mercedes-Benz 609D	North West Coach Sales	BC26F	1989	private owner, 1996
H794HEM	Mercedes-Benz 408D	Made-to-Measure	M15	1991	
A2GFF	Mercedes-Benz 811D	PMT Ami	C33F	1991	Amport & District, 1996
J121LKO	Iveco Daily 49.10	Dormobile Routemaker	B23F	1991	Stagecoach South, 1997
L35AKP	Iveco TurboDaily 59.12	Dormobile Routemaker	B27F	1993	
A2BEO	Mercedes-Benz 814D	Autobus Classique	C33F	1993	
L31ORC	Dennis Javelin GX 12SDA2125	Plaxton Premiere 350	C51F	1994	Skills, Nottingham, 2000
X924AEN	LDV Convoy	Concept Coachcraft	M16	2000	
X926AEN	LDV Convoy	Concept Coachcraft	M16	2000	
X927AEN	LDV Convoy	Concept Coachcraft	M16	2000	
X928AEN	LDV Convoy	Concept Coachcraft	M16	2000	
X929AEN	LDV Convoy	Concept Coachcraft	M16	2000	
X945AEN	LDV Convoy	Concept Coachcraft	M16	2000	
X946AEN	LDV Convoy	Concept Coachcraft	M16	2000	
X947AEN	LDV Convoy	Concept Coachcraft	M16	2000	

Previous Registrations:

A2BDO	B31XSN, C633RSG, 85D191, C633RSG	A2BTO	G840CLV
A2BEO	L177PDO	A2GFF	J387RVT

Livery: Duo-green and black or cream and black

Four buses from the A2B Travel fleet are shown in this line-up taken at its base in Prenton. On the left are the two Wadham Stringer-bodied Leyland Cub buses while on the right are the two Leyland Atlanteans, the only double-deck members of the fleet. *Richard Godfrey*

AINTREE COACHLINE

Aintree Coachline - ABC Coaches

J Cherry, 11 Clare Road, Bootle, L20 9LY

Reg	Make/Model	Body	Seating	Year	Previous Owner
OHF858S	Leyland National 11351A/1R		BC45F	1978	Merseybus, 1995
ANE2T	Leyland Titan TNLXB/1RF	Park Royal	B47/26F	1979	The Wright Company, Wrexham, 1991
YTE587V	Leyland Fleetline FE30AGR	Northern Counties	B43/32F	1979	Merseyline Travel, Garston, 2000
HKF151	Leyland Titan TNLXB/2RRSp	Leyland	BC44/26F	1981	South London, 1995
B43UCK	Leyland Tiger TRBTL11/2RH	Duple Dominant	BC47F	1984	Blue Bus, Horwich, 2000
B84SWX	Leyland Tiger TRCTL11/3RH	Plaxton Paramount 3200	C57F	1985	Arriva The Shires, 2000
B557ATX	Leyland Olympian ONLXB/1R	East Lancashire	B43/31F	1985	Cardiff Bus, 1999
B558ATX	Leyland Olympian ONLXB/1R	East Lancashire	B43/31F	1985	Cardiff Bus, 1999
C95CHM	Leyland Olympian ONLXB/1RH	Eastern Coach Works	B42/26D	1986	Go-Ahead London, 1998
D81UTF	Leyland Olympian ONLXCT/1RH	Eastern Coach Works	BC39/27F	1986	Arriva Fox County, 1998
M129UWY	Volvo B10M-62	Plaxton Premiere 350	C53F	1995	Wallace Arnold, 1997
P5ACL	Dennis Lance	Northern Counties	B49/35F	1996	
P331VWR	Volvo B10M-62	Plaxton Premiere 350	C53F	1997	Wallace Arnold, 1999
R55ACL	Dennis Arrow	East Lancashire	B49/35F	1998	
W5ACL	Dennis Trident	East Lancashire Lolyne	N51/36F	2000	
X5ACL	Iveco EuroRider 391.12.35	Beulas Stergo E	C49FT	2000	

Previous Registrations:

HKF151   KYV322X, 124CLT, NHM466X

Livery: Red & cream
Depot: Sefton Lane Industrial Estate, Maghull

Dennis Lance double-deck buses are quite rare. Pictured at Hartshead Moor is P5ACL operated by Aintree Coachlines. This vehicle carries a Northern Counties Palatine II body, the final design from the Wigan-based builder before it became part of the Henly Group, which builds buses in the UK under the Plaxton name.
Paul Wigan

ANTHONY'S TRAVEL

A A & RA Bamber, 8 Cormorant Drive, Runcorn, Cheshire, WA7 4UD

ANT856T	Neoplan N116/2	Neoplan Cityliner	C35DT	1981	Goodwin, Eccles, 1995	
TSU604	Setra S215HD	Setra	C49FT	1988	Roberts, Runcorn, 1998	
F999JGE	Mercedes-Benz 609D	Scott	BC24F	1989	Roberts, Runcorn, 1996	
A288ANT	Setra S215HD	Setra	C35FT	1990	Coliseum, Southampton, 1999	
G20ANT	Neoplan N116/3	Neoplan Cityliner	C48FT	1992	Travelrich, Clacton, 2000	
K555ANT	Leyland-DAF 400	Concept Coachcraft	M16	1993		
K22ANT	Iveco Daily 45.10	Heggie	C18F	1993	Smith, Coupar Angus, 1995	
K444ANT	Iveco Daily 49.10	Marshall C29	B23F	1993	Green Triangle, Lostock, 1999	
L111ANT	Leyland-DAF 400	Concept Coachcraft	M16	1993		
M333ANT	Mercedes-Benz 711D	Marshall C19	B27F	1994	JP Travel, Middleton, 1999	
P30ANT	LDV Convoy	Concept Coachcraft	M16	1997		
R40ANT	LDV Convoy	Concept Coachcraft	M16	1997		
S70ANT	LDV Convoy	Jaycas	M16	1998		
S80ANT	LDV Convoy	Jaycas	M16	1998		
W10ANT	LDV Convoy	Jaycas	M16	2000		

Previous Registrations:

A288ANT	G439ATR, 4358FC	K444ANT	K424GAV
ANT856T	WGT875W, PIB5898	M333ANT	M636FJF, M1JPT
G20ANT	J21XHE, 5765OZ	TSU604	E28SBO
K22ANT	K12OSB	TIB2387	E800UNB

Livery: Beige, brown, orange and cream (coaches), white and orange (minibuses)

In addition to the coaching activities, Anthony's Travel operate minibus services using a fleet of LDV Convoy minibuses. Seen in Widnes is Setra S215HD A288ANT, one of a pair and one fitted with just thirty-five seats along with refinements such as tables and servery. *British Bus Publishing*

ARRIVA NORTH WEST

ARRIVA serving Merseyside
Arriva serving the North West - Arriva serving Manchester

Arriva Liverpool Ltd, Arriva North West Ltd, Arriva Manchester Ltd,
73 Ormskirk Road, Aintree, Liverpool, L9 5AE

52	J735MFY	Mercedes-Benz 709D		Wright NimBus		B29F	1992	Amberline, 1993	
59-65		Mercedes-Benz 709D		Alexander Sprint		B25F	1994		
59	M59WKA	60	M160WTJ	61	M61WKA	64	M64WKA	65	M65WKA
70-89		Mercedes-Benz 811D		Carlyle		B33F	1989-90		
70	G100TND	78	G108TND	79	G109TND	88	G118TND	89	G119TND
77	G107TND								
108	L648DNA	Mercedes-Benz 709D		Marshall C19		B29F	1994	Star Line, 1995	
109	L649DNA	Mercedes-Benz 709D		Marshall C19		B29F	1994	Star Line, 1995	
110-119		Mercedes-Benz 811D		Plaxton Beaver		B31F	1994-95	Arriva Yorkshire, 2000	
110	N780EUA	112	L772RWW	116	L776RWW	118	L778RWW	119	L779RWW
111	L771RWW	115	L775RWW						
120-128		Mercedes-Benz 709D		Alexander Sprint		B29F	1995		
120	M120YCM	122	M122YCM	124	M124YCM	126	M126YCM	128	M128YCM
121	M121YCM	123	M123YCM	125	M125YCM				
137	K882UDB	Mercedes-Benz 709D		Plaxton Beaver		B27F	1993		
138	K884UDB	Mercedes-Benz 709D		Plaxton Beaver		B27F	1993	Star Line, 1995	
141	L642DNA	Mercedes-Benz 709D		Plaxton Beaver		B27F	1994	Star Line, 1995	
143-149		Mercedes-Benz 709D		Alexander Sprint		B27F	1994-95	Star Line, 1995	
143	M363KVR	145	M365KVR	147	M367KVR	148	M368KVR	149	M369KVR
144	M364KVR	146	M366KVR						
150	J3SLT	Mercedes-Benz 709D		Plaxton Beaver		B29F	1997	South Lancashire, 1997	

The Northwich operations of Arriva North West were transferred to Arriva Midlands North during 2000 thus reducing the numbers of minibuses that now operate in this fleet. Pictured at Warrington is Alexander-bodied Mercedes-Benz 65, M65WKA.
Paul Wigan

Twelve 8.5-metre Dennis Darts with Carlyle Dartline bodywork moved from Arriva London to Merseyside during 1999 and most of these are now based at Warrington in Arriva colours. Pictured in Liverpool is 1142, H463UGO. *Tony Wilson*

158-163

		Mercedes-Benz 709D	Alexander Sprint	B23F	1996	Timeline, Leigh, 1998
158	P178FNF	160	P180FNF	161	P181FNF	162	P182FNF	163	P183FNF

158	P178FNF	160	P180FNF	161	P181FNF	162	P182FNF	163	P183FNF
159	P179FNF								

164	P524UGA	Mercedes-Benz 709D	Plaxton Beaver	B27F	1996	Nova Scotia, Winsford, 2000
165	P525UGA	Mercedes-Benz 709D	Plaxton Beaver	B27F	1996	Nova Scotia, Winsford, 2000
166	M166LNC	Mercedes-Benz 709D	Alexander Sprint	B23F	1994	Timeline, Leigh, 1998
167	M167LNC	Mercedes-Benz 709D	Alexander Sprint	B23F	1994	Timeline, Leigh, 1998
168	M156LNC	Mercedes-Benz 709D	Alexander Sprint	B23F	1994	Timeline, Leigh, 1998
169	M157LNC	Mercedes-Benz 709D	Alexander Sprint	B23F	1994	Timeline, Leigh, 1998
170	J10SLT	Mercedes-Benz 811D	Reeve Burgess Beaver	B31F	1991	South Lancashire, 1997
171	K1SLT	Mercedes-Benz 811D	Plaxton Beaver	B31F	1993	South Lancashire, 1997
172	K2SLT	Mercedes-Benz 811D	Plaxton Beaver	B31F	1993	South Lancashire, 1997
173	K3SLT	Mercedes-Benz 811D	Plaxton Beaver	B31F	1992	South Lancashire, 1997

175-184

		Mercedes-Benz 811D	Plaxton Beaver	B31F	1996		
175	N175DWM	177	N177DWM	179	N179DWM	181	P181GND	183	P183GND
176	N176DWM	178	N178DWM	180	P180GND	182	P182GND	184	P184GND

191	K457EVC	Mercedes-Benz 811D	Wright NimBus	B31F	1993	Little White Buses, 1995
193	L193DBC	Mercedes-Benz 811D	Marshall C16	B31F	1994	Little White Buses, 1995

201-215

		Leyland Olympian ONCL10/1RZ	Northern Counties	B45/30F	1988		
201	E201WBG	204	E204WBG	207	E207WBG	210	E210WBG	214	E214WBG
202	E202WBG	205	E205WBG	208	E208WBG	212	E212WBG	215	E215WBG
203	E203WBG	206	E206WBG	209	E209WBG	213	E213WBG		

216-230

		Leyland Olympian ONCL10/1RZ	Alexander RL	B45/30F	1988		
216	E216WBG	219	E219WBG	222	E222WBG	225	E225WBG	228	E228WBG
217	E217WBG	220	E220WBG	223	E223WBG	226	E226WBG	229	E229WBG
218	E218WBG	221	E221WBG	224	E224WBG	227	E227WBG	230	E230WBG

Manchester is the most easterly depot of Arriva North West with the fleet based at a recently acquired unit to the rear of Piccadilly rail station. Based at Manchester are five of the Dennis Falcon single-deck buses many of which joined the British Bus group in the early 1990s. It carries East Lancashire bodywork, the bodybuilder being an associated company at that time. Shown here is 381, G381EKA. *Gerry Mead*

231-250

Leyland Olympian ONCL10/1RZ Alexander RL B45/30F 1989

231	F231YTJ	235	F235YTJ	239	F239YTJ	243	F243YTJ	247	F247YTJ
232	F232YTJ	236	F236YTJ	240	F240YTJ	244	F244YTJ	248	F248YTJ
233	F233YTJ	237	F237YTJ	241	F241YTJ	245	F245YTJ	249	F249YTJ
234	F234YTJ	238	F238YTJ	242	F242YTJ	246	F246YTJ	250	F250YTJ

251-270

Leyland Olympian ONCL10/1RZ Northern Counties B45/30F 1989

251	F251YTJ	255	F255YTJ	259	F259YTJ	263	F263YTJ	267	F267YTJ
252	F252YTJ	256	F256YTJ	260	F260YTJ	264	F264YTJ	268	F268YTJ
253	F253YTJ	257	F257YTJ	261	F261YTJ	265	F265YTJ	269	F269YTJ
254	F254YTJ	258	F258YTJ	262	F262YTJ	266	F266YTJ	270	F270YTJ

271-308

Volvo Olympian YN2RV18Z4 Northern Counties Palatine II B47/30F 1995-96

271	N271CKB	279	N279CKB	287	N287CKB	294	N294CKB	302	N302CKB
272	N272CKB	281	N281CKB	288	N288CKB	295	N295CKB	303	N303CKB
273	N273CKB	282	N282CKB	289	N289CKB	296	N296CKB	304	N304CKB
274	N274CKB	283	N283CKB	290	N290CKB	297	N297CKB	305	N305CKB
275	N275CKB	284	N284CKB	291	N291CKB	298	N298CKB	306	N306CKB
276	N276CKB	285	N285CKB	292	N292CKB	299	N299CKB	307	N307CKB
277	N277CKB	286	N286CKB	293	N293CKB	301	N301CKB	308	N308CKB
278	N278CKB							

361	C376CAS	Leyland Olympian ONLXB/1R	Alexander RL	BC45/27F	1986	Liverbus, 1995
362	C377CAS	Leyland Olympian ONLXB/1R	Alexander RL	B45/27F	1986	Liverbus, 1995
380	D634BBV	Leyland LX112L10ZR1	Leyland Lynx	B51F	1987	Nova Scotia, Winsford, 2000

381-388   Dennis Falcon SDA421   East Lancashire EL2000   B48F   1990

381	G381EKA	383	G383EKA	385	G385EKA	387	G387EKA	388	G388EKA
382	G382EKA	384	G384EKA	386	G386EKA				

392	G302DPA	Dennis Falcon HC SDA421	East Lancashire EL2000	B48F	1990	Southern Counties (C&NS), 1998
393	G303DPA	Dennis Falcon HC SDA421	East Lancashire EL2000	B48F	1990	Southern Counties (C&NS), 1998
394	G304DPA	Dennis Falcon HC SDA421	East Lancashire EL2000	B48F	1990	Southern Counties (C&NS), 1998
395	G305DPA	Dennis Falcon HC SDA421	East Lancashire EL2000	B48F	1990	Southern Counties (C&NS), 1998

604-625   Leyland Olympian ONLXB/1R   Eastern Coach Works   B45/32F   1983-85   Ribble, 1986

604	A140MRN	612	B151TRN	615	B155TRN	621	B965WRN	624	B968WRN
607	A146OFR	613	B153TRN	618	B962WRN	622	B966WRN	625	B969WRN
608	A147OFR	614	B154TRN	619	B963WRN	623	B967WRN		

630-635   Dennis Dominator DDA1026   East Lancashire   B43/25F   1989

630	F630BKD	632	F632BKD	633	F633BKD	634	F634BKD	635	F635BKD

646	G661DTJ	Volvo Citybus B10M-50	East Lancashire	B49/39F	1990	Southern Counties (C&NS), 1998
647	G647EKA	Volvo Citybus B10M-50	East Lancashire	B49/39F	1990	Southern Counties (C&NS), 1998
650	G650EKA	Volvo Citybus B10M-50	East Lancashire	B49/39F	1990	
651	G651EKA	Volvo Citybus B10M-50	East Lancashire	B49/39F	1990	
652	G652EKA	Volvo Citybus B10M-50	East Lancashire	B49/39F	1990	
653	G653EKA	Volvo Citybus B10M-50	East Lancashire	B49/39F	1990	

654-668   Leyland Olympian ONLXB/1R   Eastern Coach Works   B45/32F   1983-84   Crosville, 1989

654	PFM126Y	658	A140SMA	661	A151UDM	662	A153UDM	668	A142SMA
656	PFM129Y							

690-699   Volvo Citybus B10M-50   East Lancashire   B45/34F   1991   London South, 1998

690	H660GPF	692	H662GPF	695	H665GPF	697	H667GPF	699	H679GPF
691	H661GPF							

701-705   Leyland Olympian ONLXB/1RZ   Alexander RL   B45/30F   1989   Arriva Fox County, 1999

701	G521WJF	702	G522WJF	703	G523WJF	704	G524WJF	705	G525WJF

706-713   Leyland Olympian ONCL10/1RZ   Northern Counties   B47/30F   1989   Arriva Fox County, 1999

706	G506SFT	708	G508SFT	709	G509SFT	712	G512SFT	713	G513SFT

778-788   Volvo B10M-50 Citybus   Alexander Q   B55F   1992   Timeline, Leigh, 1998

778	H78DVM	785	H85DVM	786	H86DVM	787	H87DVM	788	H588DVM
779	H79DVM							

East Lancashire bodywork is fitted to many early Dennis Darts in the Arriva North West fleet. Pictured leaving Widnes bus station is 1159, M159WKA, from the 1994 order.
Cliff Beeton

| 1003 | N103YVU | Scania L113CRL | Wright Axcess-ultralow | N42F | 1996 |
| 1005 | N105YVU | Scania L113CRL | Wright Axcess-ultralow | N42F | 1996 |

1006-1034 Scania L113CRL Wright Axcess-ultralow N43F 1996

1006	N106DWM	1012	N112DWM	1018	N118DWM	1024	N124DWM	1030	N130DWM
1007	N107DWM	1013	N113DWM	1019	N119DWM	1025	N125DWM	1031	N131DWM
1008	N108DWM	1014	N114DWM	1020	N120DWM	1026	N126DWM	1032	N132DWM
1009	N109DWM	1015	N115DWM	1021	N121DWM	1027	N127DWM	1033	N133DWM
1010	N110DWM	1016	N116DWM	1022	N122DWM	1028	N128DWM	1034	N134DWM
1011	N211DWM	1017	N117DWM	1023	N123DWM	1029	N129DWM		

1035-1040 Scania L113CRL East Lancashire Flyte B47F 1996

1035	P135GND	1037	P137GND	1038	P138GND	1039	P139GND	1040	P140GND
1036	P136GND								

1041-1061 Scania L113CRL Northern Counties Paladin B42F 1997

1041	P41MVU	1046	P46MVU	1050	P250NBA	1054	R54XVM	1058	P58MVU
1042	P42MVU	1047	R47XVM	1051	R51XVM	1055	R255WRJ	1059	R59XVM
1043	P43MVU	1048	R48XVM	1052	P52MVU	1056	P56MVU	1060	P260NBA
1044	P244NBA	1049	P49MVU	1053	P53MVU	1057	R57XVM	1061	P61MVU
1045	P45MVU								

1071-1084 Scania N113CRL Wright Pathfinder B37D 1994 Arriva London, 1999

1071	RDZ1701	1074	RDZ1704	1077	RDZ1707	1080	RDZ1710	1083	RDZ1713
1072	RDZ1702	1075	RDZ1705	1078	RDZ1708	1081	RDZ1711	1084	RDZ1714
1073	RDZ1703	1076	RDZ1706	1079	RDZ1709	1082	RDZ1712		

1111	J311WHJ	Dennis Dart 9SDL3002	Plaxton Pointer	B35F	1991	Arriva London, 2000
1112	J312WHJ	Dennis Dart 9SDL3002	Plaxton Pointer	B35F	1991	Arriva London, 2000
1113	J313WHJ	Dennis Dart 9SDL3002	Plaxton Pointer	B35F	1991	Arriva London, 2000
1114	J314XVX	Dennis Dart 9SDL3011	Wright Handybus	B35F	1992	East Herts & Essex, 1998
1115	J315XVX	Dennis Dart 9SDL3011	Wright Handybus	B35F	1992	East Herts & Essex, 1998

1120-1125 Dennis Dart 9SDL3034 Northern Counties Paladin B35F 1994 Arriva London, 2000

1120	L120YVK	1122	L126YVK	1123	L151YVK	1124	L123YVK	1125	L121YVK
1121	L125YVK								

| 1135 | H95MOB | Dennis Dart 8.5SDL3003 | Carlyle Dartline | B28F | 1990 | Metroline, 1996 |

1137-1149 Dennis Dart 8.5SDL3003 Carlyle Dartline B28F* 1990 Arriva London, 1999
*1137/8 are B36F

1137	G125RGT	1140	H460UGO	1143	H465UGO	1145	H467UGO	1148	H132MOB
1138	G128RGT	1141	H461UGO	1144	H466UGO	1146	H469UGO	1149	H143MOB
1139	H458UGO	1142	H463UGO						

Six Volvo Citybuses transferred from Arriva London South to the North West fleet in 1998 to join similar buses already based on Merseyside. Pictured in Manchester is 692, H662GPF, which carries an East Lancashire body. *Gerry Mead*

Plaxton Verde bodies were the choice for the 1995 delivery of Dennis Lances and these have been joined by nine similar buses from Clydeside in 1998. All are currently allocated to Bootle depot from where 1203, M203YKA, was operating when pictured near Paradise Street bus station in Liverpool. *Tony Wilson*

1150	L150SBG	Dennis Dart 9SDL3034	East Lancashire	B32F	1993
1151	L151SBG	Dennis Dart 9SDL3034	East Lancashire	B32F	1993
1152	L152SBG	Dennis Dart 9SDL3034	East Lancashire	B32F	1993
1153	L153UKB	Dennis Dart 9SDL3034	Plaxton Pointer	B20F	1994
1154	L154UKB	Dennis Dart 9SDL3034	Plaxton Pointer	B20F	1994
1155	L155UKB	Dennis Dart 9SDL3034	Plaxton Pointer	B20F	1994
1156	L156UKB	Dennis Dart 9SDL3034	Plaxton Pointer	B20F	1994

1157-1170

				Dennis Dart 9.8SDL3040*		East Lancashire		B40F	1994-95	1170 is 9.8SDL3054
1157	M157WKA	1160	M160WKA	1163	M163WKA	1166	M166WKA	1169	M169WKA
1158	M158WKA	1161	M161WKA	1164	M164WKA	1167	M167WKA	1170	M170WKA
1159	M159WKA	1162	M162WKA	1165	M165WKA	1168	M168WKA		

1171-1187

				Dennis Dart 9.8SDL3040		Plaxton Pointer		B40F	1995
1171	M171YKA	1175	M175YKA	1179	M179YKA	1182	M182YKA	1185	M185YKA
1172	M172YKA	1176	M176YKA	1180	M180YKA	1183	M183YKA	1186	M186YKA
1173	M173YKA	1177	M177YKA	1181	M181YKA	1184	M184YKA	1187	M187YKA
1174	M174YKA	1178	M178YKA						

1188-1199

				Dennis Dart 9.8SDL3054		Plaxton Pointer		B40F	1995
1188	M188YKA	1191	M191YKA	1194	M194YKA	1196	M196YKA	1198	M198YKA
1189	M189YKA	1192	M192YKA	1195	M195YKA	1197	M197YKA	1199	M199YKA
1190	M190YKA	1193	M193YKA						

1201-1210

				Dennis Lance 11SDA3113		Plaxton Verde		B49F	1995
1201	M201YKA	1203	M203YKA	1205	M205YKA	1207	M207YKA	1209	M209YKA
1202	M202YKA	1204	M204YKA	1206	M206YKA	1208	M208YKA	1210	M210YKA

1211	M211YKD	Dennis Dart 9.8SDL3040	Plaxton Pointer	B40F	1995
1212	M212YKD	Dennis Dart 9.8SDL3040	Plaxton Pointer	B40F	1995
1213	M213YKD	Dennis Dart 9.8SDL3040	Plaxton Pointer	B40F	1995
1214	M214YKD	Dennis Dart 9.8SDL3054	Plaxton Pointer	B40F	1995
1215	M215YKD	Dennis Dart 9.8SDL3054	Plaxton Pointer	B40F	1995
1216	M216YKD	Dennis Dart 9.8SDL3054	Plaxton Pointer	B40F	1995

1217-1264

		Dennis Dart 9.8SDL3054	East Lancashire	B40F	1995

1217	M217AKB	1227	M227AKB	1237	N237CKA	1247	N247CKA	1256	N256CKA
1218	M218AKB	1228	M228AKB	1238	N238CKA	1248	N248CKA	1257	N257CKA
1219	M219AKB	1229	M229AKB	1239	N239CKA	1249	N249CKA	1258	N258CKA
1220	M220AKB	1230	M230AKB	1240	N240CKA	1250	N250CKA	1259	N259CKA
1221	M221AKB	1231	M231AKB	1241	N241CKA	1251	N251CKA	1260	N260CKA
1222	M322AKB	1232	M232AKB	1242	N242CKA	1252	N252CKA	1261	N261CKA
1223	M223AKB	1233	N233CKA	1243	N243CKA	1253	N253CKA	1262	N262CKA
1224	M224AKB	1234	N234CKA	1244	N244CKA	1254	N254CKA	1263	N263CKA
1225	M225AKB	1235	N235CKA	1245	N245CKA	1255	N255CKA	1264	N264CKA
1226	M226AKB	1236	N236CKA	1246	N246CKA				

1265	K877UDB	Dennis Dart 9.8SDL3017	Plaxton Pointer	B40F	1992	Star Line, 1995
1266	M370KVR	Dennis Dart 9.8SDL3035	Northern Counties Paladin	B40F	1994	Star Line, 1995
1267	M371KVR	Dennis Dart 9.8SDL3035	Northern Counties Paladin	B40F	1994	Star Line, 1995
1268	M372KVR	Dennis Dart 9.8SDL3035	Northern Counties Paladin	B40F	1995	Star Line, 1995
1269	M841RCP	Dennis Dart 9.8SDL3054	Northern Counties Paladin	B39F	1995	Wigan Bus Company, 1995
1270	M842RCP	Dennis Dart 9.8SDL3054	Northern Counties Paladin	B39F	1995	Wigan Bus Company, 1995
1271	M843RCP	Dennis Dart 9.8SDL3054	Northern Counties Paladin	B39F	1995	Wigan Bus Company, 1995
1273	K73SRG	Dennis Dart 9.8SDL3017	Plaxton Pointer	B43F	1993	Northumbria (Hunters), 1997
1274	K74SRG	Dennis Dart 9.8SDL3017	Plaxton Pointer	B43F	1993	Northumbria (Hunters), 1997
1275	K75SRG	Dennis Dart 9.8SDL3017	Plaxton Pointer	B43F	1993	Northumbria (Hunters), 1997
1276	J6SLT	Dennis Dart 9.8SDL3040	Plaxton Pointer	B40F	1996	South Lancashire, 1997
1277	J7SLT	Dennis Dart 9.8SDL3040	Plaxton Pointer	B38F	1996	South Lancashire, 1997
1278	J8SLT	Dennis Dart 9.8SDL3017	Plaxton Pointer	B38F	1992	South Lancashire, 1997
1279	J9SLT	Dennis Dart 9.8SDL3017	Plaxton Pointer	B38F	1992	South Lancashire, 1997
1280	L11SLT	Dennis Dart 9.8SDL3025	Plaxton Pointer	B38F	1993	South Lancashire, 1997
1281	L1SLT	Dennis Dart 9SDL3011	Plaxton Pointer	B35F	1993	South Lancashire, 1997
1282	L2SLT	Dennis Dart 9SDL3011	Plaxton Pointer	B35F	1993	South Lancashire, 1997
1285	M5SLT	Dennis Dart 9.8SDL3040	Plaxton Pointer	B40F	1994	South Lancashire, 1997

1290-1299

		Dennis Lance 11SDA3113	Plaxton Verde	B49F	1994	Clydeside, 1996

1290	M930EYS	1292	M932EYS	1294	M934EYS	1296	M936EYS	1298	M928EYS
1291	M931EYS	1293	M933EYS	1295	M935EYS	1297	M927EYS	1299	M929EYS

1300	P3SLT	Dennis Dart	Plaxton Pointer	B40F	1996	South Lancashire, 1997
1301	R301PCW	Dennis Dart SLF	Plaxton Pointer 2	N39F	1998	South Lancashire, 1997

1302-1313

		Dennis Dart SLF	Aleaxander ALX200	N35F	1998

1302	R302CVU	1305	R305CVU	1308	R308CVU	1310	R310CVU	1312	R312CVU
1303	R303CVU	1306	R606FBU	1309	R309CVU	1311	R311CVU	1313	R313CVU
1304	R304CVU	1307	R307CVU						

1314-1324

		Dennis Dart SLF	Plaxton Pointer 2	N33F	1999

1314	T314PNB	1317	T317PNB	1319	T319PNB	1321	T821PNB	1323	T323PNB
1315	T315PNB	1318	T318PNB	1320	T320PNB	1322	T322PNB	1324	T324PNB
1316	T316PNB								

1332	T62JBA	Dennis Dart SLF	Plaxton Pointer MPD	N29F	1999	Nova Scotia, Winsford, 2000
1333	T63JBA	Dennis Dart SLF	Plaxton Pointer MPD	N29F	1999	Nova Scotia, Winsford, 2000
1334	T64JBA	Dennis Dart SLF	Plaxton Pointer MPD	N29F	1999	Nova Scotia, Winsford, 2000
1335	T65JBA	Dennis Dart SLF	Plaxton Pointer MPD	N29F	1999	Nova Scotia, Winsford, 2000
1401	R151GNW	DAF DE02GSSB220	Plaxton Prestige	N38F	1998	Arriva London, 1999
1402	R152GNW	DAF DE02GSSB220	Plaxton Prestige	N32F	1998	Arriva London, 1999
1403	R153GNW	DAF DE02GSSB220	Plaxton Prestige	N33F	1998	Arriva London, 1999

1404-1415

		DAF DE02GSSB220	Alexander ALX300	N41F	2000

1404	V404ENC	1407	V407ENC	1410	V410ENC	1412	V412ENC	1414	V414ENC
1405	V405ENC	1408	V408ENC	1411	V411ENC	1413	V413ENC	1415	V415ENC
1406	V406ENC	1409	V409ENC						

1960	D108NDW	Leyland Lynx LX112TL11ZR1R	Leyland Lynx	B49F	1987	Arriva Southern Counties, 2000
1961	D155HML	Leyland Lynx LX112TL11ZR1S	Leyland Lynx	B49F	1987	Arriva Southern Counties, 2000
1962	D157HML	Leyland Lynx LX112TL11ZR1S	Leyland Lynx	B49F	1987	Arriva Southern Counties, 2000
1965	G45VME	Leyland Lynx LX2R11C15Z4S	Leyland Lynx	B49F	1989	Arriva Southern Counties, 2000

2018-2220 Leyland Titan TNLXB2RRSp Park Royal B44/30F 1979-80 London Buses, 1992-94

2018	CUL218V	2121	CUL121V	2148	CUL148V	2220	CUL220V

2201-2262 Dennis Dart SLF Plaxton Pointer 2 N39F 2000

2201	X201ANC	2214	X214ANC	2227	X227ANC	2238	X238ANC	2251	X251HJA
2202	X202ANC	2215	X215ANC	2228	X228ANC	2239	X239ANC	2252	X252HJA
2203	X203ANC	2216	X216ANC	2229	X229ANC	2241	X241ANC	2253	X253HJA
2204	X204ANC	2217	X217ANC	2231	X231ANC	2242	X242ANC	2254	X254HJA
2207	X207ANC	2218	X218ANC	2232	X232ANC	2243	X243HJA	2256	X256HJA
2208	X208ANC	2219	X219ANC	2233	X233ANC	2244	X244HJA	2257	X257HJA
2209	X209ANC	2221	X221ANC	2234	X234ANC	2246	X246HJA	2258	X258HJA
2211	X211ANC	2223	X223ANC	2235	X235ANC	2247	X247HJA	2259	X259HJA
2212	X212ANC	2224	X224ANC	2236	X236ANC	2248	X248HJA	2261	X261OBN
2213	X213ANC	2226	X226ANC	2237	X237ANC	2249	X249HJA	2262	X262OBN

2263	X263	Dennis Dart SLF	Alexander ALX200	N38F	2000
2264	X264	Dennis Dart SLF	Alexander ALX200	N38F	2000

2284-2400 Leyland Titan TNLXB2RR Leyland B44/30F 1981-82 London Buses, 1992-94

2284	KYN284X	2338	KYN338X	2353	KYN353X	2363	KYN363X	2385	KYN385X
2330w	KYN330X	2344	KYN344X	2354	KYN354X	2374	KYN374X	2400	KYN400X
2333	KYN333X	2350	KYN350X	2355	KYN355X	2376	KYN376X		

2416-2438 DAF SB120 Wright Cadet N39F On order for 2000

2416	X416AJA	2421	X421AJA	2426	X426AJA	2431	X431AJA	2435	X435AJA
2417	X417AJA	2422	X422AJA	2427	X427AJA	2432	X432AJA	2436	X436AJA
2418	X418AJA	2423	X423AJA	2428	X428AJA	2433	X433AJA	2437	X437AJA
2419	X419AJA	2424	X424AJA	2429	X429AJA	2434	X434AJA	2438	X438AJA

2443-2741 Leyland Titan TNLXB2RR Leyland B44/30F 1982-83 London Buses, 1992-94

2443	KYN443X	2468	KYN468X	2570	NUW570Y	2695	OHV695Y	2741	OHV741Y
2449	KYN449X								

2801-2822 Volvo B6BLE Wright Crusader 2 N39F 2000

2801	X801AJA	2805	X805AJA	2809	X809AJA	2814	X814AJA	2818	X818AJA
2802	X802AJA	2806	X806AJA	2811	X811AJA	2815	X815AJA	2819	X819AJA
2803	X803AJA	2807	X807AJA	2812	X812AJA	2816	X816AJA	2821	X821AJA
2804	X804AJA	2808	X808AJA	2813	X813AJA	2817	X817AJA	2822	X822AJA

When Arriva acquired MTL a comitment to introduce new buses was made. Three types are currentl being delivered, Wright-bodied DAF SB120 and Volvo B6s and Plaxton-bodied Dennis Darts. First of the Plaxton batch is 2201, X201ANC, seen complete with route-branding for the 6/7 service.
Andrew Jarosz

Following the amalgamation of the MTL and Arriva North West fleets the Atlanteans have been renumbered by the addition of 2000 to their old numbers. Pictured with its former number still displayed in 3449, GKA449L, one of the four open-top Atlanteans based in Southport. As shown on the advert panel, the route now runs south from Southport, past Ainsdale and on to Pontins camp. *Richard Godfrey*

3001-3070
Leyland Atlantean AN68D/1R   Alexander AL   B43/32F   1983-84

3001	A321GLV	3015	A335GLV	3033	A113HLV	3045	A125HLV	3057	A137HLV
3002	A322GLV	3016	A96HLV	3034	A114HLV	3046	A126HLV	3058	A138HLV
3003	A323GLV	3017	A97HLV	3035	A115HLV	3048	A128HLV	3059	A139HLV
3004	A324GLV	3018	A98HLV	3036	A116HLV	3049	A129HLV	3060	A140HLV
3005	A325GLV	3019	A99HLV	3038	A118HLV	3050	A130HLV	3061	A141HLV
3006w	A326GLV	3020	A100HLV	3039	A119HLV	3051	A131HLV	3062	A142HLV
3007w	A327GLV	3024	A104HLV	3040	A120HLV	3052t	A132HLV		
3008	A328GLV	3030	A110HLV	3041	A121HLV	3053	A133HLV	3067	A147HLV
3012	A332GLV	3031	A111HLV	3042	A122HLV	3054	A134HLV	3068	A148HLV
3013	A333GLV	3032	A112HLV	3043	A123HLV	3056	A136HLV	3070	B926KWM
3014	A334GLV								

3101-3115
Leyland Olympian ON2R50C13Z4 Northern Counties   B47/30F   1990   Arriva London, 2000

3101	H101GEV	3104	H104GEV	3107	H107GEV	3110	H110GEV	3114	H114GEV
3102	H102GEV	3105	H105GEV	3108	H108GEV	3112	H112GEV	3115	H115GEV
3103	H103GEV	3106	H106GEV	3109	H109GEV	3113	H113GEV		

3159-3168
Leyland Olympian ONCL10/2RZ Northern Counties   B51/34F   1988-89

3159	F438AKB	3161	F440AKB	3163	F442AKB	3165	F456BKF	3167	F458BKF
3160	F439AKB	3162	F441AKB	3164	F455BKF	3166	F457BKF	3168	F459BKF

3172	E913KYR	Leyland Olympian ONLXB/1RH	Northern Counties	B43/30F	1988	London Buses, 1991
3173	E926KYR	Leyland Olympian ONLXB/1RH	Northern Counties	B43/30F	1988	London Buses, 1991
3174	E916KYR	Leyland Olympian ONLXB/1RH	Northern Counties	B43/30F	1988	London Buses, 1991
3175	E928KYR	Leyland Olympian ONLXB/1RH	Northern Counties	B43/30F	1988	London Buses, 1991
3449	GKA449L	Leyland Atlantean AN68/1R	Alexander AL	O43/32F	1973	
3524	GKA524M	Leyland Atlantean AN68/1R	Alexander AL	O43/32F	1973	
3551	OLV551M	Leyland Atlantean AN68/1R	Alexander AL	O43/32F	1974	
3612	GKA37N	Leyland Atlantean AN68/1R	Alexander AL	O43/32F	1974	

3671-3683
Volvo Citybus B10M-50 — Alexander RV — B47/32F — 1989 — Arriva London, 2000

3671	F101TML	3675	F105TML	3677	F107TML	3679	F109TML	3682	F112TML
3673	F103TML	3676	F106TML	3678	F108TML	3680	F110TML	3683	F113TML
3674	F104TML								

3801-3825
MCW Metrobus DR132/16* — MCW — B46/31F — 1989 — 3801-3/5 fitted with Gardner engines *3806-15 are type DR132/17

3801	F801YLV	3806	F806YLV	3811	F811YLV	3816	F816YLV	3821	F821YLV
3802	F802YLV	3807	F807YLV	3812	F812YLV	3817	F817YLV	3822	F822YLV
3803	F803YLV	3808	F808YLV	3813	F813YLV	3818	F818YLV	3823	F823YLV
3804	F804YLV	3809	F809YLV	3814	F814YLV	3819	F819YLV	3824	F824YLV
3805	F805YLV	3810	F810YLV	3815	F815YLV	3820	F820YLV	3825	F825YLV

3826	E452SON	MCW Metrobus DR102/63	MCW	B45/30F	1987	Great Yarmouth, 1995
3827	E453SON	MCW Metrobus DR102/63	MCW	B45/30F	1987	Great Yarmouth, 1995
3828	E455SON	MCW Metrobus DR102/63	MCW	B45/30F	1987	Great Yarmouth, 1995

3881-3967
Leyland Atlantean AN68B/1R — Alexander AL — B43/32F — 1981-82

3898	XEM881W	3905	XEM905W	3910	XEM910W	3928	ACM728X	3947	ACM747X
3903	XEM903W	3906	XEM906W	3911	XEM911W	3930	ACM730X	3950	ACM750X
3904	XEM904W	3909	XEM909W	3921	ACM721X	3931	ACM731X	3953	ACM753X

3974-3991
Leyland Atlantean AN68D/1R — Alexander AL — B43/32F — 1982

3974	DEM774Y	3979	DEM779Y	3982	DEM782Y	3985	DEM785Y	3989	DEM789Y
3976	DEM776Y	3980	DEM780Y	3983	DEM783Y	3986	DEM786Y	3990	DEM790Y
3977	DEM777Y	3981	DEM781Y	3984	DEM784Y	3987	DEM787Y	3991	DEM791Y
3978	DEM778Y								

5294	BCW823V	Leyland National 2 NL106L11/1R		B44F	1980	Ribble, 1995
5295	BCW824V	Leyland National 2 NL106L11/1R		B44F	1980	Ribble, 1995
5296	DBV836W	Leyland National 2 NL106L11/1R		B44F	1980	Ribble, 1995
5297	DBV840W	Leyland National 2 NL106L11/1R		B44F	1980	Ribble, 1995

5301-5320
Scania L113CRL — Wright Axcess-ultralow — N40F — 1996

5301	P301HEM	5305	P305HEM	5309	P309HEM	5313	P313HEM	5317	P317HEM
5302	P302HEM	5306	P306HEM	5310	P310HEM	5314	P314HEM	5318	P318HEM
5303	P303HEM	5307	P307HEM	5311	P311HEM	5315	P315HEM	5319	P319HEM
5304	P304HEM	5308	P308HEM	5312	P312HEM	5316	P316HEM	5320	P320HEM

5321	N101YVU	Scania L113CRL	Wright Axcess-ultralow	N42F	1996
5322	M2SLT	Scania L113CRL	Wright Axcess-ultralow	N42F	1996
5324	N104YVU	Scania L113CRL	Wright Axcess-ultralow	N42F	1996
6036	UEM36V	Leyland National 2 NL116L11/1R		B49F	1980

Four Gas Buses are based at Southport for the tendered Park and Ride service in the town. These feature Dennis Dart chassis and Plaxton Pointer 2 bodywork decorated in a livery reflecting the use of the environmentally friendly fuel.
Reg Wilson

6101-6138 — Leyland National 2 NL116L11/1R — B49F — 1980

6101	VBG101V	6106	VBG106V	6116	VBG116V	6125	WWM908W	6134	WWM912W
6102	VBG102V	6110	VBG110V	6121	VBG121V	6129	VBG129V	6136	WWM914W
6104	VBG104V	6111	VBG111V						

6140-6172 — Leyland National 2 NL116AL11/1R — B49F* — 1981-82 — *6151 is B28DL

6140	XLV140W	6156	XLV156W	6159	XLV159W	6161	XLV161W	6169	CKB166X
6151	XLV151W	6157	XLV157W	6160	XLV160W	6168	CKB165X	6170	CKB167X
6153	XLV153W	6158	XLV158W						

6204	CEO723W	Leyland National 2 NL116L11/1R		B49F	1980	Ribble, 1995
6208	BYW430V	Leyland National 10351A/2R		B44F	1979	Parfitt's, 1995
6209	BYW432V	Leyland National 10351A/2R		B44F	1979	Parfitt's, 1995
6248	S248UVR	Dennis Dart SLF CNG	Plaxton Pointer	N41F	1999	
6249	S249UVR	Dennis Dart SLF CNG	Plaxton Pointer	N41F	1999	
6250	S250UVR	Dennis Dart SLF CNG	Plaxton Pointer	N41F	1999	
6251	S251UVR	Dennis Dart SLF CNG	Plaxton Pointer	N41F	1999	
6301	L301TEM	Volvo B10B	Alexander Strider	B49F	1994	
6302	L302TEM	Volvo B10B	Alexander Strider	B49F	1994	
6303	L303TEM	Volvo B10B	Alexander Strider	B49F	1994	

6330-6334 — DAF SB220LC550 — Ikarus CitiBus — B48F — 1993

6330	K130TCP	6331	K131TCP	6332	K132TCP	6333	K133TCP	6334	K510RJX

6402-6413 — Neoplan N4016 — Neoplan — N39F — 1994

6402	L402TKB	6405	L405TKB	6408	L408TKB	6410	L410TKB	6412	L412UFY
6403	L403TKB	6406	L406TKB	6409	L409TKB	6411	L411UFY	6413	L413TKB
6404	L404TKB	6407	L407TKB						

6501-6543 — Volvo B10B-58 — Wright Endurance — BC49F — 1994

6501	L501TKA	6510	L510TKA	6519	M519WHF	6528	M528WHF	6536	M536WHF
6502	L502TKA	6511	L511TKA	6520	M520WHF	6529	M529WHF	6537	M537WHF
6503	L503TKA	6512	L512TKA	6521	M521WHF	6530	M530WHF	6538	M538WHF
6504	L504TKA	6513	L513TKA	6522	M522WHF	6531	M531WHF		
6505	L505TKA	6514	M514WHF	6523	M523WHF	6532	M532WHF	6540	M540WHF
6506	L506TKA	6515	M515WHF	6524	M524WHF	6533	M533WHF	6541	M541WHF
6507	L507TKA	6516	M516WHF	6525	M525WHF	6534	M534WHF	6542	M542WHF
6508	L508TKA	6517	M517WHF	6526	M526WHF	6535	M535WHF	6543	M543WHF
6509	L509TKA	6518	M518WHF	6527	M527WHF				

6544-6623 — Volvo B10B-58 — Wright Endurance — BC49F — 1994-96

6544	M544WTJ	6562	M562WTJ	6578	N578CKA	6593	N593CKA	6609	N609CKA
6545	M545WTJ	6563	M563WTJ	6579	N579CKA	6594	N594CKA	6610	N610CKA
6546	M546WTJ	6564	M564YEM	6580	N580CKA	6595	N595CKA	6611	N611CKA
6547	M547WTJ	6565	M565YEM	6581	N581CKA	6596	N596CKA	6612	N612CKA
6548	M548WTJ	6566	M566YEM	6582	N582CKA	6597	N597CKA	6613	N613CKA
6549	M549WTJ	6567	M567YEM	6583	N583CKA	6598	N598CKA	6614	N614CKA
6550	M550WTJ	6568	M568YEM	6584	N584CKA	6599	N599CKA	6615	N615CKA
6551	M551WTJ	6569	M569YEM	6585	N585CKA	6601	N601CKA	6616	N616CKA
6552	M552WTJ	6570	M570YEM	6586	N586CKA	6602	N602CKA	6617	N617CKA
6553	M553WTJ	6571	M571YEM	6587	N587CKA	6603	N603CKA	6618	N618CKA
6554	M554WTJ	6572	M572YEM	6588	N588CKA	6604	N604CKA	6619	N619CKA
6556	M556WTJ	6573	M573YEM	6589	N589CKA	6605	N605CKA	6620	N620CKA
6557	M557WTJ	6574	M574YEM	6590	N590CKA	6606	N606CKA	6621	N621CKA
6558	M558WTJ	6575	M575YEM	6591	N591CKA	6607	N607CKA	6622	N622CKA
6559	M559WTJ	6576	N576CKA	6592	N592CKA	6608	N608CKA	6623	N623CKA
6561	M561WTJ	6577	N577CKA						

6901-6913 — Volvo B10B-58 — Northern Counties Paladin — B51F — 1993-95 — Liverbus, 1995

6901	K101OHF	6904	K104OHF	6907	K107OHF	6909	M109XKC	6912	M112XKC
6902	K102OHF	6905	K105OHF	6908	K108OHF	6910	M110XKC	6913	M113XKC
6903	K103OHF	6906	K106OHF						

Many of the Marshall-bodied Dennis Darts supplied to MTL now carry Arriva colours. Seen working route 53 is 7671, V671DVU, one of the type also transferred to a former North West depot, Bootle. *Cliffe Beeton*

7201-7244   Volvo B6-9.9M   Plaxton Pointer   B38F   1994

7201	L201TKA	7211	L211TKA	7220	L220TKA	7229	L229TKA	7237	L237TKA
7202	L202TKA	7212	L212TKA	7221	L221TKA	7230	L230TKA	7238	L238TKA
7203	L203TKA	7213	L213TKA	7222	L222TKA	7231	L231TKA	7239	L239TKA
7204	L204TKA	7214	L214TKA	7223	L223TKA	7232	L232TKA	7240	L240TKA
7205	L205TKA	7215	L215TKA	7224	L224TKA	7233	L233TKA	7241	L241TKA
7206	L206TKA	7216	L216TKA	7225	L225TKA	7234	L234TKA	7242	L242TKA
7208	L208TKA	7217	L217TKA	7226	L226TKA	7235	L235TKA	7243	L243TKA
7209	L209TKA	7218	L218TKA	7227	L227TKA	7236	L236TKA	7244	L244TKA
7210	L210TKA	7219	L219TKA	7228	L228TKA				

7411	K911OEM	Dennis Dart 9.8SDL3017	Plaxton Pointer	B38F	1993	Blue Triangle, 1994
7455	K955PBG	Dennis Dart 9.8SDL3017	Plaxton Pointer	B36F	1993	Blue Triangle, 1994
7487	H87MOB	Dennis Dart 8.5SDL3003	Carlyle Dartline	B28F	1990	Metroline, 1996
7491	H91MOB	Dennis Dart 8.5SDL3003	Carlyle Dartline	B28F	1990	Metroline, 1996
7496	H96MOB	Dennis Dart 8.5SDL3003	Carlyle Dartline	B28F	1990	Metroline, 1996
7520	M20GGY	Dennis Dart 9.8SDL3040	Plaxton Pointer	B40F	1994	Ogdens, Haydock, 1995
7530	M30GGY	Dennis Dart 9.8SDL3040	Plaxton Pointer	B40F	1994	Ogdens, Haydock, 1995

7531-7545   Dennis Dart 9.8   Plaxton Pointer   B38F   1996-97

7531	N531DWN	7534	P534MBU	7537	P537MBU	7540	P540MBU	7543	P543MBU
7532	N532DWN	7535	P535MBU	7538	P538MBU	7541	P541MBU	7544	P544MBU
7533	P533MBU	7536	P536MBU	7539	P539MBU	7542	P542MBU	7545	P545MBU

7546-7571   Dennis Dart 9.8   Plaxton Pointer   B38F   1998

7546	R546ABA	7551	R551ABA	7557	R557ABA	7562	R562ABA	7567	R567ABA
7547	R547ABA	7552	R552ABA	7558	R558ABA	7563	R563ABA	7568	R568ABA
7548	R548ABA	7553	R553ABA	7559	R559ABA	7564	R564ABA	7569	R569ABA
7549	R549ABA	7554	R554ABA	7560	R560ABA	7565	R565ABA	7570	R570ABA
7550	R550ABA	7556	R556ABA	7561	R561ABA	7566	R566ABA	7571	R571ABA

The former MTL colours, shown here on Neoplan 6409, L409TKB, are fast disapearing on the single-deck fleet. The vehicle was photographed in Muirhead Avenue while heading for Croxteth Park. *Richard Godfrey*

7612-7623

		Dennis Dart SLF 10.5		Marshall Capital		N38F	1999			

7612	T612PNC	7615	T615PNC	7618	T618PNC	7620	T620PNC	7622	T622PNC
7613	T613PNC	7616	T616PNC	7619	T619PNC	7621	T621PNC	7623	T623PNC
7614	T614PNC	7617	T617PNC						

7624-7676

		Dennis Dart SLF 10.5		Marshall Capital		N38F	1999-2000		

7624	V624DBN	7635	V635DVU	7646	V646DVU	7656	V656DVU	7667	V667DVU
7625	V625DVU	7636	V636DVU	7647	V647DVU	7657	V657DVU	7668	V668DVU
7626	V626DVU	7637	V637DVU	7648	V648DVU	7658	V658DVU	7669	V669DVU
7627	V627DVU	7638	V638DVU	7649	V649DVU	7659	V659DVU	7670	V670DVU
7628	V628DVU	7639	V639DVU	7650	V650DVU	7660	V660DVU	7671	V671DVU
7629	V629DVU	7640	V640DVU	7651	V651DVU	7661	V661DVU	7672	V672DVU
7630	V630DVU	7641	V641DVU	7652	V652DVU	7662	V662DVU	7673	V673DVU
7631	V631DVU	7642	V642DVU	7653	V653DVU	7663	V663DVU	7674	V674DVU
7632	V632DVU	7643	V643DVU	7654	V654DVU	7664	V664DVU	7675	V675DVU
7633	V633DVU	7644	V644DVU	7655	V655DVU	7665	V665DVU	7676	V676DVU
7634	V634DVU	7645	V645DVU						

7801-7806

		Optare MetroRider		Optare		B17F	1993-94		

7801	K801NTJ	7803	K803NTJ	7804	K804NTJ	7805	K805NTJ	7806	L806TFY
7802	K802NTJ								

7817	K817NKH	Dennis Dart 9SDL3016		Plaxton Pointer		B34F	1992	London Northern, 1994

7872-7879

		Dennis Dart SLF 9.3		Plaxton Pointer 2		N25F	1998		

7872	S872SNB	7874	S874SNB	7876	S876SNB	7878	S878SNB	7879	S879SNB
7873	S873SNB	7875	S875SNB	7877	S877SNB				

Special event vehicles:-

918	AJA118	Bristol L5G		Burlingham (1950)		B35R	1938	preservation, 1994

Ancilliary vehicles:-

916	VDB916	Leyland Leopard PSU3/3RT	Alexander Highlander	TV	1962	preservation, 1994
936	MUP713T	Bristol LH6L	Eastern Coach Works	TV	1979	Arriva North East, 1999
938	WSU442S	Leyland Leopard PSU3/3R	Alexander AYS	TV	1977	Clydeside, 1996
941	HFM186N	Leyland National 11351/1R		TV	1975	Crosville, 1989
950	WSU450S	Leyland Leopard PSU3/3R	Alexander AYS	TV	1977	Clydeside, 1996
1914	GGR406N	Leyland Leopard PSU3/3R	Plaxton/UAS	RV	1974	
1918	AJA142B	Leyland Leopard PSU3/3RT	Alexander AY/CMS	RV	1964	
1972	D89VCC	Mercedes-Benz 609D	Reeve Burgess	B20F	1987	Arriva Cymru, 1999

1973-1983	Mercedes-Benz 609D	Reeve Burgess	B20F	1987	Southern Counties, 1998

1973	E63UKL	1975	E65XKE	1978	E57UKL	1981	E54UKL	1983	E56UKL
1974	E64UKL	1977	E47UKL	1979	E44UKL	1982	E55UKL		

Allocations:-

Birkenhead (Laird Street)

MetroRider	7801	7802	7803	7804	7805	7806		
Dart	7487	7491	7496	7531	7532	7546	7547	7548
	7549	7550	7551	7552	7553	7554	7556	7557
	7558	7559	7560					
DAF SB220	6330	6331	6332	6333	6334			
Atlantean	3001	3002	3003	3004	3005	3008	3012	3013
	3041	3042	3043	3048	3049	3067	3068	3070
	3898	3905	3909	3921	3928	3930	3931	3947
	3950	3953	3974	3981	3990	3991		
Olympian	201	202	203	204	205	206	207	208
	209	210	212	213	214	215	222	223
	224	225	226	227	251	265	266	267
	268	269	270	271	272	273	274	275
	276	277	278	279	281	282	283	284
	285	286	287	288	289	290	291	292
	293	294	295	296	297	298	299	301
	302	303	304	305	306	307	308	361
	362	614	615	618	622	625	621	712
	3114	3159	3160	3161	3162	3163	3165	3166
	3166	3167	3168					

Bootle (Hawthorne Road)

Mercedes-Benz	160	166	167					
Dart	1111	1120	1121	1122	1123	1124	1150	1151
	1152	1171	1173	1176	1178	1179	1187	1191
	1192	1194	1195	1196	1997	1198	1212	1213
	1214	1216	1221	1225	1226	1227	1228	1229
	1230	1231	1232	1233	1234	1235	1236	1237
	1238	1239	1240	1241	1242	1243	1244	1245
	1246	1247	1248	1249	1250	1251	1252	1253
	1254	1255	1256	1257	1258	1259	1260	1261
	1262	1263	1264	1268	1270	1271	1314	1315
	1316	1317	1318	1319	1320	1321	1322	1323
	1324	2215	2216	2217	2218	2219	2221	2223
	2224	2226	2227	2228	2229	2231	2232	2233
	2234	2235	2236	2237	7659	7660	7661	7662
	7663	7664	7665	7667	7668	7669	7670	7671
	7672	7872	7873	7874	7875	7876	7877	7878
	7879							
Lance	1201	1202	1203	1204	1205	1206	1207	1208
	1209	1210	1291	1292	1293	1294	1295	1296
	1297	1298	1299					
Volvo B10B	6517	6518	6519	6520	6521	6522	6523	6525
	6526	6529	7530	6531	6561	6562	6563	6564
	6565	6566	6567	6568	6569	6570	6571	

MTL took delivery of large numbers of Volvo B10Bs in the mid 1990s and these carried Wright Endurance bodywork. Illustrating the type is 6619, N619CKA which shows the application of the new colours as it heads for St Helens town centre. *Cliff Beeton*

Haydock (Yew Tree Trading Estate, Kilbuck Lane)

Mercedes-Benz	108	109	175	176	177	178	179	180
	181	182	183	184				
Dart	7633							
Scania L	1006	1007	1008	1009	1010	1011	1012	1013
	1014	1015	1016	1017	1018	1019	1020	1021
	1022	1023	1024	1025	1026	1027	1028	1029
	1030	1031	1032	1033	1034			

Huyton (Wilson Road)

Dart	1171	1173	1176	1178	1179	1187	1191	1192
	1194	2201	2202	2203	2204	2207	2208	2209
	2211	2212	2213	2214	7533	7534	7535	7536
	7537	7538	7539	7540				
National	5294	5295	5296	6106	6134	6136	6208	6209
Lynx	1960	1961	1962					
Volvo B10B	6556	6557	6623	6901	6902	6903	6904	6095
	6906	6907	6908	6909	6910	6912	6913	
Titan	2148							
Olympian				3164				

Liverpool (Green Lane)

Neoplan	6402	6403	6404	6405	6406	6407	6408	6409
	6410	6411	6412	6413				
Volvo B10B	6572	6573	6575	6576	6577	6578	6579	6580
	6581	6582	6583	6584	6585	6599	6601	6603
Scania L113	5301	5302	5303	5304	5305	5306	5307	5308
	5309	5310	5311	5312	5313	5314	5315	5316
	5317	5318	5319	5320	5321	5322	5324	
Titan	2018	2220	2344	2376	2385	2570	2695	2741
Olympian	216	217	218	219	220	221	228	229
	230	241	242	243	244	245	246	247
	248	249	250	619	624			

Liverpool (Woodend Avenue, Speke)

Dart	2263	7411	7455	7543	7544	7545	7561	7562
	7563	7564	7565	7566	7567	7568	7569	7634
	7635	7636	7637	7638	7639	7640	7641	7642
	7643	7644	7645	7646	7647	7648	7649	7650
	7651	7652	7673	7674	7675	7676	7817	
DAF SB120	2416	2417	2418	2419	2422			
Volvo B6	7215	7219	7220	7221	7222	7223	7224	7225
	7226	7227	7231	7233	7234	7235	7236	7237
	7238	7241	7242	7243	7244			
Volvo B10B	6301	6302	6303	6533	6534	6535	6536	6537
	6538	6540	6541	6542	6543	6553	6554	6574
	6586	6587	6588	6589	6590	6591	6592	6593
	6594	6595	6596	6597	6598			
Atlantean	3014	3015	3016	3018	3019	3020	3024	3045
	3050	3051	3053	3056	3057	3058	3060	3061
	3062							
Titan	2121	2333	2338	2350	2353	2354	2355	2363
	2374	2400	2443	2449	2468			
Olympian	231	232	233	234	235	236	237	238
	239	240	252	253	254	255	256	257
	258	259	260	261	262	263	264	608
	612	613	701	702	703	704	705	706
	708	709	3172	3173	3174	3175		

Manchester (St Andrew's Square, Piccadilly)

Mercedes-Benz	110	111	112	115	191			
Falcon	381	382	383	386	387			
Dart	2238	2239	2241	2242	2243	2244	2246	2247
	2248	2249	2251	2252	2253	2254	2256	
Scania	1071	1072	1073	1076				
Dominator	630	632	633	634	635			
Olympian	3101	3102	3103	3104	3105	3106	3107	3108
	3109	3110	3112					

Runcorn (Beechwood)

Mercedes-Benz	121	122	125					
Dart	1157	1158	1159	1160	1161	1162	1163	1164
	1165	1166	1167	1168	1169	1170	1181	1185
	1186	1217	1218	1219	1220	1222	1223	1224
	1269							
Scania	1003	1005	1041	1042	1043	1044	1045	1046
	1047	1048	1049	1074	1075	1077	1078	1079
	1080	1081	1082	1083	1084			

St Helens (Jackson Street)

Mercedes-Benz	88	89	116	118	119			
Dart	1113	1125	1198	7520	7530	7541	7542	7612
	7613	7614	7615	7616	7617	7618	7619	7620
	7621	7622	7623					
Volvo B6	2801	2802	2803	2804	2805	2806	2607	2808
	2809	2811	2812	7201	7202	7203	7205	7206
	7209	7210	7211	7212	7213	7214	7216	7218
	7228	7229	7230	7232	7239	7240		
National	6036	6104	6111	6121	6140	6153	6156	6159
	6160	6161	6168	6170				
Volvo B10B	6501	6502	6503	6504	6505	6506	6508	6509
	6510	6511	6512	6513	6532	6602	6604	6605
	6606	6607	6608	6609	6610	6611	6612	6613
	6614	6615	6616	6617	6618	6619	6620	6621
	6622							
Atlantean	3031	3032	3033	3039	3040	3903	3904	3906
	3910	3911						

While many authorities try to encourage more use of public transport, Manchester Airport have introduced Skyline services that subsidise staff who use the bus and leave their car away from the airport. Special vinyls are carried by the vehicle allocated to the duties as shown on Alexander-bodied Dennis Dart 1310, R310CVU.

Metrobus	3801	3802	3803	3804	3805	3806	3807	3808
	3809	3810	3811	3812	3813	3814	3815	3816
	3817	3818	3819	3820	3821	3822	3823	3824
	3825	3826	3827	3828				

Skelmersdale (Neverstitch Road)

Mercedes-Benz	52	59	124	126	128	170	171	172
	173	193						
Dart	1112	1114	1115	1153	1154	1155	1156	1193
	1211	1215	1273	1274	1275	1276	1277	1278
	1279	1280	1281	1282	1285	1300		
Scania L	1035	1036	1037	1038	1039	1040	1050	1051
	1052	1053	1054	1055	1056	1057	1058	1059
	1060	1061						
Volvo Citybus	646	647	650	651	652	653	695	699
	785							

Southport (Canning Road)

Dart	6248	6249	6250	6251	7624	7625	7626	7627
	7628	7629	7630	7631	7632	7653	7654	7655
	7656	7657	7658					
Volvo B6	2813	2814	2815	2816	2817	2818	2819	2821
	2822	7204	7208	7217				
Volvo B10B	6507	6514	6515	6516	6524	6527	6528	6544
	6545	6546	6547	6548	6549	6550	6551	6552
	6558	6559						
Atlantean	3036	3977	3978	3979	3980	3982	3983	3984
	3985							
Atlantean Open-top	3449	3524	3551	3612				
Volvo Citybus	3671	3673	3674	3675	3676	3677	3679	3680
	3682							

Warrington (Athlone Road)

Mercedes-Benz	61	64	65	123	137	150		
Dart	1135	1138	1139	1140	1141	1142	1143	1144
	1145	1146	1148	1149	1172	1174	1175	1177
	1180	1182	1183	1184	1188	1189	1190	1199
Lynx	380							
Volvo Citybus	778	779	786					
Olympian	604	607	654	656	658	661	662	668

Wythenshawe (Grebba Road)

Mercedes-Benz	60	120	143	144	145	146	147	148
	149	158	159	161	162	163	168	169
Dart	1265	1266	1267	1301	1302	1303	1304	1305
	1306	1307	1308	1309	1310	1311	1312	1313
	1332	1333	1334	1335				
Falcon	384	385	388	392	393	394	395	

Unallocated -

Mercedes-Benz	70	77	78	138	141	7946	7952	
Dart	2257	2258	2259	2261	2262	2264		
National	6101	6102	6110	6116	6131	6151	6157	6158
	6161	6204						
DAF SB220	1402	1403	1404	1405	1406	1407	1408	1409
	1410	1411	1412	1413	1414			
Volvo B10M	787	788						
Atlantean	3030	3034	3035	3038	3044	3046	3047	3069
	3915	3948	3976	3986	3987	3989		
Titan	2009	2017	2148	2354				
Olympian	623							
Driving School	3052	3919	3920	3956	6125	6129		

Other vehicles in disposal pool.

1332, T62JBA is one of four Mini Pointer Darts acquired with the operations of Nova Scotia of Winsford in 2000. It is seen on lay-over in Stockport bus station having performed on local service 324.
Cliff Beeton

Gillmoss Buses

The vehicles listed below are being sold along with the Gillmoss Depot. As we close for press It has been announced that the Go-Ahead Group are preferred bidders.

309-337
Volvo Olympian YN2RV18Z4   Northern Counties Palatine II   B47/30F   1998

309	R309WVR	314	R314WVR	322	R322WVR	329	R329WVR	334	R334WVR
310	R310WVR	315	R315WVR	324	R324WVR	330	R330WVR	335	R335WVR
311	R311WVR	317	R317WVR	326	R326WVR	331	R331WVR	336	R336WVR
312	R312WVR	319	R319WVR	327	R327WVR	332	R332WVR	337	R337WVR
313	R313WVR	321	R321WVR							

2011-2177
Leyland Titan TNLXB2RRSp   Park Royal   B44/30F   1979-80   London Buses, 1992-94

2011	CUL211V	2044	WYV44T	2065	WYV65T	2116	CUL116V	2154	CUL154V
2032	EYE232V	2045	WYV45T	2070	WYV70T	2122	CUL122V	2156	CUL156V
2034	EYE234V	2046	WYV46T	2101	CUL101V	2134	CUL134V	2159	CUL159V
2039	EYE239V	2047	EYE247V	2109	CUL109V	2147	CUL147V	2177	CUL177V

2255-2259
Leyland Titan TNLXB2RR   Leyland (Park Royal kits)   B44/30F   1980-81   London Buses, 1992-93

| 2255 | GYE255W | 2256 | GYE256W | 2257 | GYE257W | 2259 | GYE259W |

2269-2391
Leyland Titan TNLXB2RR   Leyland   B44/30F   1980-82   London Buses, 1992-94

2269	GYE269W	2301	KYN301X	2316	KYN316X	2339	KYN339X	2365	KYN365X
2276	GYE276W	2304	KYN304X	2332	KYN332X	2347	KYN347X	2389	KYN389X
2278	GYE278W	2315	KYN315X	2337	KYN337X	2351	KYN351X	2391	KYN391X
2293	KYN293X								

2430-2656
Leyland Titan TNLXB2RR   Leyland   B44/30F   1982   London Buses, 1992-94

2430	KYN430X	2464	KYN464X	2499	KYN499X	2599	NUW599Y	2638	NUW638Y
2431	KYN431X	2472	KYN472X	2509	KYN509X	2612	NUW612Y	2655	NUW655Y
2450	KYN450X	2489	KYN489X	2528	KYN528X	2628	NUW628Y	2656	NUW656Y
2463	KYN463X	2494	KYN494X	2561	NUW561Y				

Following the acquisition of MTL by Arriva the company offered the authorities the sale of the Gillmoss depot to allow them to retain the remaining MTL fleet. The vehicles involved in the sale were identified with none being painted in Arriva colours. Shown here is T601JBA, the 10.8-metre Dart and one of those based at the depot.
Cliff Beeton

2682-2884		Leyland Titan TNLXB2RR*	Leyland		B44/30F	1983	London Buses, 1992-94	
2682 OHV682Y	**2703** OHV703Y	**2730** OHV730Y		**2746** OHV746Y		**2754** OHV754Y		
2692 OHV692Y	**2726** OHV726Y	**2733** OHV733Y		**2753** OHV753Y		**2884** A884SUL		
2698 OHV698Y								

3338 ?	Leyland Olympian ONLXB/1RH	Northern Counties	B43/30F	19	?, 2000
3339 ?	Leyland Olympian ONLXB/1RH	Northern Counties	B43/30F	19	?, 2000
3341 ?	Leyland Olympian ONLXB/1RH	Northern Counties	B43/30F	19	?, 2000
6169 CKB169X	Leyland National 2 NL116AL11/1R		B49F		

7245-7250		Volvo B6-9.9M		Plaxton Pointer		B38F	1994	
7245 L245TKA	**7247** L247TKA	**7248** L248TKA		**7249** L249TKA		**7250** L250TKA		
7246 L246TKA								

7301 M301YBG	Neoplan N4009	Neoplan	N21F	1995
7302 M302YBG	Neoplan N4009	Neoplan	N21F	1995
7303 M303YBG	Neoplan N4009	Neoplan	N21F	1995
7601 T601JBA	Dennis Dart SLF 10.8	Marshall Capital	N40F	1999

7602-7607		Dennis Dart SLF 8.9		Marshall Capital		N28F	1999	
7602 T602JBA	**7604** T604JBA	**7605** T605JBA		**7606** T606JBA		**7607** T607JBA		
7603 T603JBA								

7608 T608JBA	Dennis Dart SLF 10.2	Marshall Capital	N36F	1999
7609 T609JBA	Dennis Dart SLF 10.2	Marshall Capital	N36F	1999
7610 T610JBA	Dennis Dart SLF 10.2	Marshall Capital	N36F	1999
7611 T611JBA	Dennis Dart SLF 10.2	Marshall Capital	N36F	1999

7810 L9810TFY	Optare MetroRider	Optare	B17F	1994
7811 N811CKA	Optare MetroRider	Optare	B17F	1995

Livery: former MTL maroon and cream

Twenty-two Northern Counties-bodied Olympians from 1998 are based at Gillmoss and balance the ageing Leyland Titans purchased from London Buses in the early 1990s. Seen in the district with Arriva names is 309, R309WVR.
Cliff Beeton

ARROWEBROOK COACHES

A G Parsons, 2 Dingwall Drive, Greasby, Merseyside, L49 1SG

PTX466Y	Bedford YMP	Duple Dominant IV	C35F	1982	Spratt, Wreningham, 1986
882MMY	DAF MB200DKTL600	Plaxton Paramount 3500	C49FT	1983	Cooper, Killamarsh, 1989
KOI4484	DAF MB200DKFL600	Van Hool Alizée	C51FT	1984	Griffiths, Walkden, 1998
B231RRU	DAF SB2305DHS585	Plaxton Paramount 3200 II	C53F	1985	Priory Coaches, Gosport, 1990
D670SEM	Renault-Dodge S56	Northern Counties	B22F	1986	Merseybus, 1993
D672SEM	Renault-Dodge S56	Northern Counties	B22F	1986	Merseybus, 1993
D923PRJ	Freight Rover Sherpa	Made-to-Measure	M16	1987	
E463ANC	Mercedes-Benz 609D	Made-to-Measure	C24F	1988	
F368CHE	Scania K112CRB	Van Hool Alizée	C53FT	1988	Elite, Stockport, 1992
F620HGO	DAF MB230LB615	Van Hool Alizée	C52FT	1989	London Coaches, 1996
RIB5092	DAF SB3000DKV601	Van Hool Alizée	C51FT	1990	Bowers, Chapel-en-le-Frith, 1997
G227NCW	DAF MB230LT615	Van Hool Alizée	C49FT	1990	Robinsons, Great Harwood, 1999
G655EVN	CVE Omni	CVE	BC23F	1990	
G900CRW	Volvo B10M-60	Plaxton Paramount 3500 III	C57F	1990	Harry Shaw, 1994
H434DVM	Mercedes-Benz 609D	Made-to-Measure	C24F	1990	
S620KUT	Toyota Coaster BB50R	Caetano Optimo IV	C21F	1998	
S760RNE	Dennis Dart SLF	Plaxton MPD	N29F	1999	

Previous Registrations:

882MMY	VWB788Y	KOI4484	A67OWY	RIB5092	G951KJX, XJF386

Livery: White and green
Depot: Wervin Road, Croughton

Chester bus station is the location for this view of Arrowebrook Coaches' S760RNE, a Mini Pointer Dart. In addition to route 64, the company provide several vehicles for school contract work. *Andy Jarosz*

AVON COACHES

Avon Bus & Coach Co, 10 Brook Way, Birkenhead, CH43 3DT

Reg	Type	Body	Seating	Year	History
BTX206T	Leyland Titan TNLXB/1RF	Park Royal	B43/29F	1978	Red & White, 1998
CUL91V	Leyland Titan TNLXB/2RRSp	Park Royal	B44/30F	1980	London Buses, 1994
KYV482X	Leyland Titan TNLXB/2RR	Leyland	B44/24D	1982	Metroline, 1997
A209EHN	Dennis Dominator DDA167	Northern Counties	B43/31F	1983	Stagecoach Transit, 1999
A887SYE	Leyland Titan TNLXB/2RR	Leyland	B44/26D	1983	Blue Triangle, Rainham, 1999
A898SYE	Leyland Titan TNLXB/2RR	Leyland	B44/26D	1983	Blue Triangle, Rainham, 1999
C750OCN	MCW Metrobus DR102/55	MCW	B46/31F	1986	Go-Ahead North East, 2000
C776OCN	MCW Metrobus DR102/55	MCW	B46/31F	1986	Go-Ahead North East, 2000
E133SAT	Dennis Dominator DDA1014	East Lancashire	B45/31F	1987	Stagecoach Transit, 1999
E136SAT	Dennis Dominator DDA1014	East Lancashire	B45/31F	1987	Stagecoach Transit, 1999
E138SAT	Dennis Dominator DDA1014	East Lancashire	B45/31F	1987	Stagecoach Transit, 1999
E601HTF	MCW MetroRider MF158/8	MCW	B33F	1988	Reading Buses, 1999
P402KAV	Marshall Minibus	Marshall MM	N29F	1996	Go-Ahead London, 2000
P404KAV	Marshall Minibus	Marshall MM	N29F	1996	Go-Ahead London, 2000
P409KAV	Marshall Minibus	Marshall MM	N29F	1996	Go-Ahead London, 2000
R104VLX	Marshall Minibus	Marshall MM	N29F	1998	First Centrewest, 2000
R54OCK	Dennis Dart SLF	East Lancashire Spryte	N35F	1997	
S54NCW	Dennis Dart SLF	East Lancashire Spryte	N37F	1999	

Previous Registrations:
BTX206T   WDA1T

Livery: Cream and blue
Depots: North Cheshire Industrial Estate, Prenton, Birkenhead and Church Street, Bootle

The latest vehicles new to Avon Coaches are two Dennis Darts with East Lancashire Spryte bodies. Showing the route-branding carried for their duties is R54OCK. *Cliff Beeton*

BAKERS

Guideissue Ltd, Spring Grove, Congleton Road, Biddulph, Stoke-on-Trent, ST8 7RQ

1	9530RU	Volvo B10M-62	Plaxton Premiére 350	C49FT	1999	
2	5658RU	Volvo B10M-62	Plaxton Premiére 350	C49FT	1999	
3	7092RU	Volvo B10M-62	Plaxton Panther	C53F	2000	
4	3601RU	Volvo B10M-62	Plaxton Premiére 320	C57F	1996	
5	4614RU	Volvo B10M-61	Plaxton Paramount 3200 III	C53F	1987	Excelsior, Bournemouth, 1990
6	3275RU	Volvo B10M-62	Plaxton Premiére 350	C53F	2000	
7	1513RU	Volvo B10M-62	Plaxton Premiére 320	C57F	1996	
8	8150RU	Volvo B10M-62	Plaxton Premiére 320	C53F	2000	
9	1497RU	Volvo B10M-62	Plaxton Premiére 320	C53F	2000	
10	5946RU	Volvo B10M-60	Van Hool Alizée H	C49FT	1992	Shearings, 1999
11	9995RU	Volvo B10M-60	Van Hool Alizée H	C49FT	1992	Shearings, 1999
12	8399RU	Volvo B10M-60	Van Hool Alizée H	C49FT	1992	Shearings, 1999
15	3353RU	Volvo B10M-62	Plaxton Premiére 320	C49FT	1994	Excelsior, 1996
17	1879RU	Volvo B10M-62	Plaxton Premiére 320	C49FT	1994	Excelsior, 1996
18	3471RU	Mercedes-Benz 412D	Olympus	M16	2000	
19	6577RU	Mercedes-Benz 410D	Autobus Classique	M16	1992	
20	3102RU	Mercedes-Benz Vario O814	Autobus Nouvelle 2	BC24F	1998	
21	G689OHE	Mercedes-Benz 811D	Reeve Burgess Beaver	B20FL	1990	Tellings Golden Miller, Byfleet, 2000
22	G690OHE	Mercedes-Benz 811D	Reeve Burgess Beaver	B20FL	1990	Tellings Golden Miller, Byfleet, 2000
23	R578GDS	Mercedes-Benz Vario O810	Plaxton Beaver 2	B31F	1997	Superior Travel, Greenock, 1999
24	J206KTT	Mercedes-Benz 709D	Reeve Burgess Beaver	B25F	1991	Plymouth Citybus, 1999
25	R114DNV	Iveco TurboDaily 59.12	Marshall	B27F	1997	MK Metro, 1999
26	R115DNV	Iveco TurboDaily 59.12	Marshall	B27F	1997	MK Metro, 1999

Bakers recently joined the Status Bus and Coach Group and some vehicles from other members of the group, such as MK Metro and Tellings, have found a home here. The coach fleet have used a selection of xxxxRU index plates for many years. New in 1996 for the coaching fleet, 4, 3601RU, is seen in the simple yet attractive colours applied to the Plaxton Premiére 320. *Cliff Beeton*

Yellow and blue colours are carried by the minibus fleet. Seen working route 823 to Leek is Mercedes-Benz Vario 29, T129XVT which carries a Plaxton Beaver body. *Cliff Beeton*

27	9423RU	Mercedes-Benz 811D	Optare StarRider	BC29F	1989
28	5621RU	Mercedes-Benz 609D	Whittaker Europa	BC21F	1999
29	T129XVT	Mercedes-Benz Vario O810	Plaxton Beaver 2	B31F	1999
30	3093RU	Volvo B10M-62	Plaxton Premiére 350	C49FT	1997
31	7025RU	Volvo B10M-62	Plaxton Premiére 350	C49FT	1997
32	6280RU	Volvo B10M-62	Plaxton Premiére 350	C49FT	1997
33	3563RU	Volvo B10M-62	Plaxton Premiére 350	C37FT	1997
34	3566RU	Volvo B10M-62	Plaxton Premiére 350	C49FT	1999
35	8830RU	Mercedes-Benz 811D	Optare StarRider	BC29F	1992

Previous registrations

1497RU	From new	5658RU	From new
1513RU	From new	5946RU	J217NNC
1879RU	XEL55S, L327ERU	6280RU	From new
3093RU	From new	6577RU	From new
3102RU	From new	7025RU	From new
3275RU	From new	7092RU	From new
3353RU	XEL6S, L326ERU	8150RU	From new
3471RU	From new	8399RU	J218NNC
3563RU	From new	8830RU	From new
3566RU	From new	9423RU	From new
3601RU	From new	9530RU	From new
4614RU	D255HFX, 4614RU, D780FVT	9595RU	D126VPR
5621RU	G429NET	9995RU	J220NNC

Livery: Duo green or white with green relief (coaches), yellow and blue (buses)
Depots: Wallis Street, Biddulph and Highway Garage, Rudyard
Note: Bakers is a Status Bus and Coach Group company

BENNETT'S TRAVEL

Bennett's Travel Cranberry Ltd, Cranberry, Cotes Heath, Staffs, ST21 6SQ

ECS889V	Leyland Fleetline FE30AGR	Northern Counties	B44/31F	1979	Derby, 1995
DUI4760	Leyland Leopard PSU5C/4R	Plaxton Supreme III	C57F	1978	Sutton, Hutton Roof, 1996
AFH198T	Leyland Leopard PSU5C/4R	Duple Dominant II	C57F	1979	Oakley Coaches, 1989
BNB242T	Leyland Leopard PSU5C/4R	Duple Dominant II	C50F	1979	Ribble, 1991
FGC309T	Leyland Leopard PSU5C/4R	Plaxton Supreme III	C57F	1978	Plimmer, Cheadle, 1997
LHA452V	Ford R1114	Duple Dominant II	C53F	1980	Central, Walsall, 1986
UUY600V	Leyland Leopard PSU3E/4R	Duple Dominant II	C53F	1980	Barry Raybould, Walsall, 1996
XJG812V	Leyland Leopard PSU5C/4R	Duple Dominant II	C53F	1980	Lucas, Kingsley, 1994
GCS47V	Leyland Leopard PSU3E/4R	Alexander AY	B53F	1980	Stagecoach Western, 2000
GCS53V	Leyland Leopard PSU3E/4R	Alexander AY	B53F	1980	Stagecoach Western, 2000
MAB181X	Bedford YNT	Duple Dominant IV Express	C53F	1982	Hayton's, Burnage, 1996
RJR247Y	Bedford YNT	Duple Dominant III Express	B53F	1982	South Mimms Coaches, 1996
FKK847Y	MCW Metroliner CR126	MCW	B47F	1983	Fitzgerald, Sheffield, 1999
YPD108Y	Leyland Tiger TRCTL11/2R	Duple Dominant II Express	C53F	1983	Stanley Gath, Thornhill Lees, 1998
5457NF	Bedford YNT	Wright Contour	C48FT	1983	Patel, Leicester, 1992
A754DUY	Bedford YNT	Wright Contour	C53F	1984	Eltenton, Nuneaton, 1992
A309KDD	Quest D	Locomotors	BC30FL	1984	non pcv, 1995
B224WEU	Leyland Tiger TRCTL11/3RH	Duple Laser 2	C57F	1984	Stonehouse Coaches, 1995
NIB3264	Leyland Royal Tiger RT	Leyland Doyen	C47FT	1984	DA Travel, Blurton, 1994
D961UDY	Mercedes-Benz L608D	Reeve Burgess	B20F	1986	Crosville Wales, 1995
D148VRP	Mercedes-Benz L608D	Alexander AM	BC19F	1986	Buckinghamshire Road Car, 1996
E67NVT	Leyland Royal Tiger RT	Leyland Doyen	C53FT	1987	Daybird, Roadline, Killamarsh, 1998
SDZ6287	Volvo B10M-60	Plaxton Paramount 3500 III	C51F	1989	Capitol, Cwmbran, 1998
M562TJL	Mercedes-Benz 814D	Autobus Classique	C33F	1995	Perruzza, Kendal, 1999
N295DWE	Mercedes-Benz 811D	Mellor	B31F	1996	Phoenix, Blackpool, 1998
T48JBA	Dennis Dart SLF	Plaxton MPD	N29F	1999	

Previous registrations:

5457NF	XNT141Y, URH341, UAB586Y	MAB181X	PNT844X, LSV548
A754DUY	RPP514	NIB3264	B289AMG
DUI4760	BGJ315S	SDZ6287	G118XRE
E67NVT	E42JRF, 2335PL	YPD108Y	YPD108Y, WRC751
FKK847Y	FKK847Y, ESU247		

Livery: Cream and dark brown

Bennett's operate a rare Quest D which was designed as a replacement for the Ford PCV R-series chassis. Making A309KDD doubly interesting is that it carries Locomotors bodywork, a firm who mostly specialised in airside related vehicles.
David Hall

BENNETT'S of WARRINGTON

B A Bennett & D B Bennett, The Garage, Athlone Road, Warrington, WA2 8JJ

SND290X	Leyland Leopard PSU5D/4R	Duple Dominant IV	C53F	1981	Tansey, Warrington, 2000
TXI8757	Volvo B10M-61	Jonckheere Jubilee P90	C49/9FT	1983	ABC, Leicester, 1999
MIL2654	DAF MB230DKFL615	Jonckheere Jubilee	C51FT	1987	Daisy, Broughton, 1998
E607ARJ	Peugeot-Talbot Freeway	Talbot	B14F	1988	Flanagan, Grappenhall, 1999
G34UKP	Renault Master T35	Oatia	M16	1990	Locations Transport, Withington, '99
H968LSF	Mercedes-Benz 408D	Wright Wishaw	M15L	1990	Ferguson, East Whitburn, 1999
J626BWB	Talbot Freeway	TBP	B16F	1991	Derbyshire CC, 2000
J918LEM	Volvo B10M-60	Plaxton Expressliner	C46FT	1991	Moore, Davenport, 1997
K19AMB	Volvo B10M-60	Plaxton Premiére 350	C50FT	1992	Aintree Coachline, 2000
M886SKU	LDV 400	Autobus Classique	M16	1994	Hilton, Newton-le-Willows, 2000

Previous Registrations:

MIL2654	E222GNV	TXI8757	MRP837Y, GSV957, LHO942Y

Livery: White and blue or various

Bennett's of Warrington operate J626BWB, a Talbot Freeway with TBP tri-axle bodywork, which is seen outside its base in Warrington. The Freeway is frequently found with social services operators, including local authorities, as a result of the easy access for wheelchairs through double rear doors where a ramp, not a lift, is fitted. *Andy Jarosz*

BETTABUS

J Rowlands, Cartmel Grange Lane, Gateacre, Liverpool, L25 5JZ

ANA553Y	Leyland Atlantean AN68D/1R	Northern Counties	B43/32F	1982	McColl, Balloch, 2000
A698HNB	Leyland Atlantean AN68D/1R	Northern Counties	B43/32F	1984	Liverpool Motor Services, 2000

Livery: Orange and brown
Depot: Weaver Industrial Estate, Blackburne Street, Garston

Bettabus operates two Leyland Atlanteans new to Greater Manchester Transport on route 13. Pictured complete with GMS fleet numbers and colours is ANA553Y. *Cliff Beeton*

BOSTOCK'S

Bostocks Coaches Ltd, Spragg Street Garage, Congleton, Cheshire, CW12 1QH

BRC681T	Leyland Atlantean AN68A/1R	Northern Counties	B47/31D	1979	Holmeswood Coaches, 1998
SMB601V	Leyland Leopard PSU5D/5R	Duple Dominant II	C57F	1980	
LHE254W	Leyland Leopard PSU5D/4R	Plaxton Supreme IV	C57F	1981	Holmeswood Coaches, 1998
BCA126W	Leyland Tiger TRCTL11/3R	Duple Dominant II	C57F	1981	
DCA522X	Bedford YMQ	Plaxton Supreme IV	C45F	1982	
KLG106Y	Bedford YMP	Plaxton Supreme V	C45F	1982	
LCA183Y	Volvo B10M-61	Duple Goldliner IV	C49FT	1983	
RIB8747	Leyland Olympian ONTL11/2R	Eastern Coach Works	C45/27F	1984	Oare's of Holywell, 1998
LIB6438	Leyland Tiger TRCLXCT/3R	Plaxton Paramount 3500 II	C53F	1985	Mayne, Manchester, 1999
LIB6440	Leyland Tiger TRCLXCT/3R	Plaxton Paramount 3500 II	C53F	1985	Mayne, Manchester, 1999
C120PNV	Leyland Tiger TRCTL11/3RZ	Plaxton Paramount 3200 II E	C53F	1986	
ALZ6244	Scania K112CRB	Van Hool Alizée H	C53F	1987	Hilton, Newton-le-Willows, 2000
HOI7544	Scania K112CRB	Van Hool Alizée DH	C51FT	1987	LB Hackney, 2000
D438TMB	Bedford YNV Venturer (Cum)	Duple 320	C57F	1987	
F773GNA	Leyland Tiger TRCTL11/3ARZ	Plaxton Paramount 3200 III	C53F	1989	Andrews, Groby, 2000
F523UVW	Volvo B10M-61	Plaxton Paramount 3200 III	C53F	1989	Arriva The Shires, 2000
F572UPB	Volvo B10M-61	Plaxton Paramount 3200 III	C53F	1989	Arriva The Shires, 2000
NIL5675	Volvo B10M-60	Plaxton Paramount 3500 III	C53F	1989	Wallace Arnold, 1993
152ENM	Volvo B10M-60	Plaxton Paramount 3500 III	C49FT	1990	Holmeswood Coaches, 2000
H2HWD	Scania K113TRB	Van Hool Astrobel	C57/14FT	1990	Holmeswood Coaches, 2000
J91JFR	Dennis Javelin 12SDA2129	Plaxton Paramount 3200 III	C57F	1991	Reynolds Diplomat, Bushey, 2000
J287NNC	Scania K93CRB	Plaxton Premiére 320	C57F	1992	Holmeswood Coaches, 1998
J288NNC	Scania K93CRB	Plaxton Premiére 320	C57F	1992	Holmeswood Coaches, 1998
J220XKY	Scania K93CRB	Van Hool Alizée H	C55F	1992	Holmeswood Coaches, 1999
ESK807	Volvo B10M-60	Van Hool Alizée	C49FT	1993	Holmeswood Coaches, 2000
L388YNV	Dennis Javelin 12SDA2131	Plaxton Premiére 320	C57F	1994	Country Lion, Northampton, 2000
L6HWD	Dennis Javelin 10SDA2139	Berkhof Excellence 1000L	C39FT	1994	Holmeswood Coaches, 2000
M31KAX	Mercedes-Benz 711D	Autobus Classique	C25F	1994	Roberts, Maerdy, 2000
M848LTX	Toyota Coaster HZB50R	Caetano Optimo III	C21F	1995	Capitol, Cwmbran, 1998
M43HSU	Volvo B10M-62	Van Hool Alizée HE	C49FT	1995	Park's of Hamilton,1998
M335KRY	Volvo B10M-62	Jonckheere Deauville P599	C51FT	1995	Chambers, Moneymore, 1999
N784ORV	Dennis Javelin GX 12SDA2134	Caetano Algarve 2	C51FT	1995	Holmeswood Coaches, 2000
N910DWJ	Dennis Javelin 10SDA2163	Berkhof Excellence 1000L	C39FT	1996	Buddens, Romsey, 1998
N897KFA	Dennis Javelin GX 12SDA2159	Plaxton Premiére 350	C49FT	1996	Happy Days, Woodseaves, 2000
N899KFA	Dennis Javelin GX 12SDA2159	Plaxton Premiére 350	C53FT	1996	Happy Days, Woodseaves, 2000
R7BOS	Scania K113CRB	Van Hool Alizée HE	C49FT	1997	Holmeswood Coaches, 2000
S9BOS	MAN 11.220 HOCL-R	Berkhof Axial 30	C35F	1998	
S8BOS	Dennis Javelin 10m	Berkhof Axial 50	C39FT	1999	

Special event vehicle

765JTU	Bedford SB1	Plaxton Consort IV	C41F	1960	

Previous Registrations:

152ENM	G802GPG, ESK807, G881RRN	J91JFR	J91JFR, VJI9414
ALZ6244	D38GAJ	L388YNV	A8CLN
ESK807	K816HUM	LIB6438	C348YBA
F523UVW	F451PSL, NXI9006	LIB6440	C426YBA
F572UPB	F452PSL, NXI9007	M43HSU	LSK514
F773GNA	F773GNA, MEY892	NIL5675	F447DUG
HOI7544	E125BRG, TTC86, A15LBH, E656LLR	R7BOS	R5HWD
H2HWD	H134ACU, KSU464, H681FCU, H10WLE, H163POF	RIB8747	A105FPL

Livery: Maroon (buses & some coaches); white, newer coaches.
Note: This operator is in a group headed by Holmeswood Coaches.

Bostocks Coaches became part of the Holmeswood Coaches group in 1998, since when all but eight vehicles in the fleet have been replaced. Representing the fleet is RIB8747, a Leyland Olympian with the Eastern Coach Works body style developed to meet NBC's need for interurban service vehicles. The type mostly entered service on city commuter routes. Recent single-deck arrivals carry a base livery of white with vinyls. ESK807 is a Volvo B10M with Van Hool Alizée bodywork. *Cliff Beeton*

BOWKER BUS & COACH

G A Bowker, 52 Cranberry Road, Alsager, Stoke-on-Trent, ST7 2LE

MPY908P	Volvo B58-61	Plaxton Supreme III	C53F	1976	Ashall, Manchester, 1997
IIL6436	AEC Reliance 6U2R	Plaxton Supreme III	C53F	1977	Gretton, Peterborough, 1997
IIJ145	Leyland Leopard PSU3C/4R	Plaxton Supreme III Express	C53F	1977	Ashall, Manchester, 1998
XWX182S	Leyland Leopard PSU3E/4R	Duple Dominant II	C53F	1978	Ashall, Manchester, 1998
EEC909W	Iveco 60F10	Harwin	C25F	1981	Bailey, Blackburn, 1999
TOS799X	Leyland Leopard PSU3F/5R	Plaxton Supreme V	C53F	1982	Ashall, Manchester, 1998
WRA688Y	Leyland Leopard PSU5D/4R	Duple Dominant IV	C53F	1982	Ashall, Manchester, 1998

Previous Registrations

EEC909W	EEC909W, GSK305	IIL6436	SPC722R, RNC478, SFL460R
IIJ145	SOJ702S	TOS799X	LTY559X, MNX30S

Livery: Maroon and cream
Depots: Lawton Hall Estate, Church Lawton and Fairlands, Kidsgrove.

XWX182S is seen here representing Bowkers Bus & Coach. This Leyland Leopard was new to Wallace Arnold and was one of several Duple Dominant II bodies supplied to the tour operator alongside Plaxton Supremes. It operated initially as a 49-seater until the start of the 1981 season when it reverted to 53. It was sold in 1983.
Cliff Beeton

BOYDONS

DR DM RM & GM Boydon, Winkhill Filling Station, Winkhill, Leek, ST13 7PP

SIB7882	AEC Reliance 6U3ZR	Plaxton Supreme IV	C57F	1979	George, Hare Street, 1988
GSU7T	AEC Reliance 6U3ZR	Plaxton Supreme IV	C51F	1979	Flear Coaches, Middlesbrough, 1985
NIL7716	AEC Reliance 6U3ZR	Plaxton Supreme IV Express	C53F	1979	Eynons, Trimsaran, 1986
NIL8905	AEC Reliance 6U3ZR	Plaxton Supreme IV	C57F	1979	Grange, East Ham, 1990
SIB3053	AEC Reliance 6U3ZR	Plaxton Supreme IV	C53F	1980	Dudley Coachways, 1993
4195PX	Leyland Tiger TRCTL11/3R	Plaxton Paramount 3500	C49FT	1982	Cadishead Coaches, 1993
TIB2865	Leyland Tiger TRCTL11/3R	Plaxton Paramount 3200	C57F	1982	Walls of Wigan, 1993
MIB4964	Leyland Tiger TRCTL11/3R	Plaxton Paramount 3500	C50F	1983	Bordian, Darwen, 1989
VIB6165	Leyland Tiger TRCTL11/3R	Plaxton Paramount 3500	C53F	1983	Gelsthorpe, Mansfield, 1995
GIL1909	Leyland Tiger TRCTL11/3R	Plaxton Paramount 3200	C57F	1984	Britannia, Telford, 1999
556DHO	DAF SB2300DHTD585	Plaxton Paramount 3200	C53FT	1984	Rons, Ashington, 2000
RIB8034	Mercedes-Benz L608D	Mellor	C21F	1985	Booth, Bury, 1992
TOI6161	Toyota Coaster HB31R	Caetano Optimo	C18F	1989	Elite, Stockport, 1999
RIL7382	Mercedes-Benz 811D	Carlyle C16	B33F	1990	Roseville, Newcastle-u-Lyme, 2000

Previous Registrations:

556DHO	B697VCX	RIL7382	G110TND
4195PX	WBV540Y	SIB3053	PRO445W
GIL1909	A834PPP	SIB7882	EBM446T
MIB4964	THL293Y	TIB2865	CLD886Y
NIL7716	XBX831T	TOI6161	G946VBC
NIL8905	EBM449T	VIB6165	BAJ632Y, 540CCY, SWN885Y
RIB8034	C612ADB		

Livery: White, red, yellow and orange.

The Boydons fleet has developed from being mostly AEC-based through to Leyland Tiger. All full-size coaces now carry Plaxton bodywork. Illustrating the livery is Paramount 3500 VIB6165. *Cliff Beeton*

C M T

CMT Buses - ABC Buses

C & M Travel, D3 Liver Industrial Estate, Long Lane, Aintree, Liverpool, L4 7ES

1002	PTT79R	Leyland National 11351A/1R	B50F	1976	Wingates Tours, Melling, 1993
1036	HSC110T	Leyland National 11351A/1R	B49F	1978	Wigan Bus Company, 1994
1037	HSC113T	Leyland National 11351A/1R	B49F	1978	Wigan Bus Company, 1994
1071	NPK249R	Leyland National 10351A/1R	B41F	1976	County, 1993
1072	SPC266R	Leyland National 10351A/1R	B41F	1977	County, 1993
1073	SPC284R	Leyland National 10351A/1R	B41F	1977	County, 1993
1074	SPC286R	Leyland National 10351A/1R	B41F	1977	County, 1993
1075	SPC291R	Leyland National 10351A/1R	B41F	1977	County, 1993
1076	SPC278R	Leyland National 10351A/1R	B41F	1977	County, 1993
1077	SPC267R	Leyland National 10351A/1R	B41F	1977	County, 1993
1078	LPB222P	Leyland National 10351/1R	B41F	1976	County, 1993
1079	UPB309S	Leyland National 10351A/1R	B41F	1977	County, 1993
1080	UPB317S	Leyland National 10351A/1R	B41F	1977	County, 1993
1082	UPB308S	Leyland National 10351A/1R	B41F	1977	County, 1993
1091	ERP552T	Leyland National 11351A/1R	B49F	1979	United Counties, 1993
1092	ERP553T	Leyland National 11351A/1R	B49F	1979	United Counties, 1993
1094	KRP564V	Leyland National 11351A/1R	B47F	1979	United Counties, 1993
1095	MNH571V	Leyland National 11351A/1R	B49F	1979	United Counties, 1993
1096	MNH576V	Leyland National 11351A/1R	B49F	1979	United Counties, 1993
1097	PJT272R	Leyland National 11351A/1R	B49F	1977	Quickstep, 1994
1098	PEV695R	Leyland National 11351A/1R	B49F	1976	Quickstep, 1994

An extensive fleet of Leyland Nationals is progressively being replaced by new buses as well as the Leyland Lynx. Seen on route 86 is 2055, F204MBT. This is one of eleven Lynx acquired from Sovereign Bus in 2000 along with two from fellow Blazefield subsidiary Harrogate and District. *Phillip Stephenson*

The new Volvo buses delivered to CMT reflect the development of the low-floor models. From the 1997 build is 2029, R869LHG, which has a Volvo B10L chassis and a Wright Liberator body. It is seen in Walton returning to Liverpool centre on route 345. *Richard Godfrey*

2001	M647YLV	Volvo B10B	Wright Endurance	B49F	1995
2002	M648YLV	Volvo B10B	Wright Endurance	B49F	1995
2003	M649YLV	Volvo B10B	Wright Endurance	B49F	1995
2004	M650YLV	Volvo B10B	Wright Endurance	B49F	1995
2005	N652CHF	Dennis Dart 9.8SDL3054	Northern Counties Paladin	B40F	1995
2006	N653CHF	Dennis Dart 9.8SDL3054	Northern Counties Paladin	B40F	1995
2007	N654CHF	Dennis Dart 9.8SDL3054	Northern Counties Paladin	B40F	1995
2008	N655CHF	Dennis Dart 9.8SDL3054	Northern Counties Paladin	B40F	1995
2009	N656CHF	Dennis Dart 9.8SDL3054	Northern Counties Paladin	B40F	1995
2010	N657CHF	Dennis Dart 9.8SDL3054	Northern Counties Paladin	B40F	1995
2011	N658CHF	Dennis Dart 9.8SDL3054	Northern Counties Paladin	B40F	1995
2012	N659EKD	Volvo B10B	Wright Renown	B51F	1996
2013	N660EKD	Volvo B10B	Wright Renown	B51F	1996

2014-2025

| | Dennis Dart SLF | | Wright Crusader | | N36F | | 1997 | |

2014	P909YCW	2017	P912YCW	2020	P915YCW	2022	P917YCW	2024	P919YCW
2015	P910YCW	2018	P913YCW	2021	P916YCW	2023	P918YCW	2025	P920YCW
2016	P911YCW	2019	P914YCW						

2026-2035

| | Volvo B10L | | Wright Liberator | | N44F | | 1997-98 | |

| 2026 | R866LHG | 2028 | R868LHG | 2030 | R870LHG | 2032 | R872LHG | 2034 | R874LHG |
| 2027 | R867LHG | 2029 | R869LHG | 2031 | R871LHG | 2033 | R873LHG | 2035 | R875LHG |

2036-2045

| | Volvo B10BLE | | Wright Renown | | N44F | | 1998 | |

| 2036 | S447KCW | 2038 | S449KCW | 2040 | S451KCW | 2042 | S453KCW | 2044 | S455KCW |
| 2037 | S448KCW | 2039 | S450KCW | 2041 | S452KCW | 2043 | S454KCW | 2045 | S456KCW |

2046	F279AWW	Leyland Lynx LX112L10ZR1S	Leyland Lynx	B49F	1989	Arriva Yorkshire, 1999
2047	F296AWW	Leyland Lynx LX112L10ZR1S	Leyland Lynx	B49F	1989	Arriva Yorkshire, 1999
2048	F303AWW	Leyland Lynx LX112L10ZR1S	Leyland Lynx	B49F	1989	Arriva Yorkshire, 1999

2049	W465CRN	Volvo B10BLE	Wright Renown	N44F	2000	
2050	W466CRN	Volvo B10BLE	Wright Renown	N44F	2000	
2051	W467CRN	Volvo B10BLE	Wright Renown	N44F	2000	
2052	W468CRN	Volvo B10BLE	Wright Renown	N44F	2000	
2053	G202URO	Leyland Lynx LX2R11C15Z4S	Leyland Lynx	B49F	1989	Sovereign, 2000
2054	F203MBT	Leyland Lynx LX112TL11ZR1R	Leyland Lynx	B51F	1989	Sovereign, 2000
2055	F204MBT	Leyland Lynx LX112TL11ZR1R	Leyland Lynx	B51F	1989	Sovereign, 2000
2056	F205MBT	Leyland Lynx LX112TL11ZR1R	Leyland Lynx	B47F	1989	Sovereign, 2000
2057	F206MBT	Leyland Lynx LX112TL11ZR1R	Leyland Lynx	B51F	1989	Sovereign, 2000
2058	F207MBT	Leyland Lynx LX112TL11ZR1R	Leyland Lynx	B49F	1989	Sovereign, 2000
2059	F208MBT	Leyland Lynx LX112TL11ZR1R	Leyland Lynx	B51F	1989	Sovereign, 2000
2060	E324SWY	Leyland Lynx LX112LXCTZR1R	Leyland Lynx	B49F	1987	Harroigate & District, 2000
2061	E325SWY	Leyland Lynx LX112LXCTZR1R	Leyland Lynx	B49F	1987	Harroigate & District, 2000
2062	E840EUT	Leyland Lynx LX112TL11ZR1R	Leyland Lynx	B51F	1987	Sovereign, 2000
2063	F358JVS	Leyland Lynx LX112TL11ZR1R	Leyland Lynx	B49F	1988	Sovereign, 2000
2064	F359JVS	Leyland Lynx LX112TL11ZR1R	Leyland Lynx	B49F	1988	Sovereign, 2000
2065	E371YRO	Leyland Lynx LX112TL11ZR1R	Leyland Lynx	B51F	1987	Sovereign, 2000
6001	CBV305S	Leyland Atlantean AN68A/2R	East Lancashire	B50/36F	1977	ABC Travel, Ainsdale, 1999
6002	GFV151W	Leyland Atlantean AN68A/2R	East Lancashire	B50/36F	1981	ABC Travel, Ainsdale, 1999
6003	D6359WNU	DAF MB230DKFL615	Plaxton Paramount 3500 III	C53F	1987	ABC Travel, Ainsdale, 1999
6004	F354DVR	Ford Transit VE6	Mellor	B16F	1988	ABC Travel, Ainsdale, 1999
6005	J44ABC	Optare MetroRider MR01	Optare	B33F	1992	ABC Travel, Ainsdale, 1999
6006	J55ABC	Mercedes-Benz 709D	Alexander Sprint	BC25F	1991	ABC Travel, Ainsdale, 1999
6008	J800ABC	DAF SB220LC550	Optare Delta	B49F	1992	ABC Travel, Ainsdale, 1999
6009	K400ABC	Optare MetroRider MR01	Optare	B33F	1992	ABC Travel, Ainsdale, 1999
6013	L5ABC	Optare MetroRider MR09	Optare	B22F	1993	ABC Travel, Ainsdale, 1999
6014	L6ABC	Optare MetroRider MR09	Optare	B22F	1993	ABC Travel, Ainsdale, 1999
6015	L700ABC	DAF SB220LC550	Optare Delta	B49F	1994	ABC Travel, Ainsdale, 1999
6016	M7ABC	Optare MetroRider MR31	Optare	B24F	1995	ABC Travel, Ainsdale, 1999
6017	M77ABC	Optare MetroRider MR31	Optare	B24F	1995	ABC Travel, Ainsdale, 1999
6018	M777ABC	Optare MetroRider MR31	Optare	B24F	1995	ABC Travel, Ainsdale, 1999
6019	N600ABC	DAF SB220LC550	Northern Counties Paladin	B49F	1996	ABC Travel, Ainsdale, 1999
6020	N66ABC	Mercedes-Benz 811D	Marshall C16	BC33F	1996	ABC Travel, Ainsdale, 1999
6021	N8ABC	Optare MetroRider MR31	Optare	B24F	1996	ABC Travel, Ainsdale, 1999
6022	N9ABC	Optare MetroRider MR31	Optare	B24F	1996	ABC Travel, Ainsdale, 1999
6023	P222ABC	Optare Excel L1070	Optare	N36F	1997	ABC Travel, Ainsdale, 1999
6024	P333ABC	Optare Excel L1070	Optare	N36F	1997	ABC Travel, Ainsdale, 1999
6025	R11ABC	Optare Solo M850	Optare	N25F	1998	ABC Travel, Ainsdale, 1999
6026	S22ABC	Optare Solo M850	Optare	N25F	1998	ABC Travel, Ainsdale, 1999
6027	S33ABC	Optare Solo M850	Optare	N25F	1998	ABC Travel, Ainsdale, 1999
6028	S44ABC	Optare Solo M850	Optare	N25F	1998	ABC Travel, Ainsdale, 1999
6029	S111ABC	Optare Solo M850	Optare	N25F	1998	ABC Travel, Ainsdale, 1999
6030	T552ADN	Optare Solo M850	Optare	N25F	1999	ABC Travel, Ainsdale, 1999

Special event vehicle

	TCK821	Leyland Titan PD3/5	Metro-Cammell	B41/31F	1963	ABC Travel, Ainsdale, 1999

Ancillary vehicle

1087	AYR303T	Leyland National 10351A/2R		TV	1978	Dee Ward, Market Harborough, 1993

Previous Registrations:

J800ABC   J365BNW

Livery: Red (CMT buses); white and blue (coaches); red and cream (ABC buses)

CHESTER CITY TRANSPORT

Chester City Transport Ltd, Station Road, Chester, CH1 3AD

1	B201EFM	Leyland Olympian ONLXB/1R	Northern Counties	BC43/30F	1985	
2	B202EFM	Leyland Olympian ONLXB/1R	Northern Counties	BC43/30F	1985	
3	B203EFM	Leyland Olympian ONLXB/1R	Northern Counties	BC43/32F	1985	
4	B204EFM	Leyland Olympian ONLXB/1R	Northern Counties	BC43/32F	1985	
5	VRA124Y	Leyland Olympian ONLXB/1R	Northern Counties	B43/28F	1982	Derby, 1987
6	VRA125Y	Leyland Olympian ONLXB/1R	Northern Counties	B43/28F	1982	Derby, 1987
7	UWW1X	Leyland Olympian ONLXB/1R	Roe	B47/29F	1982	West Yorkshire PTE, 1987
8	UWW2X	Leyland Olympian ONLXB/1R	Roe	B47/29F	1982	West Yorkshire PTE, 1987
9	F209JMB	Leyland Olympian ONCL10/2RZ	Northern Counties	BC45/32F	1989	
10	F210JMB	Leyland Olympian ONCL10/2RZ	Northern Counties	BC45/33F	1989	
11	F882VSJ	Leyland Olympian ONCL10/1RZ	Leyland	B47/31F	1988	A1 (McKinnon), Ardrossan, 1991
12	A976OST	Leyland Olympian ONLXB/1R	Alexander RL	B45/30F	1984	Highland Scottish, 1991
13	C378CAS	Leyland Olympian ONLXB/1RH	Alexander RL	B45/30F	1986	Highland Scottish, 1991
14	C379CAS	Leyland Olympian ONLXB/1RH	Alexander RL	B45/30F	1986	Highland Scottish, 1991
15	C380CAS	Leyland Olympian ONLXB/1RH	Alexander RL	B45/30F	1986	Highland Scottish, 1991
24	XFM211	Leyland Tiger TRCTL11/3R	Duple Dominant IV	C55F	1983	Kirkham, Oswaldtwistle, 1988
25	E25BTU	Dennis Javelin 11SDL1905	Duple 320	C55F	1988	
28w	A54KVM	Leyland Tiger TRCTL11/3R	Plaxton Paramount 3200	C55F	1984	GM Buses, 1989
29	E43SBO	Dennis Javelin 11SDA1906	Duple 320	C51F	1988	Bebb, Llantwit Fardre, 1989
30	E126LAD	Hestair Duple SDA1512	Duple 425	C53FT	1988	Swanbrook, Cheltenham, 1993
41	E41YMB	Renault-Dodge S56	Northern Counties	BC23F	1988	

51-60

		Dennis Dart 9SDL3011	Plaxton Pointer	B35F	1991-93					
51	J51EDM	53	J53EDM	55	J155EDM	57	K57LLG	59	K59LLG	
52	J52EDM	54	J54EDM	56	K56LLG	58	K58LLG	60	L160PDM	

61	L61PDM	Dennis Dart 9SDL3021	Plaxton Pointer	B35F	1993	
62	L62PDM	Dennis Dart 9SDL3021	Plaxton Pointer	B35F	1993	
63	L63SFM	Dennis Dart 9SDL3031	Plaxton Pointer	B35F	1994	
64	L64SFM	Dennis Dart 9SDL3031	Plaxton Pointer	B35F	1994	
65	M165XMA	Dennis Dart 9SDL3031	Plaxton Pointer	B35F	1994	
66	M166XMA	Dennis Dart 9SDL3031	Plaxton Pointer	B35F	1994	
67	N459EEY	Dennis Dart 9.8SDL3054	Plaxton Pointer	B40F	1996	Caelloi, Pwllheli, 1998
77	TWH694T	Leyland Fleetline FE30AGR	Northern Counties	B43/32F	1978	GM Buses, 1990
78	HDB124V	Leyland Fleetline FE30AGR	Northern Counties	B43/32F	1980	GM Buses, 1990
79	BCB613V	Leyland Fleetline FE30AGR	Northern Counties	B43/32F	1980	GM Buses, 1990

In the early 1990s Chester City Transport replaced several older double-deck buses with more modern, mid-life Leyland Olympians and Lions. Purchased from the A1 co-operative is Workington-built Olympian 11, F882VSJ. It is seen at Chester bus station.
Cliff Beeton

Open-top tours of Chester are operated in association with Guide Friday and use City of Chester vehicles. Illustrating one of the converted Fleetlines is 95, SDM95V which was passing along John Street when photographed. *Richard Godfrey*

81-86

	Scania L113CRL			Wright Access-ultralow		N42F	1997		
81	R81EMB	83	R83EMB	84	R84EMB	85	R85EMB	86	R86EMB
82	R82EMB								

87-98

	Leyland Fleetline FE30AGR			Northern Counties		O43/16F*	1978-80	*94 is B43/29F	
87	CFM87S	92	KFM192T	95	SDM95V	96	SDM96V	98	SDM98V
90	KFM190T	94	SDM94V	97	SDM97V				

99-103

	Dennis Dominator DD121B			Northern Counties		B43/29F	1981		
99	YMA99W	100	YMA100W	101	YMA101W	102	YMA102W	103	YMA103W

104-112

	Dennis Dominator DDA150*			Northern Counties		B43/29F	1982-83	*110-112 are DDA170	
104	HMA104X	106	HMA106X	108	KLG108Y	110	A110UCA	112	A112UCA
105	HMA105X	107	KLG107Y	109	KLG109Y	111	A111UCA		

121w	OCS34X	Dennis Dominator DDA151	East Lancashire	B45/31F	1981	A1 (Duff), Ardrossan, 1988
131	A105KRN	Dennis Dominator DDA158	East Lancashire	B43/33F	1983	Hyndburn, 1990
132	A106KRN	Dennis Dominator DDA158	East Lancashire	B43/33F	1983	Hyndburn, 1990
133	B107UFV	Dennis Dominator DDA950	East Lancashire	B43/33F	1985	Hyndburn, 1990
134	B108UFV	Dennis Dominator DDA950	East Lancashire	B43/33F	1985	Hyndburn, 1990
135	JSL282X	Dennis Dominator DD139	East Lancashire	B50/33F	1981	Brighton, 1991
137w	JSL284X	Dennis Dominator DD139	East Lancashire	B50/33F	1981	Brighton, 1991
238	E38YFM	Renault-Dodge S56	Northern Counties	B22F	1988	
249	P149LMA	Marshall Mini	Marshall MM	B29F	1996	
250	P150LMA	Marshall Mini	Marshall MM	B29F	1996	
255	F505CBO	MCW MetroRider MF150/105	MCW	B25F	1987	Oxford Cityline, 1998

Two Leyland National buses joined the Chester City Transport fleet in 1999 are are allocated to school contracts. Now carrying fleet livery and seen at the city's bus station is 318, LAG188V. *Cliff Beeton*

269-276

		Optare MetroRider MR09		Optare		B23F	1990	Oxford Cityline, 1998
269	G769WFC	271	G771WFC	273	G773WFC	275	G775WFC	276	G776WFC
270	G770WFC	272	G772WFC	274	G774WFC			

318	LAG188V	Leyland National 2 NL116L11/1R				B52F	1980	Stagecoach East Midland, 1999
320	HWJ620W	Leyland National 2 NL116L11/1R				B52F	1980	Stagecoach East Midland, 1999

368-374

		Dennis Dart SLF		Marshall Capital		N37F	1999	
368	V368KLG	370	V370KLG	372	V372KLG	373	V373KLG	374	V374KLG
369	V369KLG	371	V371KLG					

781-785

		Volkswagen LT46		Constables		B10FL	2000	
781	W781NFG	782	W782NFG	783	W783NFG	784	W784NFG	785	W785NFG

Special event vehicle

47	DFM347H	Guy Arab V		Northern Counties		B41/32F	1969

Previous Registrations:

A54KVM	XFM211, A54KVM	XFM211	A157MCK

Livery: Cream and maroon; white, red and blue (Chester Park & Ride); cream,blue and yellow (Diamond Service).

CITY BUS

City Bus - City Coach

J C Bleasdale, 99-103 Stanhope Street, Liverpool, L8 5RE

Reg	Make	Body	Seating	Year	History
EMB370S	Leyland National 11351A/1R		B49F	1978	Crosville Wales, 1991
EON830V	Leyland National 2 NL116L11/1R		BC39F	1980	Stevensons, 1992
KWA23W	Leyland National 2 NL116L11/1R		B48DL	1980	Mainline, 1996
GUW489W	Leyland National 2 NL106AL11/2R		B41F	1981	Merseybus, 1998
LCW731W	Leyland Leopard PSU5D/4R	Plaxton Supreme IV	C57F	1981	Burnley & Pendle, 1994
MEF825W	Bristol VRT/SL3/6LXB	Eastern Coach Works	B43/31F	1981	Northumbria, 1994
SVL174W	Bristol VRT/SL3/6LXB	Eastern Coach Works	B43/31F	1981	RoadCar, 1995
KYV319X	Leyland Titan TNLXB2RR	Leyland	B44/26D	1981	Metroline, Harrow, 1997
KYV343X	Leyland Titan TNLXB2RR	Leyland	B44/24D	1981	Metroline, Harrow, 1997
917MMB	Leyland Tiger TRCTL11/3R	Plaxton Supreme V	C53F	1982	Robinsons, Gt Harwood, 1990
A209OKJ	MCW Metrobus DR102/42	MCW	B46/31F	1984	Arriva Southern Counties (KNS), 2000
B131SED	Leyland National 2 NL116TL11/1R		B52F	1985	Arriva Cymru, 1999
JSV343	Aüwaerter Neoplan N722/3	Plaxton Paramount 4000 II	C53/18CT	1986	Dodsworth, Boroughbridge, 1995
D32MWN	Leyland Lynx LX112TL11ZR1	Leyland Lynx	B51F	1987	Whitelaw, Stonehouse, 1993
D390SGS	Freight Rover Sherpa	Dormobile	B16F	1987	Eagles & Crawford, Mold, 1992
F631BKD	Dennis Dominator DDA1026	East Lancashire	B43/25F	1990	Arriva Southern Counties (WS), 2000
P445SWX	MAN 11.190 HOCL-R	Optare Vecta	B39F	1996	
R102HUA	Optare MetroRider MR11	Optare	B28F	1997	
S511KFL	Dennis Dart SLF	Marshall Capital	N37F	1998	
S512KFL	Dennis Dart SLF	Marshall Capital	N37F	1998	
W991XDM	Dennis Dart SLF	Plaxton MPD	N28F	2000	

Previous Registrations:
917MMB   LEC198X   JSV343   C753CWX   LCW731W   LHE253W, XSU910

Livery: Blue and white.
Depots: Stanhope Street, Liverpool and Parliament Street, Liverpool

Three low-floor Dennis Darts can be found in the City Bus fleet, two bodied by Marshall while the latest arrival is a shorter version, the Mini Pointer Dart. Seen working the Vauxhall Circular is S511KFL. *R L Wilson*

CLOWES

GA & KM Clowes & M Barks, Barrow Moor Farm, Barrow Moor, Longnor, Buxton, SK17 0QP

RAW32R	Bedford YMT	Duple Dominant	C53F	1977	Bryant's Coaches, Williton, 1989
VFV8V	Leyland Leopard PSU3E/4R	Duple Dominant II Express	C53F	1979	Happy Days, Woodseaves, 1996
YXI6366	DAF MB200DKTL600	Plaxton Supreme IV	C53F	1981	Happy Days, Woodseaves, 1995
YXI6367	Volvo B10M-56	Plaxton Supreme IV Express	C45F	1982	McCarthy & Lomas, 1994
VRY1X	DAF MB200DKTL600	Smit Euro Hi-Liner	C53F	1982	Robin Hood, Rushton, 1990
YOI7373	Leyland Tiger TRCTL11/3R	Plaxton Viewmaster IV	C53F	1982	Golden Boy, Hoddesdon, 1996
DLB790Y	Bova EL26/581	Bova Europa	C53F	1983	Proctor, Bedale, 1996
D959WJH	Freight Rover Sherpa	Dormobile	BC16F	1986	Bowes, Chapel-en-le-Frith, 2000
D710SKU	Freight Rover Sherpa	Crystals	M16	1986	private owner, 1988
RIB3524	Neoplan N216H	Neoplan Jetliner	C53F	1986	Robin Hood, Rudyard, 1993
ELZ2972	Leyland Cub	Wright Wishaw	BC29F	19--	Motherwell DC, 1999
E208HRY	Iveco Daily 49.10	Carlyle Dailybus 2	B25F	1988	Arriva Fox County, 1998
E78DMA	Neoplan N216H	Neoplan Jetliner	C51FT	1988	Hardings, Huyton, 2000
RIB8636	DAF MB230LB615	Duple 340	C53F	1989	Robin Hood, Rudyard, 1999
G36HDW	Freight Rover Sherpa	Carlyle Citybus 2	B20F	1990	A Line, Bedworth, 1997

Previous Registrations:

E78DMA	E94VWA, TOP11, E815XKD, NSU160		
ELZ2972	?	YOI7373	DNK581Y
RIB3524	C718JTL	YXI6366	GTC820X
RIB8636	F671TRE	YXI6367	KNP2X

Livery: White, green and orange.

Clowes depot is located to the far east of the area coverred by this publication. Fom the remote depot school contract journeys provide one of the main sources of work. Representing the fleet is YXI6367, a Plaxton Supreme IV Express-bodied Volvo B10M. *Cliff Beeton*

COPELAND'S TOURS

Copeland Tours (Stoke on Trent) Ltd, Uttoxeter Road, Meir, Stoke-on-Trent   ST1 3ER

MIB537	Leyland Leopard PSU3C/4R	Plaxton Paramount 3200 (1984)	C53F	1975	Tims Travel, Sheerness, 1999
MIB520	Ford R1114	Plaxton Supreme III	C43DL	1977	
MIB542	Bedford YMT	Plaxton Supreme IV	C53F	1980	Inland Travel, Flimwell, 1999
MIB864	DAF MB200DKTL600	Jonckheere Bermuda	C55F	1982	Slatepearl, Trentham, 1985
MIB614	Leyland Tiger TRCTL11/3R	Plaxton Paramount 3200 E	C50FT	1983	Wessex, Bristol, 1991
MIB302	DAF MB200DKFL600	Plaxton Paramount 3200	C53F	1983	Hunter, Leeds, 1996
MIB104	DAF MB200DKFL600	Plaxton Paramount 3200	C48FT	1983	Bruce, Pitscottie, 1994
MIB268	DAF MB200DKFL600	Van Hool Alizée	C50FT	1983	Smithson, Spixworth, 1996
PDZ6269	Leyland Tiger TRCTL11/3R	Plaxton Paramount 3500	C49FT	1984	Essbee, Coatbridge, 1998
MIB615	DAF MB200DKFL600	Plaxton Paramount 3200	C42FTL	1984	Kinch, Barrow-on-Soar, 1988
MIB279	DAF MB230DKFL615	Plaxton Paramount 3500 III	C53F	1987	Stevensons, 1994
MIB761	Toyota Coaster HB31R	Caetano Optimo	C21F	1989	Kinch, Barrow-on-Soar, 1993
MIB346	Hestair Duple SDA1512	Duple 425	C53FT	1989	Grimshaw, Burnley, 1994
MIB746	Mercedes-Benz 811D	Wadham Stringer Wessex	B31F	1989	Brighton & Hove, 1999
MIB116	Mercedes-Benz 811D	Wadham Stringer Wessex	B31F	1989	Brighton & Hove, 1999
MIB783	Mercedes-Benz 811D	Wadham Stringer Wessex	B31F	1989	Brighton & Hove, 1999

Previous Registrations:

MIB104	TTG244Y	MIB520	TRE202R, 111WEH
MIB116	F45XPR	MIB536	B489TYG, A12ESS, B141DCX, PDZ6269
MIB236	-	MIB537	MUS103P, TFA13, OVT253P, GSK664
MIB246	-	MIB542	JJF880V, SDY788, 405HPJ, TCT51, LKE869V
MIB268	KYC729Y, FIL7622	MIB614	EAH892Y, CIW6752, FFA270Y
MIB270	-	MIB615	A102HJF
MIB278	-	MIB746	F49XPR
MIB279	D606YCX, AAX568A, LUY742, D138DFP	MIB761	G860WBC
MIB302	ANA459Y, WSV539	MIB864	YRF754Y, 470WYA
MIB346	F545YCK	MIB783	F43XPR

Copeland's Tours have a fleet that carry MIB index marks, the company holding additional numbers on retention. *One of Copelands* **DAF coaches is shown here. MIB268 carries a Van Hool Alizée body.** *Cliff Beeton*

D&G BUS COMPANY

D&G Bus & Coach Ltd, St Martins Road, Longton, Stoke-on-Trent, ST3

1	C135VRE	Mercedes-Benz L608D	PMT Hanbridge	B19F	1986	PMT, 1998
2	C420VVN	Mercedes-Benz L608D	Reeve Burgess	B20F	1986	Webber, Bodmin, 1999
3	D302SDS	Renault-Dodge S56	Alexander AM	B25F	1987	Countybus, Seighford, 1998
4	D525RCK	Mercedes-Benz L608D	Reeve Burgess	B20F	1986	Stagecoach Western, 1999
5	RBZ4209	Mercedes-Benz L608D	Reeve Burgess	B20F	1987	Stagecoach Western, 1999
6	D142RAK	Renault-Dodge S56	Reeve Burgess	B25F	1987	Pete's Travel, West Bromwich, 1999
7	D395KND	Renault-Dodge S56	Mellor	BC25F	1987	Milne, Macduff, 1999
8	H744VHS	Mercedes-Benz 609D	Scott	BC20F	1990	Pete's Travel, West Bromwich, 1999
9	F94JGE	Mercedes-Benz 609D	North West Coach Sales	BC24F	1989	Pete's Travel, West Bromwich, 1999
10	D431TCA	Renault-Dodge S56	Northern Counties	B22F	1987	Pete's Travel, West Bromwich, 1999
11	D865NVS	Renault-Dodge S56	Reeve Burgess	B25F	1986	Pete's Travel, West Bromwich, 1999
12	D787NDV	Ford Transit 190	Mellor	B16F	1987	Pete's Travel, West Bromwich, 1999
14	D636NOD	Ford Transit 190	Mellor	B16F	1987	Pete's Travel, West Bromwich, 1999
15	D226PPU	Mercedes-Benz L608D	Reeve Burgess	B20F	1986	Crawley Luxury Coaches, 1999
16	D51RLG	Mercedes-Benz L608D	PMT Hanbridge	B20F	1986	Crawley Luxury Coaches, 1999
17	D513FAE	Mercedes-Benz L608D	Dormobile	B20F	1986	Webber, Bodmin, 1999
	D131VRP	Mercedes-Benz L608D	Dormobile	B20F	1986	Bakers, Biddulph, 2000
	D511RCK	Mercedes-Benz L608D	Reeve Burgess	BC19F	1986	?, 2000

Previous registrations:

D525RCK	D525RCK, RBZ5459	RBZ4209	D42UAO

Livery: Blue
Depots: St Martin's Road Longton and New Road, Tean

D&G Bus Company operate a fleet of minibuses that include several of the body styles that were involved in the large expansion of minibus operations in the late 1980s. Purchased by National Bus and now number 17 in this fleet, D513FAE was allocated new to Bristol Omnibus and carries the Dormobile conversion of the Mercedes-Benz L608D panel van. *Cliff Beeton*

DAVID TANNER TRAVEL

D Tanner, 10 Cowley Street, St Helens, Merseyside, WA10 2SR

E202EPB	Iveco Daily 49.10	Robin Hood City Nippy	B25F	1987	Stagecoach South, 1996
E972DNK	MCW MetroRider MF150/81	MCW	B23F	1988	Arriva The Shires, 1998
E992DNK	MCW MetroRider MF150/83	MCW	B23F	1988	Arriva The Shires, 1998
E233DTV	MCW MetroRider MF150/93	MCW	B23F	1988	Yorkshire Traction, 2000
F162AWO	MCW MetroRider MF154/20	MCW	B31F	1989	Cardiff Bus, 2000
F473MDN	Renault-Dodge S56	Northern Counties	B23F	1989	Clarke, Threshfield, 1999
F474MDN	Renault-Dodge S56	Northern Counties	B23F	1989	Clarke, Threshfield, 1999
F345VEF	Renault-Dodge S56	Northern Counties	B23F	1989	Stagecoach Transit, 1996
P746HND	Dennis Dart SLF	Plaxton Pointer 2	N39F	1997	Swanbrook, Cheltenham, 1999

Previous registrations:

F473MDN   F341VEF, VIA179   F474MDN   F337VEF, VIA485

Livery: Various

When photographed in St Helens, David Tanner's E972DNK still carried the livery of Luton & District, having finished its time with Arriva The Shires in the Gade Valley. It is one of a pair that have recently been joined by similar MetroRiders from Cardiff and Yorkshire Traction. *Richard Godfrey*

DOBSON'S

Dobson Buses Ltd, 258 Manchester Road, Lostock Gralam, Northwich, CW9 7PL

OCU820R	Leyland Fleetline FE30AGR	Alexander AL	B44/29F	1977	Stagecoach Busways, 1999
ANA215T	Leyland Atlantean AN68A/1R	Northern Counties	B43/32F	1978	Bellamy, Nottingham, 2000
NNN476W	Leyland Atlantean AN68C/1R	Roe	B46/34F	1981	Bailey, Hucknall, 2000
YLW895X	Bedford YMQ	Lex Maxeta	B37F	1981	Weybus, Weymouth, 1997
YAJ155Y	Leyland Fleetline FE30AGR	Northern Counties	B43/31F	1982	Stagecoach Transit, 1999
A503FSS	Dennis Lancet SDA516	Alexander P	B53F	1984	Zak'z, Birmingham, 2000
F248HDB	Peugeot-Talbot Pullman	Talbot	B22F	1988	Walsh, Halifax, 1996
F958HTO	Iveco Daily 49.10	Robin Hood City Nippy	B25F	1989	Douglas, Weymouth, 2000
G602SJA	Peugeot-Talbot Pullman	Talbot	B22F	1989	Ludlows, Halesowen, 1994
G879SKE	Peugeot-Talbot Pullman	Talbot	B22F	1990	Arriva Southern Counties (KS), 1998
J332LVM	Peugeot-Talbot Pullman	Talbot	B22F	1991	
J387PVR	Peugeot-Talbot Pullman	Talbot	B22F	1992	
L483DOA	Peugeot-Talbot Pullman	TBP	B22F	1993	
N263FMA	Iveco TurboDaily 59.12	Mellor	BC31F	1996	

Previous Registrations:
YLW895X   LCY299X, SVO89, GGK236X, RIB7018

Livery: White(minibuses)
Depot: Wincham Park, Chapel Street, Wincham

Dobson's operate town services in Northwich using a fleet of Peugeot-Talbot Pullman minibuses. Shown here is G602SJA. The operator's school services saw expansion during 1999 with the arrival of two double-deck buses. *Cliff Beeton*

EXPRESS TRAVEL

Express Travel Ltd, Woodend Avenue, Speke, Liverpool, L24 9NB

K20AMB	Volvo B10M-60	Plaxton Expressliner II	C46FT	1992
K504WNR	Volvo B10M-60	Plaxton Expressliner II	C46FT	1993
K506WNR	Volvo B10M-60	Plaxton Expressliner II	C46FT	1993
L705PHE	Volvo B10M-62	Van Hool Alizée	C38FT	1994
L706PHE	Volvo B10M-62	Van Hool Alizée	C38FT	1994
L707PHE	Volvo B10M-62	Van Hool Alizée	C38FT	1994
L708PHE	Volvo B10M-62	Van Hool Alizée	C38FT	1994
L709PHE	Volvo B10M-62	Van Hool Alizée	C38FT	1994
L710PHE	Volvo B10M-62	Van Hool Alizée	C38FT	1994
L711PHE	Volvo B10M-62	Van Hool Alizée	C38FT	1994
L712PHE	Volvo B10M-62	Van Hool Alizée	C38FT	1994
L713PHE	Volvo B10M-62	Van Hool Alizée	C38FT	1994
L714PHE	Volvo B10M-62	Van Hool Alizée	C38FT	1994
P454DCW	Dennis Dart SLF	East Lancashire Spryte	N31F	1997
P455DCW	Dennis Dart SLF	East Lancashire Spryte	N31F	1997
P456DCW	Dennis Dart SLF	East Lancashire Spryte	N31F	1997
P457DCW	Dennis Dart SLF	East Lancashire Spryte	N31F	1997
P458DCW	Dennis Dart SLF	East Lancashire Spryte	N31F	1997
P459DCW	Dennis Dart SLF	East Lancashire Spryte	N31F	1997
P460DCW	Dennis Dart SLF	East Lancashire Spryte	N31F	1997
P461DCW	Dennis Dart SLF	East Lancashire Spryte	N31F	1997
P842WUG	Volvo B10M-62	Van Hool Alizée HE	C50FT	1997
S509NFR	Dennis Dart SLF	East Lancashire Spryte	N30F	1999
T840CCK	Dennis Dart SLF	East Lancashire Spryte	N30F	1999
T841CCK	Dennis Dart SLF	East Lancashire Spryte	N30F	1999

Livery: Blue, white and red.

In addition to their National Express contracts, Express Travel also operate contracts for Merseytravel using a fleet of East Lancashire Spryte-bodied Dennis Darts. Seen working route 176 is P460OCW. *Cliff Beeton*

FIRST PMT

Crosville - Flexi - Pennine - PMT - Red Rider

PMT Ltd, Hobson Street, Burslem, Stoke-on-Trent ST6 2AQ

22	H202JHP	Peugeot-Talbot Pullman	Talbot	B8FL	1990	Midland Red West, 1995
23	H203JHP	Peugeot-Talbot Pullman	Talbot	B22F	1990	Midland Red West, 1995
24	ERF24Y	Leyland Tiger TRCTL11/3R	Plaxton Paramount 3500	C53F	1983	
25	M25YRE	Peugeot Boxer	TBP	M9	1995	
26	M26YRE	Peugeot Boxer	TBP	M9	1995	
27	M27YRE	Peugeot Boxer	TBP	M9	1995	
28	M28YRE	Peugeot Boxer	TBP	M9	1995	
29	C770PUJ	Renault Master T35	Renault	M9L	1986	WYM Ambulance, 1996
30	D810NWW	Renault Master T35	Renault	M9L	1987	WYM Ambulance, 1996
31	T131ARE	Mercedes-Benz 614	Minibus Options	M14L	1999	
32	T132ARE	Mercedes-Benz 614	Frank Guy	M14	1999	
33	T133ARE	Mercedes-Benz 614	Frank Guy	M14	1999	
34	T134ARE	Mercedes-Benz 614	Frank Guy	M14	1999	
35	T135ARE	Mercedes-Benz 614	Minibus Options	M14	1999	
36	T136ARE	Mercedes-Benz 614	Minibus Options	M14	1999	
44	FXI8653	Leyland Tiger TRCTL11/3R	Plaxton Paramount 3500 III	C53F	1988	
45	WJI5239	Leyland Tiger TRCTL11/3R	Plaxton Paramount 3200 E	C53F	1984	The Shires, 1998
46	507EXA	Volvo B10M-61	Jonckheere Deauville P599	C51FT	1989	First Aberdeen (M), 2000
47	XRF1X	Leyland Tiger TRCTL11/3ARZA	Plaxton Paramount 3200 III	C53F	1988	First Yorkshire (C), 2000

51-56		Tecnobus U500EUK		Tecnobus Gulliver			B9C	1998	LHD Electric
51	S251AFA	**53**	S253AFA	**54**	S254AFA	**55**	S255AFA	**56**	S256AFA
52	S252AFA								

57-72		Optare Solo M850		Optare			N27F	1999	
57	T157BBF	**61**	T161BBF	**64**	T164BBF	**67**	T167BBF	**70**	V470GBF
58	T158BBF	**62**	T162BBF	**65**	T165BBF	**68**	T168BBF	**71**	V71GEH
59	T159BBF	**63**	T163BBF	**66**	T166BBF	**69**	V69GEH	**72**	V472GBF
60	T160BBF								

73-78		Optare Solo M850		Optare			N27F	2000	
73	W473SVT	**75**	W475SVT	**76**	W476SVT	**77**	W477SVT	**78**	W478SVT
74	W474SVT								

88	C108SFP	Mercedes-Benz L307D	Reeve Burgess	M12	1985	Goldcrest, Birkenhead, 1990

Six Tecnobus Gulliver minibuses are operated by First PMT on behalf of Merseytravel, the tendering authority for the region. Seen at Birkenhead is 53, S253AFA. The service links the shopping centre with the Woodhead Ferry terminal.
Cliff Beeton

First PMT dedicate several buses to school duties which the group are looking to expand using special school buses similar to those used in the USA. Transferred from Brewers in 1997, 297, HHJ374Y carries an Alexander TE body is seen preparing to set out on route 30 to Bradwell. The vehicle is currently allocated to Crewe.
Cliff Beeton

89-99

								Optare Solo M850	Optare			N27F	2000	
89	X289XFA	92	X292XFA	94	X294XFA	96	X296XFA	98	X298XFA
91	X291XFA	93	X293XFA	95	X295XFA	97	X297XFA	99	X299XFA

100	F100UEH	Mercedes-Benz 609D	PMT	C24F	1989	
101	G101EVT	Mercedes-Benz 609D	PMT	C21F	1990	
102	F452YHF	Mercedes-Benz 811D	North West Coach Sales	C24F	1989	C & M, Aintree, 1992
104	F713OFH	Mercedes-Benz 307D	North West Coach Sales	M9L	1989	van, 1992
107	XRF2X	Mercedes-Benz 811D	Optare StarRider	BC29F	1988	Leon's, Stafford, 1997
109	F217OFB	Mercedes-Benz 307D	North West Coach Sales	M12L	1989	van, 1992
110	H189CNS	Mercedes-Benz 814D	Dormobile Routemaker	C33F	1991	Executive Travel, 1994
114	G805AAD	Mercedes-Benz 308	North West Coach Sales	M12L	1989	van, 1992
115	B115NBF	Mercedes-Benz L608D	PMT Hanbridge	C21FL	1984	
117	V117DLH	Iveco Daily 49.10	Whitacre	M12	1999	
178	F166DNT	Ford Transit VE6	Dormobile	M15L	1989	Derwen Coll, Gobowen, 1994

224-230

						MCW MetroRider MF150/118	MCW			B25F*	1988	Crosville, 1990 *225/8/30 B23F
224	F88CWG	226	F106CWG	228	F108CWG	229	F109CWG	230	F110CWG
225	F95CWG	227	F107CWG							

231	L231NRE	Optare MetroRider	Optare	B31F	1994	

232-258

										Mercedes-Benz Vario O810	Plaxton Beaver 2			B27F	1997	
232	R232ERE	238	R238ERE	244	R244ERE	249	R249ERE	254	R254ERE
233	R233ERE	239	R239ERE	245	R245ERE	250	R250ERE	255	R255ERE
234	R234ERE	240	R240ERE	246	R246ERE	251	R251ERE	256	R256ERE
235	R235ERE	241	R241ERE	247	R247ERE	252	R252ERE	257	R257ERE
236	R236ERE	242	R242ERE	248	R248ERE	253	R253ERE	258	R258ERE
237	R237ERE	243	R243ERE							

For 2000 and 2001 the minibus requirement of FirstGroup is being met by the Opatre Solo. Seen with Red Rider names is 62, T162BBF. The use of alphabetic prefixes to fleet numbers has now ceased. *Cliff Beeton*

259-270

Mercedes-Benz Vario O814 — Plaxton Beaver 2 — B27F — 1998

259	S259SFA	**262**	S262SFA	**265**	S265SFA	**267**	S267SFA	**269**	S269SFA
260	S260SFA	**263**	S263SFA	**266**	S266SFA	**268**	S268SFA	**270**	S270SFA
261	S261SFA	**264**	S264SFA						

295	BVP782V	Leyland Leopard PSU3E/4R	Plaxton Supreme IV Express	C53F	1979	Midland Red West, 1996
297	HHJ374Y	Leyland Tiger TRCTL11/2R	Alexander TE	C49F	1983	Brewers, 1997
299	G67RND	Leyland Tiger TRBL10/3ARZA	Alexander N	B55F	1989	First Manchester, 1999

310-318

Leyland Swift LBM6T/2RS — PMT Knype — BC37F* — 1988-89 — *312/8 are BC35F

310	F310REH	**312**	F312REH	**313**	F313REH	**317**	F317REH	**318**	G318YVT
311	F311REH								

320	E342NFA	Leyland Swift LBM6T/2RS	PMT Knype	B37F	1988	PMT demonstrator, 1988
321	L321HRE	Optare MetroRider MR17	Optare	BC30F	1993	
322	L269GBU	Optare MetroRider	Optare	B28F	1993	
323	L323NRF	Optare MetroRider MR17	Optare	B29F	1994	

330-352

Mercedes-Benz 811D — PMT Ami — B28F — 1989-90

330	G330XRE	**335**	G335XRE	**340**	G340XRE	**343**	G343CBF	**346**	G346CBF
331	G331XRE	**336**	G336XRE	**341**	G341XRE	**344**	G344CBF	**349**	G549ERF
332	G332XRE	**338**	G338XRE	**342**	G342CBF	**345**	G345CBF	**352**	H352HRF
334	G334XRE	**339**	G339XRE						

354	H354HVT	Mercedes-Benz 811D	Reeve Burgess Beaver	B33F	1990
355	H355HVT	Mercedes-Benz 811D	Reeve Burgess Beaver	B33F	1990
356	H356HVT	Mercedes-Benz 811D	Reeve Burgess Beaver	B33F	1990
357	H357HVT	Mercedes-Benz 811D	Reeve Burgess Beaver	B33F	1990

358-363 Mercedes-Benz 811D | PMT Ami | B29F | 1990

358	H358JRE	360	H160JRE	361	H361JRE	362	H362JRE	363	H363JRE
359	H359JRE								

365 G495FFA | Mercedes-Benz 811D | PMT Ami | B28F | 1990

366-371 Mercedes-Benz 811D | PMT Ami | B29F | 1991

366	H366LFA	368	H368LFA	369	H369LFA	370	H370LFA	371	H371LFA
367	H367LFA								

372	H372MEH	Mercedes-Benz 811D	Whittaker-Europa	B31F	1991
373	H373MVT	Mercedes-Benz 811D	PMT Ami	B29F	1991
374	K374BRE	Mercedes-Benz 811D	Autobus Classique	B29F	1992
375	K375BRE	Mercedes-Benz 811D	Autobus Classique	B29F	1992
376	J751AAW	Mercedes-Benz 709D	Dormobile Routemaker	BC25F	1991	Stonier, 1994

377-383 Optare MetroRider MR15 | Optare | B30F | 1994

377	M377SRE	379	M379SRE	381	M381SRE	382	M382SRE	383	M383SRE
378	M378SRE	380	M380SRE						

384-390 Optare MetroRider MR15 | Optare | B29F | 1996

384	P384MEH	386	P386MEH	388	P388MEH	389	P389MEH	390	P390MEH
385	P385MEH	387	P387MEH						

391-396 Optare MetroRider MR15 | Optare | B29F | 1997

391	R391ERE	393	R393ERE	394	R394ERE	395	R395ERE	396	R396ERE
392	R392ERE								

405-429 Mercedes-Benz 709D | Plaxton Beaver | B22F | 1996

405	N405HVT	410	N410HVT	415	P415NFA	420	P420MEH	425	P425MEH
406	N406HVT	411	N411HVT	416	P416NFA	421	P421MEH	426	P426MEH
407	N407HVT	412	N412HVT	417	P417NFA	422	P422MEH	427	P427MEH
408	N408HVT	413	P413NFA	418	P418NFA	423	P423MEH	428	P428MEH
409	N409HVT	414	P414NFA	419	P419NFA	424	P424MEH	429	P429MEH

430-448 Mercedes-Benz 709D | Plaxton Beaver | B24F | 1992

430	J430WFA	436	K436XRF	439	K439XRF	444	K544XRF	446	K446XRF
431	J431WFA	437	K437XRF	441	K441XRF	445	K445XRF	448	K448XRF
434	K434XRF	438	K438XRF	442	K442XRF					

451	D451ERE	Mercedes-Benz L609D	PMT Hanbridge	B20F	1987
454	D454ERE	Mercedes-Benz L609D	PMT Hanbridge	B20FL	1987
460	E760HBF	Mercedes-Benz L609D	PMT Hanbridge	B20F	1988
467	E767HBF	Mercedes-Benz 709D	PMT	B21F	1988
483	H483JRE	Mercedes-Benz 609D	Whittaker Europa	B20F	1990
484	J484PVT	Mercedes-Benz 709D	PMT	B25F	1991
485	J485PVT	Mercedes-Benz 709D	Whittaker (PMT)	B25F	1992
486	J486PVT	Mercedes-Benz 709D	Whittaker (PMT)	B25F	1992

487-498 Mercedes-Benz 709D | Dormobile Routemaker | B24F* | 1993 | *488/9 are B27F

487	K487CVT	490	K490CVT	493	L493HRE	495	L495HRE	497	L497HRE
488	K488CVT	491	K491CVT	494	L494HRE	496	L496HRE	498	L498HRE
489	K489CVT	492	K492CVT						

532	G532CVT	Renault-Dodge S56	PMT	B25F	1990	
533	H722CNC	Renault S75	Northern Counties	B17FL	1990	First Manchester, 1998
534	H723CNC	Renault S75	Northern Counties	B17FL	1990	First Manchester, 1998

Recent transfers into PMT have seen several Dennis Dominators delivered to the Wirral for school contracts operated by Crosville. Pictured between duties is 693, F145MBC. *Andrew Jarosz*

553-563

| | | | | | | | | | | Mercedes-Benz 709D | | Marshall C19 | | B23F | 1994 |

553	L553LVT	556	L556LVT	558	L558LVT	560	M660SRE	562	M562SRE
554	L554LVT	557	L557LVT	559	M559SRE	561	M561SRE	563	M563SRE
555	L455LVT								

564-573

Mercedes-Benz 709D   Plaxton Beaver   B24F   1994

564	M564SRE	566	M566SRE	568	M568SRE	570	M570SRE	572	M572SRE
565	M565SRE	567	M567SRE	569	M569SRE	571	M571SRE	573	M573SRE

574-594

Mercedes-Benz 709D   Plaxton Beaver   B22F   1995

574	N574CEH	579	N579CEH	583	N583CEH	587	N587CEH	591	N591CEH
575	N575CEH	580	N580CEH	584	N584CEH	588	N588CEH	592	N592CEH
576	N576CEH	581	N581CEH	585	N585CEH	589	N589CEH	593	N593CEH
577	N577CEH	582	N582CEH	586	N586CEH	590	N590CEH	594	N594CEH
578	N578CEH								

608	VCA452W	Bristol VRT/SL3/501(6LXB)	Eastern Coach Works	B43/31F	1980	Crosville, 1990
609	VCA464W	Bristol VRT/SL3/501(6LXB)	Eastern Coach Works	B43/31F	1980	Crosville, 1990
610	WTU465W	Bristol VRT/SL3/501(6LXB)	Eastern Coach Works	B43/31F	1980	Crosville, 1990
614	WTU483W	Bristol VRT/SL3/501(6LXB)	Eastern Coach Works	B43/31F	1981	Crosville, 1990
618	YBW489V	Bristol VRT/SL3/6LXB	Eastern Coach Works	B43/31F	1979	Thames Transit, 1989
622	GBF78N	Bristol VRT/SL2/6G	Eastern Coach Works	O43/31F	1974	
625	AHW203V	Bristol VRT/SL3/6LXB	Eastern Coach Works	B43/27D	1980	City Line, 1994
626	ANA616Y	Leyland Atlantean AN68D/1R	Northern Counties	B43/32F	1983	First Manchester, 1999
627	A658HNB	Leyland Atlantean AN68D/1R	Northern Counties	B43/32F	1983	First Manchester, 1999
628	AHU514V	Bristol VRT/SL3/6LXB	Eastern Coach Works	B43/27D	1980	First Hampshire, 1999

690-694

Dennis Dominator DDA1024   East Lancashire   B46/33F   1989   First Capital, 2000

690	F140MBC	691	F141MBC	692	F142MBC	693	F145MBC	694	F147MBC

698	F296PTP	Dennis Dominator DDA1023	East Lancashire	B45/31F	1988	First Capital, 2000
699	F298PTP	Dennis Dominator DDA1023	East Lancashire	B45/31F	1988	First Capital, 2000
700	K174EUX	Volvo Olympian YN2RV18V3	Alexander RH	B42/32F	1994	SBS, Singapore, 1999

Batches of Optare Delta and Leyland Lynx buses were supplied to PMT in 1990 for evaluation. These were fitted with high-back seating and can still be found in the fleet. Shown working the X64 service to Shrewsbury is 804, H804GRE. Arriva Midlands North also operate this service using a vehicle based at the other end of the route.
Cliff Beeton

701-731

Bristol VRT/SL3/501   Eastern Coach Works   B43/31F*   1979-80 *723 is BC39/28F
*728 is B39/29F

| 701 | GRF701V | 708 | GRF708V | 723 | MFA723V | 729 | NEH729W | 731 | NEH731W |
| 707 | GRF707V | 709 | GRF709V | 728 | NEH728W | | | | |

733-747

Leyland Olympian ONLXB/1R   Eastern Coach Works   B45/32F*   1983-84   *seating varies

733	A733GFA	736	A736GFA	739	A739GFA	742	A742GFA	745	A745JRE
734	A734GFA	737	A737GFA	740	A740GFA	743	A743JRE	746	A746JRE
735	A735GFA	738	A738GFA	741	A741GFA	744	A744JRE	747	A747JRE

748	EWY78Y	Leyland Olympian ONLXB/1R	Roe		B47/29F	1983	Turner, Brown Edge, 1988
749	EWY79Y	Leyland Olympian ONLXB/1R	Roe		B47/29F	1983	Turner, Brown Edge, 1988
750	GFM101X	Leyland Olympian ONLXB/1R	Eastern Coach Works(1985)	B45/32F	1982	Crosville, 1990
751	GFM102X	Leyland Olympian ONLXB/1R	Eastern Coach Works	B45/32F	1982	Crosville, 1990
752	GFM103X	Leyland Olympian ONLXB/1R	Eastern Coach Works	B45/32F	1982	Crosville, 1990

753-762

Leyland Olympian ONCL11/1RZ   Leyland   B47/29F*   1989   *seating varies

| 753 | G753XRE | 755 | G755XRE | 757 | G757XRE | 759 | G759XRE | 761 | G761XRE |
| 754 | G754XRE | 756 | G756XRE | 758 | G758XRE | 760 | G760XRE | 762 | G762XRE |

763-782

Leyland Olympian ONLXB/1R   Eastern Coach Works   B45/32F   1982-83   Crosville, 1990

763	GFM104X	767	GFM109X	770	KFM113Y	774	MTU122Y	779	A137SMA
764	GFM105X	768	KFM111Y	772	KFM115Y	775	MTU123Y	781	A143SMA
765	GFM106X	769	KFM112Y	773	MTU120Y	776	MTU124Y	782	A144SMA
766	GFM108X								

The acquisition of the English operations of Crosville substantially increased the number of Olympians with PMT from the initial ten. Many of these are now transferred to other depots including 779, A137SMA, which is based at Burslem. It is seen shortly after a repaint. *Cliff Beeton*

784-799
Leyland Olympian ONLXB/1R — Eastern Coach Works — B45/32F — 1984-85 — Crosville, 1990

784	A146UDM	788	A159UDM	791	A162VDM	794	A165VDM	797	A168VFM
785	A156UDM	789	A160UDM	792	A163VDM	795	A166VFM	798	A169VFM
786	A157UDM	790	A161VDM	793	A164VDM	796	A167VFM	799	A170VFM
787	A158UDM								

801-809
DAF SB220LC550 — Optare Delta — BC48F — 1990

801	H801GRE	803	H803GRE	805	H805GRE	807	H807GRE	809	H809GRE
802	H802GRE	804	H804GRE	806	H806GRE	808	H808GRE		

810-821
Scania L113CRL — Wright Axcess-ultralow — N40F — 1998

810	R810NVT	813	S813AEH	816	S816AEH	818	S818AEH	820	S820AEH
811	R811NVT	814	S814AEH	817	S817AEH	819	S819AEH	821	S821AEH
812	R812NVT	815	S815AEH						

822-832
Scania L94UB — Wright Axcess Floline — N43F — 1999 — 822-9 Yorkshire, 1999

822	T822SFS	825	T825SFS	827	T827SFS	829	T829SFS	831	V831GBF
823	T823SFS	826	T826SFS	828	T828SFS	830	V830GBF	832	V832GBF
824	T824SFS								

833-838
Scania L113CRL — Wright Axcess-ultralow — N40F — 1998 — First Yorkshire, 2000

833	R438ALS	835	R440ALS	836	R441ALS	837	R442ALS	838	S443BSG
834	R439ALS								

842	D752DLO	Leyland Lynx LX112TL11ZR1S	Leyland Lynx	B49F	1987	CentreWest, 1999
843	D875ELL	Leyland Lynx LX112TL11ZR1R	Leyland Lynx	B48F	1987	Essex Buses, 1999
844	F102GRM	Leyland Lynx LX112L10ZR1R	Leyland Lynx	B48F	1988	CentreWest, 1999
845	F361YTJ	Leyland Lynx LX112L10ZR1R	Leyland Lynx	B51F	1988	Topp-Line, Wavertree, 1994
846	F362YTJ	Leyland Lynx LX112L10ZR1R	Leyland Lynx	B51F	1988	Topp-Line, Wavertree, 1994
847	F363YTJ	Leyland Lynx LX112L10ZR1R	Leyland Lynx	B51F	1988	Topp-Line, Wavertree, 1994
848	F364YTJ	Leyland Lynx LX112L10ZR1R	Leyland Lynx	B51F	1988	Topp-Line, Wavertree, 1994

849	F608WBV	Leyland Lynx LX112L10ZR1S	Leyland Lynx			B52F	1988	Westbus, Ashford, 1993	
850	G136YRY	Leyland Lynx LX112L10ZR1R	Leyland Lynx			B51F	1990	Westbus, Ashford, 1993	

851-861

		Leyland Lynx LX2R11C15Z4S	Leyland Lynx			BC48F	1990		
851	H851GRE	854	H854GRE	856	H856GRE	858	H858GRE	860	H860GRE
852	H852GRE	855	H855GRE	857	H857GRE	859	H859GRE	861	H861GRE
853	H853GRE								

862	L862HFA	Dennis Lance 11SDA3112	Northern Counties Paladin			BC47F	1993		

863-867

		Dennis Lance 11SDA3113	Plaxton Verde			BC45F	1995		
863	N863CEH	864	N864CEH	865	N865CEH	866	N866CEH	867	N867CEH

868	P868MBF	Dennis Lance	Northern Counties Paladin			B43F	1997		
869	P869MBF	Dennis Lance	Northern Counties Paladin			B43F	1997		
870	P870MBF	Dennis Lance	Northern Counties Paladin			B43F	1997		

871-878

		Scania L113CRL	Wright Axcess-ultralow			N51F	1997		
871	R871ERE	873	R873ERE	875	R875ERE	877	R877ERE	878	R878ERE
872	R872ERE	874	R874ERE	876	R876ERE				

879	R879HRF	Scania L113CRL	Wright Axcess-ultralow			N40F	1998		
880	R880HRF	Scania L113CRL	Wright Axcess-ultralow			N40F	1998		
881	R881HRF	Scania L113CRL	Wright Axcess-ultralow			N40F	1998		
883	TJI4828	Volvo B10M-60	Jonckheere Deauville			C53F	1989	CentreWest (Bee Line), '98	
884	D497NYS	Volvo B10M-61	Duple Dominant			B55F	1986	First Essex, 1999	
885	D499NYS	Volvo B10M-61	Duple Dominant			B55F	1986	First Essex, 1999	
888	F160XYG	Leyland Olympian ONCL10/1RZ	Northern Counties			B45/29F	1988	First Yorkshire (C), 1999	
889	F156XYG	Leyland Olympian ONCL10/1RZ	Northern Counties			B45/29F	1988	Yorkshire Rider (C), 1999	
890	F158XYG	Leyland Olympian ONCL10/1RZ	Northern Counties			B45/29F	1988	Yorkshire Rider (C), 1999	

For a while PMT used a livery based on silver-grey for the limited-stop services. Several Olymians carried the scheme and so did Lance 867, N867CEH one of five with Plaxton bodywork delivered to the company when under Badgerline control. FirstGroup was formed following the merger of Badgerline with GRT, the Aberdeen-based group. *Cliff Beeton*

891	A171VFM	Leyland Olympian ONLXB/1R	Eastern Coach Works		B45/32F	1984	Crosville, 1990
892	B181BLG	Leyland Olympian ONLXB/1R	Eastern Coach Works		B45/32F	1984	Crosville, 1990
893	B182BLG	Leyland Olympian ONLXB/1R	Eastern Coach Works		B45/32F	1984	Crosville, 1990
894	B188BLG	Leyland Olympian ONLXB/1R	Eastern Coach Works		B45/32F	1985	Crosville, 1990
895	B195BLG	Leyland Olympian ONLXB/1R	Eastern Coach Works		B45/32F	1985	Crosville, 1990
896	B199DTU	Leyland Olympian ONLXB/1R	Eastern Coach Works		B45/32F	1985	Crosville, 1990
897	B200DTU	Leyland Olympian ONLXB/1R	Eastern Coach Works		BC42/32F	1985	Crosville, 1990
898	B201DTU	Leyland Olympian ONLXB/1R	Eastern Coach Works		BC42/32F	1985	Crosville, 1990
899	B202DTU	Leyland Olympian ONLXB/1R	Eastern Coach Works		BC42/32F	1985	Crosville, 1990

901-920

Dennis Dart 9SDL3011 Plaxton Pointer BC35F 1991-92

901	J901SEH	905	J905SEH	909	J909SEH	913	J913SEH	917	J917SEH
902	J902SEH	906	J906SEH	910	J910SEH	914	J914SEH	918	J918SEH
903	J903SEH	907	J907SEH	911	J911SEH	915	J915SEH	919	K919XRF
904	J904SEH	908	J908SEH	912	J912SEH	916	J916SEH	920	K920XRF

921-929

Dennis Dart 9SDL3016 Plaxton Pointer BC35F 1992

921	K921XRF	923	K923XRF	925	K925XRF	927	K927XRF	929	K929XRF
922	K922XRF	924	K924XRF	926	K926XRF	928	K928XRF		

931	L931HFA	Dennis Dart 9SDL3034	Plaxton Pointer	BC35F	1993
932	L932HFA	Dennis Dart 9SDL3034	Plaxton Pointer	BC35F	1993
933	L933HFA	Dennis Dart 9SDL3034	Plaxton Pointer	BC35F	1993
934	L934HFA	Dennis Dart 9SDL3034	Plaxton Pointer	BC35F	1993
935	L935HFA	Dennis Dart 9.8SDL3025	Marshall C36	BC36F	1993
936	L936HFA	Dennis Dart 9.8SDL3025	Marshall C36	BC36F	1993

937-942

Dennis Dart 9SDL3034 Plaxton Pointer BC35F 1994

937	L937LRF	939	L939LRF	940	L940LRF	941	L941LRF	942	L942LRF
938	L938LRF								

Four of the five recently delivered Dennis Darts are allocated to Chester where 992, X992FFA is seen shortly after entering service. Vehicles based at Chester usually carry the Crosville local name. *Andrew Jarosz*

In the spring of 2000 the Leyland Olympians that operate on the Alton Towers service received special liveries using the corporate colours applied in traditional styling. Seen leaving Hanley bus station with a heavy load is 756, G756XRE. *Cliff Beeton*

943-952

Dennis Dart 9SDL3040 — Marshall C37 — BC35F 1994

943	M943SRE	945	M945SRE	947	M947SRE	949	M949SRE	952	M952SRE
944	M944SRE	946	M946SRE	948	M948SRE	951	M951SRE		

953-972

Dennis Dart 9.8SDL3054 — Plaxton Pointer — BC36F 1995

953	M953XVT	957	M957XVT	961	M961XVT	965	M965XVT	969	M969XVT
954	M954XVT	958	M958XVT	962	M962XVT	966	M966XVT	970	M970XVT
955	M955XVT	959	M959XVT	963	M963XVT	967	M967XVT	971	M971XVT
956	M956XVT	960	M960XVT	964	M964XVT	968	M968XVT	972	M972XVT

973	P973MBF	Dennis Dart	Plaxton Pointer	B36F	1997
974	P974MBF	Dennis Dart	Plaxton Pointer	B36F	1997
975	P975MBF	Dennis Dart	Plaxton Pointer	B36F	1997
976	P976MBF	Dennis Dart	Plaxton Pointer	B36F	1997

977-981

Dennis Dart SLF — Plaxton Pointer 2 — N37F 1998

977	R977NVT	978	R978NVT	979	R979NVT	980	R980NVT	981	R981NVT

982-989

Dennis Dart SLF — Alexander ALX200 — N37F 1999

982	T982LBF	984	T984LBF	986	T986LBF	988	V988GBF	989	V989GBF
983	T983LBF	985	T985LBF	987	T987LBF				

991-995

Dennis Dart SLF — Alexander ALX200 — N37F 2000

991	X991FFA	992	X992FFA	993	X993FFA	994	X994FFA	995	X995FFA

The Cheshire & Merseyside Bus Handbook

Ancillary vehicles:-

TLL16	GSU845T	Leyland Leopard PSU3E/3R	Alexander AYS	TV	1979	KCB Network, 1996
TLL17	GSU838T	Leyland Leopard PSU3E/3R	Alexander AYS	TV	1979	Greater Manchester, 1997
TLL18	EGB50T	Leyland Leopard PSU3E/3R	Alexander AY	TV	1978	Northampton, 1998
TLL19	MDT238W	Leyland Leopard PSU3E/3R	Duple Dominant II	TV	1981	First Mainline, 2000
G128	C128VRE	Mercedes-Benz L608D	PMT Hanbridge	B-F	1985	
G182	D182BEH	Mercedes-Benz L608D	PMT Hanbridge	B20F	1986	
G210	C706JMB	Mercedes-Benz L608D	Reeve Burgess	B19F	1986	Crosville, 1990
TMM440	K440XRF	Mercedes-Benz 709D	Plaxton Beaver	B24F	1992	
TWC314	F314REH	Leyland Swift LBM6T/2RS	PMT Knype	TV	1989	
TWC315	F315REH	Leyland Swift LBM6T/2RS	PMT Knype	TV	1989	
TWC316	F316REH	Leyland Swift LBM6T/2RS	PMT Knype	TV	1989	
TVG611	WTU472W	Bristol VRT/SL3/501(6LXB)	Eastern Coach Works	TV	1980	Crosville, 1990

Previous Registrations:

507EXA	G845GNV, FSU333, G845GNV, PSU627	J751AAW	J920HGD, XRF1X
C770PUG	C477EUA, 507EXA	K174EUX	SBS7204J(Singapore)
D810NWW	D810NWW, FXI8653	TJI4828	F758OJH
D875ELL	D806NDW, 810DYE	WJI5239	A155EPA
FXI8653	E44JRF	XRF1X	F619XWY
F102GRM	F102GRM, 292CLT	XRF2X	E950LEH
GBF78N	GBF78N, 507EXA		

Allocations

Adderley Green (Dividy Road) - PMT

Outstation:- Leek

Mercedes-Benz	232	248	254	255	256	257	258	259
	260	261	262	263	264	265	266	267
	268	269	270	430	431	577	578	579
	580	581	582	583	584	585	586	587
	590							
Iveco	117							
Renault	533							
MetroRider	378	379	380	381	382	383	391	392
	393	394	395	396				
Solo	73	89	91	92	93	94	95	96
	97	98	99					
Dart	902	903	926	927	928	929	939	953
	954							
Optare Delta	803	804	805	806	807	808	809	
Lynx	852	853	854	855	856	857		
Scania L113	813	814	815	816	817	818	819	820
	821	833	834	835	836	837	838	878

Burslem (Scotia Road) - PMT

Mercedes-Benz	245	247	355	441	553	554	555	556
	557	558	559	560	561	562	563	569
	570	571						
Dart	914	915	916	917	932	957	958	959
	961	962	982	983	984			
Lance	863	864	865	866	867	868	869	870
Lynx	858	859						
Scania L94	822	823	824	825	826	827	828	829
	830	831	832					
Bristol VR	709	728						
Olympian	746	747	779	784	785	787		

Cheadle (Brookhouse Industrial Estate) - PMT

Dart	921	922	924	938	940	941	942	953
	963	985	986	987	988	989	991	
Olympian	739	758	761					

Three Northern Counties-bodied Volvo Olympians latterly with First Yorkshire joined PMT in 1999. All are now allocated to Dukinfield for the Pennine operation, but 889, F156XYG, was pictured at Hanley while working to Audley Wereton before its re-allocation. The reported transfer of the Pennine operation to First Manchester has not taken place and, for the time being, it will remain part of PMT. *Cliff Beeton*

Chester (Liverpool Road) - Crosville

Mercedes-Benz	359	411	415	416	444	566		
Solo	57	58	59	65	66	67	68	69
	70	71	72					
MetroRider	224	225	227	228	230	321		
Dart	907	912	913	918	931	933	937	992
	993	994	995					
Tiger	24							
Lynx	847							
Scania	810	871	872	873				
Bristol VR	618	729						
Olympian	745	751	763	769	775	796	798	799
	898	899						

Crewe (Second Avenue, Crewe Gates Farm) - PMT

Mercedes-Benz	31	32	33	34	35	36	342	354
	573							
Leopard	295							
Tiger	297							
Lynx	860	861						
Bristol VR	625	628	701	707	723	731		
Olympian	744	760	773	774	776	781	786	788

Dukinfield (Rothesay Garage, Broadway) - Pennine

Mercedes-Benz	357	358	360	361	375	405	410	422
	423	424	425	426	427	436	488	
MetroRider	322	323						
Dart	944	946	947	948	965	966		
Tiger	299							
Volvo	884							
Lynx	842	843	844	846	849	851		
Atlantean	626	627						
Olympian	700	733	740	741	743	748	749	768
	888	889	890					

Ellesmere Port (Wellington Road) - Crosville

Mercedes-Benz	407	408	409	412	434
MetroRider	377	389	390		
Solo	66	67			
Dart	901	904	934	960	
Bristol VR	608	609	610	614	
Olympian	745	891			

Moreton (Tarren Way Industrial Estate) - Red Rider

Mercedes-Benz	593							
Solo	60	61	62	63	64			
Renault Master	29							
Renault S75	534							
MetroRider	231							
Dart	969	970	971	972				
Olympian	734	752	753	754	755	764	765	766
	768	772	791	792	794	795	893	894
	895	896	897					

Newcastle-under-Lyme (Liverpool Road) - Flexi

Iveco/Ford	178							
Peugeot	25	26	28					
Mercedes-Benz	100	101	102	107	109	110	332	334
	341	345	366	376	437	438	439	446
	448	451	454	460	467	490	491	494
	498							
Swift	312	318						
Tiger	44	45	47					
Volvo	46	883						
Bristol VR (Opentop)	622							

Newcastle-under-Lyme (Liverpool Road) - PMT

Mercedes-Benz	233	234	235	236	237	238	239	240
	241	242	243	244	246	250	251	252
	253	330	338	339	370	371	373	406
	413	414	417	418	419	420	421	428
	429	442	564	565	567	572	573	574
	575	576	588	589	591	592	593	594
Solo	74	75	76	77	78			
Dart	902	903	909	910	911	919	920	925
	943	955	964	973	974	975	976	
Optare Delta	801	802						
Lynx	845							
Volvo	885							
Olympian	738	742	756	757	759	762		

65

PMT have an accessible coaching operation under the Flexi name. Illustrating the livery used is 46, 507EXA, a Volvo B10M with Jonckheere Deauville bodywork recently transferred from First Aberdeen where it operated with the Mairs fleet. *Cliff Beeton*

Rock Ferry (New Chester Road) - Crosville

Tecnobus	51	52	53	54	55	56		
Mercedes-Benz	374							
MetroRider	384	385	386	387	388			
Dart	905	906	908	935	936	945	949	951
	952	956	967	968	977	978	979	980
	981							
Lance	862							
Lynx	848	850						
Scania	811	812	874	875	876	877	879	880
	881							
Olympian	750	767	770	782	892			
Dennis Dominator	690	691	692	693	694	698	699	

Unallocated

Mercedes-Benz	88	104	114	115	331	335	336	340
	343	344	346	349	352	356	362	363
	365	367	368	369	372	445	483	484
	485	486	487	489	492	493	495	496
	497	568						
Peugeot	22	23	27					
Renault	30	532						
Swift	310	311	313	317	320			
Bristol VRT	708							
On loan to First Capital								
Olympian	735	736	737	789	793	796	797	

GREENBUS

L McVey, 22 Sixth Avenue, Fazakerley, Liverpool, L9 9DU

F276LND	Mercedes-Benz 307D	Northern Counties	M12L	1989	Furlong, Kirkby, 1999
J444ABC	Optare MetroRider MR01	Optare	B33F	1992	CMT (ABC), Aintree, 1999
T36CCK	Dennis Dart SLF	Plaxton MPD	N29F	1999	
T37CCK	Dennis Dart SLF	Plaxton MPD	N29F	1999	

Livery: Green and yellow
Depot: Hanson Road, Aintree

The Fazakerley-based operator Greenbus employes two Mini Pointer Darts on Merseytravel route 121 from Aintree Station. Pictured in Muirhead Avenue, Norris Green is T36CCK which illustrates the livery carried by the pair. *Richard Godfrey*

HALTON

Halton Borough Transport Ltd, Moor Lane, Widnes, Halton, WA8 7AF

1-14			Dennis Dart SLF		Marshall Capital		N39F	1998-99		
1	R712MEW	4	S196FFM	7	S195FFM	10	T759LFM	13	V994LLG
2	R713MEW	5	S197FFM	8	T757LFM	11	T760LFM	14	V995LLG
3	R714MEW	6	S194FFM	9	T758LFM	12	V993LLG		

15-22			Dennis Dart SLF		Marshall Capital		N41F*	2000	15-7 are N43F; 20 is N26F and 8.8m	
15	W471VMA	17	W986XMA	19	X965ULG	21	X967ULG	22	X968ULG
16	W987XMA	18	W985XMA	20	X966ULG		

35	H35HBG	Leyland Lynx LX2R11C15Z4R	Leyland Lynx II	B51F	1991
36	J249KWM	Leyland Lynx LX2R11C15Z4R	Leyland Lynx II	B51F	1991
37	J250KWM	Leyland Lynx LX112L10ZR1R	Leyland	B51F	1991
38	J251KWM	Leyland Lynx LX2R11C15Z4R	Leyland Lynx II	B51F	1991
46	J628LHF	Leyland Lynx LX2R11C15Z4R	Leyland Lynx II	B51F	1992
47	J630LHF	Leyland Lynx LX2R11C15Z4R	Leyland Lynx II	B51F	1992
48	J629LHF	Leyland Lynx LX2R11C15Z4R	Leyland Lynx II	B51F	1992
49	J929MKC	Leyland Lynx LX2R11C15Z4R	Leyland Lynx II	B51F	1992

Halton operates a fleet of Leyland Lynx that meets its requirement for larger capacity single-decks. Pictured at St Helens is 61, J924MKC, which features the ramp floor between the lower level and the higher floor over the rear axle. An alternative to the ramp was a step which is identified by the last character of the chassis code. Unlike the National which was integral the Lynx was available for others to body. An early prototype Lynx body built on a Tiger chassis has just been located in Australia. *Gerry Mead*

The Cheshire & Merseyside Bus Handbook

Recent arrivals with Halton have been Marshall-bodied Dennis Darts. In principal, two lengths have been supplied, though number 20 is an 8.8-metre version. Pictured in Roe Street is number 2, R713MEW.
Tony Wilson

52	J925MKC	Leyland Lynx LX2R11C15Z4R	Leyland Lynx II	B51F	1992
53	K852MTJ	Leyland Lynx LX2R11C15Z4R	Leyland Lynx II	B51F	1992
57	K853MTJ	Leyland Lynx LX2R11C15Z4R	Leyland Lynx II	B51F	1992
58	J921MKC	Leyland Lynx LX2R11C15Z4S	Leyland Lynx II	B51F	1992
59	J922MKC	Leyland Lynx LX2R11C15Z4S	Leyland Lynx II	B51F	1992
60	J923MKC	Leyland Lynx LX2R11C15Z4R	Leyland Lynx II	B51F	1992
61	J924MKC	Leyland Lynx LX2R11C15Z4R	Leyland Lynx II	B51F	1992
62	J926MKC	Leyland Lynx LX2R11C15Z4R	Leyland Lynx II	B51F	1992
63	J927MKC	Leyland Lynx LX2R11C15Z4R	Leyland Lynx II	B51F	1992
64	J928MKC	Leyland Lynx LX2R11C15Z4R	Leyland Lynx II	B51F	1992

67-78

Dennis Dart 9.8SDL3054   Marshall C37   B40F   1994-96

67w	M579WLV	70w	M582WLV	73	M71AKA	75	M74AKA	77	N672CLV
68w	M580WLV	71	M583WLV	74	M73AKA	76	N671CLV	78	N673CLV
69w	M581WLV	72	M584WLV						

79-90

Dennis Dart SLF   Marshall Capital   N39F   1997

79	P341OEW	82	P344OEW	85	R402XFL	87	R407XFL	89	R409XFL
80	P342OEW	83	P345OEW	86	R403XFL	88	R408XFL	90	R410XFL
81	P343OEW	84	R401XFL						

Ancillary Vehicle

| 98w | KTB748F | Leyland Leopard PSU4/1R | East Lancashire | RV | 1968 |

Livery: Red and white

HAPPY AL's

T A Cullinan, Corporation Road, Birkenhead, Wirral, CH41 8EQ

1	ALZ3537	Bristol VRT/SL3/6LXB	Eastern Coach Works	B43/27D	1980	Oxford Bus Company, 1993
2	ALZ3542	Bristol VRT/SL3/6LXB	Eastern Coach Works	BC39/27F	1979	Badgerline, 1992
3	ALZ6403	Bristol VRT/SL3/6LXB	Eastern Coach Works	B43/31F	1980	RoadCar, 1995
4	XAZ1361	Leyland Atlantean AN68C/1R	Roe	B43/31F	1982	KHCT, 1994
5	XAZ1362	Leyland Atlantean AN68C/1R	Roe	B43/31F	1982	KHCT, 1994
6	XAZ1363	Leyland Atlantean AN68C/1R	Roe	B43/31F	1982	KHCT, 1994
7	XAZ1364	Leyland Atlantean AN68C/1R	Roe	B43/31F	1982	KHCT, 1994
8	XAZ1865	Leyland Atlantean AN68C/1R	Roe	B43/31F	1982	KHCT, 1994
9	XAZ1370	Leyland Atlantean AN68C/1R	Roe	B43/31F	1982	KHCT, 1994
10	XAZ1371	Bristol VRT/SL3/6LXB	Eastern Coach Works	B43/27D	1981	Oxford Bus Company, 1993
11	XAZ1372	Bristol VRT/SL3/6LXB	Eastern Coach Works	B43/27D	1980	Oxford Bus Company, 1993
12	XAZ1373	Bristol VRT/SL3/6LXB	Eastern Coach Works	B43/27D	1980	Oxford Bus Company, 1993
13	ALS645V	Bristol VRT/SL3/6LXB	Eastern Coach Works	B43/30F	1980	City Line, 1993
14	KSD102W	Volvo-Ailsa B55-10	Alexander AV	B44/35F	1980	Avon Buses, Prenton, 1995
15	PFC513W	Bristol VRT/SL3/6LXB	Eastern Coach Works	B43/27D	1981	Oxford Bus Company, 1993
17	MNS48Y	Dennis Dominator DD162	Alexander RL	B45/34F	1983	Kelvin Central, 1995
18	MNS51Y	Dennis Dominator DD162	Alexander RL	B45/34F	1983	Kelvin Central, 1995
19	A9ALS	Leyland Olympian ONLXB/1R	Eastern Coach Works	BC42/29F	1985	Crosville Wales, 1990
20	A13ALS	Leyland Olympian ONTL11/2R	Eastern Coach Works	C45/28F	1985	Thamesway, 1991
21	A14ALS	Leyland Olympian ONTL11/2R	Eastern Coach Works	C45/25F	1985	Thamesway, 1991
22	A16ALS	Leyland Olympian ONLXB/1R	Eastern Coach Works	BC42/29F	1985	Crosville Wales, 1990
23	A17ALS	Leyland Olympian ONLXB/1R	Eastern Coach Works	BC42/29F	1985	Crosville Wales, 1990
24	ALZ7211	Bristol VRT/SL3/6LXB	Eastern Coach Works	B43/27D	1980	Oxford Bus Company, 1993
25	A518VKG	Leyland Olympian ONLXB/1R	East Lancashire	B43/31F	1984	Cardiff Bus, 1999
26	A519VKG	Leyland Olympian ONLXB/1R	East Lancashire	B43/31F	1984	Cardiff Bus, 1999
27	ALZ3566	Leyland National 11351A/1R		B49F	1979	Mainline, Sheffield, 1997
28	ALZ4516	Leyland National 2 NL116AL11/1R		B52F	1980	Stagecoach Busways, 1996
29	ALZ6293	Leyland National 2 NL106AL11/1R		B44F	1981	Avon Buses, Prenton, 1997
30	ALZ9284	Leyland National 11351/1R (Volvo)		B52F	1974	Volvo demonstrator, 1998
31	ALZ9286	Leyland National 11351A/1R (Volvo)		B49F	1976	Volvo demonstrator, 1998
32	ALZ9328	Leyland National 11351A/1R (Volvo)		B49F	1979	Volvo demonstrator, 1998
33	A12ALS	Leyland National 2 NL116L11/1R		B52F	1986	Avon Buses, Prenton, 1996
34	A133FDC	Leyland National 2 NL116AHLXCT/1R		B49F	1983	Avon Buses, Prenton, 1997
35	N17ALS	DAF DE02LTSB220	Ikarus CitiBus	B49F	1996	
36	N18ALS	DAF DE02LTSB220	Ikarus CitiBus	B49F	1996	
37	N900ALS	Volvo B6LE	Wright Crusader	NC35F	1996	Ralph's, Langley, 1997
38	N100ALS	Volvo B6LE	Wright Crusader	NC35F	1996	Ralph's, Langley, 1997
39	R14ALS	Optare Excel L1150	Optare	N41F	1997	
40	R15ALS	Optare Excel L1150	Optare	N41F	1997	

Two Optare Excel low-floor buses were acquired by Happy Al's in 1997 and remain the newest buses in the fleet. Illustrating the type is R15ALS, pictured working to Arrowe Park Hospital on a Merseytravel service.
Cliff Beeton

42	ALZ1221	Van Hool T815	Van Hool Alicron	C53F	1986	Windmill, Copford, 1988
43	ALZ4161	Van Hool T815	Van Hool Alicron	C49FT	1986	Windmill, Copford, 1988
44	A18ALS	Leyland Royal Tiger RTC	Leyland Doyen	C53F	1987	Sinclair, Greenhead, 1993
45	A19ALS	Leyland Royal Tiger RTC	Leyland Doyen	C53F	1987	Lancaster, 1993
46	A20ALS	Neoplan N122	Neoplan Skyliner	C51/18CT	1987	Express Travel, Perth, 1994
47	XAD835	Volvo B58-56	Plaxton Supreme III	C53F	1976	Taj, Walsall, 1995
48	ALZ3102	Van Hool T815	Van Hool Alizée	C49FT	1991	Warrington, 1994
49	ALZ2928	Leyland Royal Tiger RTC	Leyland Doyen	C53F	1988	West Riding, 1989
50	ALZ3561	Van Hool T815	Van Hool Alizée	C49FT	1991	Warrington, 1994
5	HPV849	DAF SBR2300DHS570	Van Hool Astrobel	C57/14CT	1987	Hardings Tours, Huyton, 2000
56	MIL9765	DAF SBR3000DKZ570	Plaxton Paramount 4000 III	C55/19CT	1990	Dunn Line, Nottingham, 1999
57	B553ATX	Leyland Olympian ONLXB/1R	East Lancashire	B43/31F	1984	Cardiff Bus, 2000
60	C560GWO	Leyland Olympian ONLXB/1R	East Lancashire	B43/27F	1986	Cardiff Bus, 2000
61	C561GWO	Leyland Olympian ONLXB/1R	East Lancashire	B43/27F	1986	Cardiff Bus, 1999
62	C562GWO	Leyland Olympian ONLXB/1R	East Lancashire	B43/27F	1986	Cardiff Bus, 1999
63	C563GWO	Leyland Olympian ONLXB/1R	East Lancashire	B43/27F	1986	Cardiff Bus, 1999
64	C564GWO	Leyland Olympian ONLXB/1R	East Lancashire	B43/27F	1986	Cardiff Bus, 1999
65	C565GWO	Leyland Olympian ONLXB/1R	East Lancashire	B43/27F	1986	Cardiff Bus, 1999
67	C567GWO	Leyland Olympian ONLXB/1R	East Lancashire	B43/27F	1986	Cardiff Bus, 1999

Previous Registrations:

A9ALS	C205GTU	ALZ6403	HWJ929W
A10ALS	-	ALZ7211	KJO509W
A12ALS	C974PFS	ALZ9284	GBF74N
A13ALS	B692BPU	ALZ9286	UHG728R
A14ALS	B695BPU	ALZ9328	EUM888T
A16ALS	C206GTU	HPV849	E325EVH
A17ALS	C207GTU	MIL9765	G778HOV, 245DOC
A18ALS	E44MMT, PJI3749	N17ALS	N31FWU
A19ALS	D457EEG, IIL4012	N18ALS	N32FWU
A20ALS	E91VWA	N100ALS	N902NNR
ALS645V	AHU518V	N900ALS	N901NNR
ALZ1221	TJF757, C384AAD, BAZ4772, C769WKS	XAD835	MNR738P
ALZ2928	E49TYG, A10ALS	XAZ1361	WAG369X
ALX3102	H7CLW	XAZ1362	WAG371X
ALZ3537	KJO508W	XAZ1363	WAG372X
ALZ3542	TWS907T	XAZ1364	WAG375X
ALZ3561	H6CLW	XAZ1365	WAG380X
ALZ3566	CWX666T	XAZ1370	WAG382X
ALZ4161	C426VAY, 196COY, C426VAY	XAZ1371	PFC511W
ALZ4516	SNS822W	XAZ1372	KJO503W
ALZ6293	JCK846W	XAZ1373	KJO506W

Livery: White, red, orange and yellow.

While the East Lancashire Greenway upgrade to the Leyland National included body modifications other suppliers retained the National styling. Volvo introduced a pack that included upgrades to many engineering parts inlcuding a new engine. Three of the buses that promoted this product are now with Happy Al's, inlcuding ALZ9286, once new to Ribble.
R L Wilson

71

HARDINGS

Hardings Tours Ltd, 60 St Johns Road, Huyton, Liverpool, L36 5SY

NIL2994	Scania K112CRB	Van Hool Alizée	C49FT	1988	Dodds of Troon, 1996
MIL2267	Scania K113CRB	Van Hool Alizée	C55F	1989	Wingate Travel, 1996
K3SUP	Scania K113CRB	Plaxton Premiére 350	C49FT	1993	Supreme, Hadleigh, 1996
K756YFR	Volvo B10M-60	Jonckheere Deauville P599	C53F	1993	Redline, Penwortham, 1998
K806KWX	Volvo B10M-60	Jonckheere Deauville P599	C53F	1993	Allan, Castleford, 1999
K807KWX	Volvo B10M-60	Jonckheere Deauville P599	C53F	1993	Allan, Castleford, 1999
L401LHE	Scania K113CRB	Van Hool Alizée	C49FT	1994	
L402LHE	Scania K113CRB	Van Hool Alizée	C49FT	1994	
L403LHE	Scania K113CRB	Van Hool Alizée	C49FT	1994	
M208PAN	Scania K113CRB	Berkhof Excellence 1000L	C51FT	1994	
M397ACK	Volvo B10M-62	Plaxton Premiére 350	C49FT	1994	Redline, Penwortham, 1998
N205VRX	Volvo B10M-62	Berkhof Excellence 1000L	C51FT	1995	
N206VRX	Volvo B10M-62	Berkhof Excellence 1000L	C51FT	1995	
R880SDT	Scania L94IB	Irizar Intercentury 12.32	C53F	1997	
R890SDT	Scania L94IB	Irizar Intercentury 12.32	C53F	1997	
T741JHE	Scania L94IB	Van Hool T9 Alizée	C49FT	1999	
T742JHE	Scania L94IB	Irizar Intercentury 12.32	C53F	1999	

Previous Registrations:

K3SUP	K991HVO	M397ACK	M112SFV, 4RN, A14RED
K756YFR	K923RGE, 14RED	MIL2267	F600GET
K806KWX	K842HUM, UOI880	NIL2994	E760RCS
K807KWX	K837HUM, OIJ1721		

Livery: White, red, orange and yellow
Depots: St Johns Road, Huyton and Wilson Road, Huyton

Scania's arrangement with Irizar has seen a large number of this combination supplied to operators in northern Europe, including Britain. Two heights of the model are built with the lower-height Intercentury that continues to use the many panels common with the Century 12.35 & 12.37 models. R880SDT is shown here.
David Donati collection

HELMS of EASTHAM

Helms Coaches Ltd, 11 Clare Road, Bootle, L20 9LY

Reg	Chassis	Body	Seating	Year	History
SCN254S	Leyland Atlantean AN68A/2R	Alexander AL	B49/37F	1978	Liverpool MS, Aintree, 1999
SCN266S	Leyland Atlantean AN68A/2R	Alexander AL	B49/37F	1978	Wilson, Strathaven, 2000
SCN276S	Leyland Atlantean AN68A/2R	Alexander AL	B49/37F	1978	Liverpool MS, Aintree, 1999
DOC31V	Leyland National 2 NL116L11/1R		B50F	1980	Teamdeck, Hanley, 2000
EKA224Y	Dennis Lancet SD510	Duple Dominant	BC31F	1983	Knotty Bus, Cotes Heath, 1999
A116ESA	Leyland Tiger TRBTL11/2R	Alexander P	B53F	1983	Stagecoach Bluebird Buses, 1999
A118ESA	Leyland Tiger TRBTL11/2R	Alexander P	B53F	1983	Stagecoach Bluebird Buses, 1999
A53HRE	Leyland Tiger TRCTL11/2R	Plaxton Paramount 3200 E	C53F	1984	Hulleys of Baslow, 2000
FAZ3525	Volvo B10M-61	Van Hool Astral	C47/11FT	1984	Elite, Stockport, 1995
B552ATX	Leyland Olympian ONLXB/1R	East Lancashire	B43/31F	1984	Cardiff Bus, 1999
B554ATX	Leyland Olympian ONLXB/1R	East Lancashire	B43/31F	1984	Cardiff Bus, 1999
B555ATX	Leyland Olympian ONLXB/1R	East Lancashire	B43/31F	1984	Cardiff Bus, 1999
B111KPF	Leyland Tiger TRCTL11/3RH	Berkhof Everest 370	C53F	1984	Aintree Coachline, 1999
B85SWX	Leyland Tiger TRCTL11/3RH	Plaxton Paramount 3200 E	C53F	1985	Arriva The Shires (Southend), 2000
B132SED	Leyland National 2 NL116L11/1R		B49F	1985	Arriva Cymru, 2000
D711SKB	Leyland Lynx LX563TL11FR1	Leyland Lynx	B51F	1986	Arriva Cymru, 2000
E641VFY	Leyland Lynx LX112TL11ZR1R	Leyland Lynx	B51F	1987	Arriva Cymru, 2000
G802XLO	Volvo B10M-60	Plaxton Paramount 3200 III	C53F	1990	Claremont, Worcester Park, 1999
K505WNR	Volvo B10M-60	Plaxton Première 350	C53F	1993	Aintree Coachline, 2000
K88ABC	Volvo B10M-60	Plaxton Première 320	C50F	1993	CMT, Aintree, 2000
K888ABC	Volvo B10M-60	Plaxton Première 320	C50F	1993	CMT, Aintree, 2000
L20ABC	Volvo B10M-60	Plaxton Première 320	C53F	1993	CMT, Aintree, 2000

Previous registrations

FAZ3525	A525WGK, ROI5103, A797KFP	K88ABC	K847HUM	
JIL4404	SND300X	L20ABC	L52CNY	

Livery: Cream and red
Depot: Hooton Park Stables, Eastham, Wirral

Recent arrivals with Helms of Eastham are three former Cardiff Bus Leyland Olympians with East Lancashire bodywork. Representing the type is B555ATX. In October 2000, two Leyland Lynx were added to the fleet.
Phillip Stephenson

HOLLINSHEADS

Hollinshead Coaches Ltd, Wharf Road, Biddulph, Stoke-on-Trent, ST8 6AQ

FFR486S	Bedford YMT	Plaxton Supreme III	C53F	1978	Murray, Blackpool, 1993
GBW100V	Bedford YMT	Plaxton Supreme IV	C53F	1980	Tours, Isle of Man, 1988
NIB8318	Leyland Tiger TRCTL11/3RZ	Plaxton Paramount 3200	C53F	1985	Mosley, Barugh Green, 1995
NIB8317	Leyland Tiger TRCTL11/3R	Plaxton Paramount 3200 II	C53F	1986	Mosley, Barugh Green, 1995
RIL1023	Bedford YNT	Plaxton Paramount 3200 II	C53F	1986	Grayline, Bicester, 1993
RIL1015	Volvo B10M-61	Plaxton Paramount 3500 III	C53F	1987	Stevensons, Uttoxeter, 1992
RIL1016	Volvo B10M-61	Plaxton Paramount 3200 III	C53F	1989	Dunn-Line, Nottingham, 1994
RIL1017	Volvo B10M-60	Plaxton Paramount 3500 III	C53F	1991	Southern Coaches, Barrhead, 1997
J10BUS	Volvo B10M-60	Plaxton Paramount 3500 III	C53F	1992	Irving, Carlisle, 1999
P223YGG	Volvo B10M-62	Van Hool Alizée	C53F	1997	Trathens, Plymouth, 1999

Previous registrations

GBW100V	CJO321V, 786AFC, GBW100V, 4356MAN, BMN111A		
NIB8317	C770KHL	RIL1016	F869RFP
NIB8318	B849EHE	RIL1017	H830AHS
RIL1015	D805SGB	RIL1023	C502JCY

Livery: Red and cream

The Hollinsheads coach operation compises a fleet of fifty-three seat coaches mostly built by Plaxton. Representing the fleet is NIB8317 which is one of two Leyland Tiger chassis operated. *Cliff Beeton*

HUGGINS

JW DJ & I Huggins & D Simmons, 21 Tarran Way North, Moreton, Wirral, CH46 4UA

NIL7948	Leyland Fleetline FE30AGR	Northern Counties	B47/31D	1977	Darlington, 1995	
RIL9164	Leyland Leopard PSU5D/5R	Wadham Stringer Vanguard	B40F	1981	MoD, 1995 (50AC10)	
RIL9157	Leyland Atlantean AN68D/1R	Northern Counties	B43/32F	1983	Stagecoach Manchester, 1997	
RIL9158	Leyland Atlantean AN68D/2R	East Lancashire	BC45/32F	1983	Stagecoach Ribble, 1997	
A8GGT	Leyland Tiger TRCTL11/3R	Plaxton Paramount 3200 E	C57F	1983	Stagecoach Midland Red, 1999	
A725THV	MCW Metrobus DR101/18	MCW	B41/28D	1984	London United, 1998	
C749OCN	MCW Metrobus DR102/25	MCW	B46/31F	1986	Go-Ahead Northern, 1999	
C770OCN	MCW Metrobus DR102/25	MCW	B46/31F	1986	Go-Ahead Northern, 1999	
C772OCN	MCW Metrobus DR102/25	MCW	B46/31F	1986	Go-Ahead Northern, 1999	
C773OCN	MCW Metrobus DR102/25	MCW	B46/31F	1986	Go-Ahead Northern, 1999	
C774OCN	MCW Metrobus DR102/25	MCW	B46/31F	1986	Go-Ahead Northern, 1999	
RIL9160	Dennis Javelin 11SDA1905	Duple 320	C53F	1987	Dennis demonstrator, 1992	
E511PWR	Volkswagen LT55	Optare City Pacer	BC25F	1987	County, 1993	
E413DMA	Leyland Tiger TRCTL11/3LZ	Plaxton Derwent 2	BC56F	1987	MoD, 1997 (87KF10)	
E222FLD	Scania N112DRB	Van Hool Alizée L	C47F	1987	Heyfordian, Upper Heyford, 1997	
E564MAC	Peugeot-Talbot Pullman	Talbot	B22F	1988	Barrow, 1989	
E571MAC	Peugeot-Talbot Pullman	Talbot	BC20F	1988	Barrow, 1990	
RIL9161	Dennis Javelin 11SDL1905	Duple 320	C55F	1989	Quo Vadis, Stanwell Moor, 1993	
G574BHP	Peugeot-Talbot Freeway	Talbot	B16FL	1990	Shropshire CC, 1997	
G909GOL	Peugeot-Talbot Freeway	Talbot	B16FL	1990	Derbyshire CC, 1997	
RIL9162	Leyland Tiger TR2R62C21Z5/8	Plaxton Paramount 3200 III	C51FT	1991	Cyril Evans, Senghenydd, 1999	
RIL9163	Leyland Tiger TRCL10/3ARZA	Plaxton Paramount 3200 III	C53F	1991	Metropolitan Police, 1997	
J915HGD	Peugeot-Talbot Pullman	TBP	B23F	1991	Shropshire CC, 1997	
K943EWG	Peugeot-Talbot Pullman	TBP	B16FL	1993	Derbyshire CC, 1999	
K603OCA	Dennis Javelin	Wadham Stringer Vanguard II	BC40F	1993	MoD, 1999 ( )	

Previous registrations

A8GGT	A202RHT		RIL9161	G857VAY
NIL7948	UTV210S		RIL9162	H258GRY
RIL9157	ANA646Y		RIL9163	J932CYK
RIL9158	BFV222Y			
RIL9160	E321FPE			

Livery: White and duo-blue

Displaying the Manchester-style destination blinds is Northern Counties-bodied Atlantean ANA646Y which arrived in the Huggins fleet in 1997 and has subsequently been re-registered RIL9157.
R L Wilson

HUXLEY

J F Huxley, Rose Cottage, Greaves Lane East, Threapwood, Malpas, Cheshire, SY14 7AT

YBN630V	Leyland Leopard PSU3E/4R	Plaxton Supreme IV Express	C53F	1979	West Sussex CC, 1998
YBN632V	Leyland Leopard PSU3E/4R	Plaxton Supreme IV Express	C51F	1980	Aintree Coachline, Bootle, 1992
NLS987W	Leyland National 2 NL116L11/1R		B52F	1980	Stagecoach Midland Red, 1999
GUW441W	Leyland National 2 NL106AL11/2R		B44F	1981	Arriva The Shires, 2000
HUF625X	Leyland National 2 NL116AL11/1R		B49F	1982	Stagecoach South (C), 1999
HIL3935	Volvo B10M-61	Van Hool Alizée	C48FT	1982	Appleby, Conisholme, 1991
MFE504	Volvo B10M-61	Van Hool Alizée	C46FT	1982	Tellings, Byfleet, 1988
HIL3931	DAF MB200DKFL600	Van Hool Alizée	C48FT	1983	Bridges, Saham Toney, 1989
YWO182	Bova EL26/581	Bova Europa	C53F	1984	County, Leicester, 1990
ESK879	Leyland Tiger TRCTL11/3R	Plaxton Paramount 3200 E	C53F	1984	Arriva The Shires, 1998
HIL3934	Leyland Tiger TRCTL11/3RH	Plaxton Paramount 3500 II	C46FT	1985	Stagecoach Midland Red, 1999
D111OWG	Renault-Dodge S56	Reeve Burgess	B25F	1986	Arriva Fox County, 1998
D120WCC	Freight Rover Sherpa	Carlyle	B18F	1987	Amberline, 1992
E417EPE	Renault-Dodge S56	Northern Counties	B29F	1987	Arriva Fox County, 1998
E631BVK	Renault-Dodge S56	Alexander AM	B25F	1987	James, Tamworth, 2000
E337WYS	Renault-Dodge S56	Alexander AM	B20F	1988	Wilson, Carnwarth, 1998
E199XWG	Renault-Dodge S56	Reeve Burgess	B25F	1988	A-Line, Bedworth, 1998
E602HTF	MCW MF154/8	MCW	B33F	1988	Reading Buses, 1999
F111YVP	MCW MF158/16	MCW	B31F	1988	Stagecoach East London, 1996

Previous Registrations:

ESK879	A150EPA, HIL3935		HIL3935	VAT222W, AAG275X, ESK879
HIL3931	KOO760Y, HOI2804		LIL4398	JDT433N, 2749MAN, JDT433N
HIL3932	-		MFE504	From new
HIL3934	C212PPE, 9737VC, C212PPE		YWO182	B245YKX, 5946PP, B319RJF

Livery: Yellow and white or brown and cream.

Huxley operate coaches from Malpas, not far from a similar operation owned by the Meredith family. Huxley now operate three Leyland Nationals around the Cheshire countryside, though HUF625X, a National 2 model new to Southdown, was photographed in Chester. *Cliff Beeton*

JIM STONES COACHES

J Stones, The Jays, Light Oaks Lane, Glazebury, Cheshire, WA3 5LH

A499MHG	Leyland-DAB 9.948L	DAB	B41F	1984	Leyland Vehicles, 1986
B500MPY	Leyland-DAB Tiger Cub	DAB/Eastern Coach Works	B46F	1985	Tees, 1993
B10JYM	Leyland Tiger TRCTL11/3LZ	East Lancashire Spryte (1998)	B53F	1985	MoD 1996 (37KC41)
B11JYM	Leyland Tiger TRCTL11/3LZ	East Lancashire Spryte (1998)	B53F	1986	MoD 1997 (69KE46)
B16TYG	Leyland Tiger TRCTL11/3LZ	Plaxton Derwent 2	B54F	1989	MoD 1996 (03KJ36)
T294ROF	Mercedes-Benz Vario O814	Plaxton Beaver 2	B31F	1999	
BUS1N	Dennis Dart SLF	Plaxton MPD	N28F	1999	
BUS1T	Dennis Dart SLF	Plaxton MPD	N28F	1999	
B1BUS	Dennis Dart SLF	Plaxton MPD	N28F	1999	
M1BUS	Dennis Dart SLF	Plaxton MPD	N28F	1999	
BUS1S	Dennis Dart SLF	Plaxton MPD	N28F	2000	
B1JYM	Dennis Dart SLF	Plaxton MPD	N28F	2000	
J5BUS	Dennis Dart SLF	Plaxton MPD	N28F	2000	
T1KET	Dennis Dart SLF	Plaxton MPD	N28F	2000	
H1JYM	Dennis Dart SLF	Plaxton Pointer 2	N--F	2000	

Previous Registrations:

A499MHG	A499MHG, BUS1T	B500MPY	B500MPY, B1BUS
B11JYM	C529GVU		

Livery: Blue and white
Depot: Hope Carr Way, Leigh

Jim Stones' fleet has displaced most of the Mercedes-Benz Vario buses with Dennis Darts. These carry the rear number plate within the advert panel incorporating the cherished number into the message. Typical is *BUS1T to Leigh with Jim Stones*. Now the oldest buses in the fleet are two built by Leyland-DAB as possible replacements for the Bristol LH before the B-series National was built. The only two on country, they are used sparingly to help their preservation. On a rare trip to Stockport A499MHG is seen when still carrying BUS1T.
Richard Godfrey

LADYLINE

H Lomas, Mount Pleasant Farm, Key Green, Congleton, CW12 3PZ

OJD55R	Bristol LH6L	Eastern Coach Works	B39F	1976	Go-Ahead (OK), 1997
YFB971V	Leyland National 11351A/1R		B52F	1979	Stephenson, Rochford, 1997
AUP369W	Leyland Atlantean AN68B/1R	Roe	B43/30F	1980	Go-Ahead (Coastline), 1999
MRY7W	Bedford YMT	Plaxton Supreme IV	C53F	1980	Bovington Massey, Romford, 1992
FBX562W	Bedford YMQ	Duple Dominant	B50F	1980	E Jones & Son, Ponciau, 1994
TJI8791	Van Hool T815	Van Hool Alizée	C49FT	1982	Hookways Greenslades, Meeth, 2000
B822GPT	Bedford YMP	Plaxton Paramount 3200	C31F	1984	Plaza, Birmingham, 2000
B87CDS	Bedford YNT	Wright Contour	C53F	1985	AAA Coaches, Edinburgh, 1994
B532SAJ	DAF MB200DKFL600	Duple Carribean	C49FT	1985	Bowers, Chapel-en-le-Frith, 1998
E577ANE	Renault-Dodge S56	Northern Counties	B25F	1988	A-Line, Bedworth, 1999
E291TAX	Renault-Dodge S56	Northern Counties	B25F	1988	Garside, Adlington, 1999
F145GVO	Renault-Dodge S56	Northern Counties	B25F	1988	A-Line, Bedworth, 1999
E291TAX	Renault-Dodge S56	Northern Counties	B25F	1988	Garside, Adlington, 1999
F872TNH	Toyota Coaster HB31R	Caetano Optimo	C21F	1988	Gastonia, Cranleigh, 1997

Previous Registrations:

B532SAJ	B157PDC, RSK170	TJI8971	FGE834X, 6400VT, 6853TU, HSV989

Livery: Orange and blue

Based in Congleton, Cheshire, Ladyline Travel operate several minibuses on local service. Illustrated here is F145GVO, which carries Northern Counties bodywork on its Renault-Dodge S56 chssis cowl. *Cliff Beeton*

LANCASHIRE ROSE

J & M Pugh, 75 Eastham Crescent, Clock Face, St Helens, WA9 4ER

D611AFR	MCW MetroRider MF151/5	MCW	BC23F	1987	Blackburn, 1999
D893DSF	Renault-Dodge S56	Alexander AM	B25F	1987	Nip-On, St Helens, 1999
F623UBV	MCW MetroRider MF159/3	MCW	B33F	1988	Blackburn, 1999
G82KUB	Mercedes-Benz 811D	Optare StarRider	B30F	1989	Irvine, Law, 1999

Livery: Turquoise and white.

New to London Buses, Ladyline OJD55R is a Bristol LH with Eastern Coachworks body. Interestingly, the nearside destination retains OK Travel lettering.
Cliff Beeton

Sole double-deck with Ladyline is Roe-bodied Atlantean AUP369W. It is seen here in an all-over orange scheme applied since it was acquired from the Go-Ahead group.
Cliff Beeton

LIVERPOOL MOTOR SERVICES

D Forrest, Regent House, Long Lane, Aintree, L9 7BP

SDC146H	Leyland Atlantean PDR1A/1	Northern Counties	B43/31F	1970	Avon Buses, Prenton, 1998
479BOC	Leyland Leo' PSU3B/4R(TL11)	Duple 320 (1987)	C51F	1973	Arriva Midlands North, 2000
ULO441R	Bristol LHS6L	Plaxton Supreme III	C35F	1976	Helms, Bootle, 2000
OSR197R	Bristol VRT/LL3/6LXB	Alexander AL	B49/35F	1977	Stagecoach Ribble, 1999
LWU470V	Bristol VRT/SL3/6LXB	Eastern Coach Works	B43/31F	1980	Stagecoach Devon, 1998
DBV834W	Leyland National 2 NL106L11/1R		B44F	1980	Stagecoach Western Buses, 1999
NKU197X	Dennis Dominator DDA133	Alexander RH	B46/32F	1981	Stagecoach Fife, 2000
A207OKJ	MCW Metrobus DR102/42	MCW	B46/31F	1984	Arriva Southern Counties, 2000
A762NNA	Leyland Atlantean AN68D/1R	Northern Counties	B43/32F	1984	West Lancashire, Formby, 1999
A764NNA	Leyland Atlantean AN68D/1R	Northern Counties	B43/32F	1984	Stagecoach Manchester, 2000
A941SYE	Leyland Titan TNLXB/2RR	Leyland	B44/32F	1984	Avon Buses, Prenton, 2000
B551ATX	Leyland Olympian ONLXB/1R	East Lancashire	B43/31F	1985	Cardiff Bus, 1999
D32RWC	Leyland Lynx LX112TL11FR1	Leyland Lynx	B49F	1986	Arriva Cymru, 2000
D706YHK	Leyland Olympian ONLXB/1RH	Eastern Coach Works	B42/26D	1987	Stagecoach London, 2000
E404EPE	Renault-Dodge S56	Northern Counties	B22F	1987	Hunt, Alford, 2000

Special event vehicles

240AJB	AEC Regent V 2DRA	Park Royal	B41/32F	1962	UK AEA, Harwell, 1996
NMY655E	AEC Routemaster R2RH	Park Royal	B32/24F	1967	Merseybus, 1996
CWM154C	Leyland Titan PD2/40	Weymann Orion	O37/27F	1965	Merseybus, 1996
TCK847	Leyland Titan PD3/5	MCW	B41/31F	1963	preservation, 1996

Previous registrations

479BOC	AJA360L		ULO441R	PNM35R	WPX448
D706YHK	D260FYM, VLT20				

Livery: Green and Cream.
Depot: Hanson Road, Liverpool and Long Lane, Aintree

Liverpool Motor Services have adopted a new cream and green livery along with a LMS motif as shown here on Atlantean A762NNA which orginated with Greater Manchester Transport.
Andrew Jarosz

LOCAL MOTION

Local Motion - Ravel Travel

DR & TA Beardsmore, 15 Roberts Drive, Rudheath, Northwich, CW9 7JZ
A & D Beardsmore, 9 St John's Close, Rudheath, Northwich, CW9 7JZ

SIB6715	Leyland National 1051/1R/0402	East Lancashire Greenway (1992)	B41F	1973	Arriva North East, 2000
AFE805A	Leyland National 11351/1R		BC52F	1974	Nova Scotia, Winsford, 1998
PDZ6265	Leyland National 11351/1R (V)	East Lancashire Greenway (1994)	B49F	1975	Arriva Southern Counties (C&NS), 2000
WJI3507	Leyland National 11351/1R		B49F	1976	Nova Scotia, Winsford, 1998
WJI3508	Leyland National 11351/1R		B49F	1976	Nova Scotia, Winsford, 1998
SJI5066	Leyland National 11351/1R (V)	East Lancashire Greenway (1994)	B49F	1977	Arriva Southern Counties (C&NS), 2000
UMB338R	Bristol VRT/SL3/501	Eastern Coach Works	B43/31F	1977	Crosville Wales, 1996
WDM347R	Bristol VRT/SL3/501	Eastern Coach Works	B43/31F	1977	Happy Days, Woodseaves, 1993
AHG948R	Leyland Leopard PSU3E/4R	Plaxton Supreme III	C53F	1977	Maypole Coaches, Lathom, 1998
CBV124S	Leyland Atlantean AN68A/1R	East Lancashire	B45/31F	1978	Roadliner, Crewe, 1999
WJI3499	Leyland National 11351A/1R		B49F	1978	Nova Scotia, Winsford, 1998
XAK457T	Leyland National 11351A/1R		B52F	1978	Swanbrook, Cheltenham, 1998
XOV750T	Leyland National 11351A/1R		B49F	1979	Travel West Midlands, 1997
WTU496W	Bristol VRT/SL3/501	Eastern Coach Works	B43/31F	1981	Ashall, Manchester, 1999
JCK852W	Leyland Nat 2 NL106AL11(G)	East Lancashire Greenway (1991)	B41F	1981	Arriva Southern Counties (WS), 2000
SIB6710	Leyland Nat 2 NL106AL11/1R	East Lancashire Greenway (1992)	B41F	1981	Arriva North East, 2000
B576DRS	Dennis Dorchester SDA810	Plaxton Paramount 3500 II	C55F	1985	Philhaines, Frampton West, 2000
F786ROO	Renault Master	Videotech	M8L	1989	Dean, Anderton, 1996

Previous Registrations:

AFE805A	GPC733N	SJI5066	NEN961R
B576DRS	B200CGA, VLT226	WJI3499	JBR687T
PDZ6265	GPJ891N	WJI3507	NOE549R
SIB6710	DBV844W	WJI3508	NOE557R
SIB6715	TPD176M		

Livery: Red and cream

Five Greenway conversions of Leyland Nationals currently work in the Local Motion fleet. New to London & Country as SN76, SIB6715 is seen in fleet livery as it headed for Weaverham.
Cliff Beeton

MAGHULL COACHES

B K Reilley, 1 Canal Street, Bootle, L20 8AE

M1	E233NFX	Freight Rover Sherpa	Carlyle Citybus 2	B20F	1987	Midland Red North, 1994
M2	E230NFX	Freight Rover Sherpa	Carlyle Citybus 2	B20F	1987	Midland Red North, 1994
M3	F945CUA	Freight Rover Sherpa	Carlyle Citybus 2	B20F	1988	P&O Lloyd, Bagilt, 1995
M4	F872XOE	Freight Rover Sherpa	Carlyle Citybus 2	B20F	1988	McLaughlin, Penwortham, 1995
M5	F208AKG	Freight Rover Sherpa	Carlyle Citybus 2	B20F	1988	Shamrock, Pontypridd, 1995
M6	F216AKG	Freight Rover Sherpa	Carlyle Citybus 2	B20F	1988	Shamrock, Pontypridd, 1995
M7	E141RAX	Freight Rover Sherpa	Carlyle Citybus 2	B20F	1987	Dalybus, Eccles, 1995
M8	F226AWO	Freight Rover Sherpa	Carlyle Citybus 2	B20F	1988	ABC Travel, Ainsdale, 1995
M9	G267GKG	Freight Rover Sherpa	Carlyle Citybus 2	B20F	1989	Merry Hill Minibuses, 1998
M10	H714LOL	Freight Rover Sherpa	Carlyle Citybus 2	B20F	1990	Merry Hill Minibuses, 1998
M13	F126JGS	Ford Travsit VE6	Chassis Developments	M16	1988	Lumley, Speke, 1991
M14	ANA116Y	Mercedes-Benz L608D	Reeve Burgess	BC19F	1983	Murray, Huyton Quarry, 1994
M15	WAV122X	Mercedes-Benz L508D	Reeve Burgess	BC19F	1982	Carnochan, Lockerbie, 1994

RFM267L	Daimler Fleetline CRL6	Park Royal	B44/32F	1973	A1A, Birkenhead, 2000
JWM689P	Leyland Atlantean AN68/1R	East Lancashire	B43/32F	1976	Merseybus, 1999
BFR303R	Leyland Atlantean AN68A/2R	East Lancashire	B50/36F	1977	Toxteth Community Council, 1992
JIL8627	Leyland Leopard PSU3E/4R	Duple Dominant II	C53F	1979	C&S, Heathfield, 1999
KIB7027	Leyland Leopard PSU5C/4R	Duple Dominant II	C55F	1979	Grayline, Bicester, 1998
MCN548W	Leyland Atlantean AN68A/1R	Northern Counties	B43/32F	1981	Stagecoach Manchester, 1997
RUT131W	DAF MB200DKTL600	Jonckheere Bermuda	C51F	1981	Clyde, East Kilbride, 1989
PXI6348	DAF MB200DKTL600	Jonckheere Bermuda	C53F	1982	Harris, Windsor, 1987
OOP958X	Leyland Tiger TRCTL11/3R	Duple Goldliner	C50FT	1982	Travel West Midlands, 1995
951RMX	Neoplan N122/3	Neoplan Skyliner	C53/20CT	1982	Yelloway Trathens, 1989
B354WUL	Ford Transit 190	Dormobile	M10L	1985	Eldonian Housing, Liverpool, 1996
F349DMS	Mercedes-Benz 609D	Whittaker Europa	BC24F	1989	Hill, St Helens, 1999
GIL6343	TAZ D3200	TAZ Dubrava	C49FT	1989	Lamb, Morecambe, 2000
F465LTU	TAZ D3200	TAZ Dubrava	C53F	1989	A2B Travel, Prenton, 1997
F819RJF	TAZ D3200	TAZ Dubrava	C49FT	1989	Hardings, Huyton, 1996
F793TBC	TAZ D3200	TAZ Dubrava	C53F	1989	Patrick, Osgathorpe, 2000
G707VRY	TAZ D3200	TAZ Dubrava	C49FT	1989	Hegarty, Blackpool, 1998
G712VRY	TAZ D3200	TAZ Dubrava	C49FT	1990	Hardings, Huyton, 1998
L331BFX	MAN 16.290 HOCL-R	Berkhof Excellence 1000	C49FT	1993	Yellow Coaches, Bournemouth, 1999

Previous registrations

951RMX	BDV867Y	KIB7027	EAP937V
F349DMS	F859BCW, JIW6434	OOP958X	VSS2X, WLT702
F870ONR	A2BDO, F465LTU	PXI6348	WRK2X
GIL6343	F877ONR	RUT131W	OFP73W, 531PP
JIL8627	EWW216T	RFM267L	MLK652L, AIA1120

Livery: Turquoise and white.

MARK PERRY TRAVEL

D Coleman, Tomaria Cottage, Halebank Road, Widnes, WA8 8NJ

MNC519W	Leyland Atlantean AN68A/1R	Northern Counties	B43/32F	1980	Castle, Speke, 1999
WWM920W	Leyland Atlantean AN68B/1R	Willowbrook	B45/33F	1980	Castle, Speke, 1999
AFY191X	Leyland Atlantean AN68B/1R	Willowbrook	B45/33F	1982	Castle, Speke, 1999
D317SDS	Renault-Dodge S56	Alexander AM	B25F	1987	Mainline, 1997
D681SEM	Renault-Dodge S56	Alexander AM	B23F	1987	Mainline, 1997

Livery: Two-tone blue and white.
Depot: Golden Triangle Industrial Estate, Widnes

Maghull Coaches operate minibus services alongside traditional coaching. Imports from Jonckheere started with the Bermuda and this fleet contains two examples built on DAF MB200 coaches. Shown here in full fleet colours is RUT131W.

Perrys Travel's AFY191X is from a batch of Willowbrook-bodied Atlanteans built for Merseyside PTE. It is seen on rail replacement services outside Crewe station. For much of the time the trio of Atlanteans are to be found undertaking school contract duties. *Cliff Beeton*

MATTHEWS TRAVEL

G Matthews, Darlingtons Industrial Estate, Chester Road, Heswall, Wirral, L60 3RG

HIL8334	Volvo B10M-61	Plaxton Paramount 3500	C53FT	1984	Brentwood Coaches, 1997
367TYD	Volvo B10M-61	Van Hool Alizée	C50DTL	1988	Yorks, Northampton, 2000
E848AAW	Mercedes-Benz 809D	Reeve Burgess Beaver	BC23F	1988	Blue Buses, Bucknell, 1996
284NHY	Mercedes-Benz 609D	North West Coach Sales	BC23F	1988	Matthew, Parkgate, 1996
F731FDV	Mercedes-Benz 709D	Reeve Burgess Beaver	BC23F	1989	Stagecoach Devon, 1999
F759FDV	Mercedes-Benz 709D	Reeve Burgess Beaver	BC23F	1989	Stagecoach Devon, 1999
J38VDW	Iveco Daily 49.10	Carlyle Dailybus 2	B25F	1992	Caeliol, Pwllheli, 1996
L406LHE	Scania K113CRB	Irizar Cenury 12.35	C49FT	1994	Bowers, Birmingham, 1999

Previous Registrations:

284BHY	F944YKD		E848AAW	E700HLB, 6727VT
387TYD	E268OMT		HIL8334	A705XMH, 999BWC

Livery: Cream (coaches); blue and white (buses)

Matthews Travel are one of several operators that provide services connecting Wirral towns with Chester. Seen at the southern end of its route is Iveco Daily J38VDW which is fitted with a Carlyle Dailybus body.
Andrew Jarosz

MEREDITH'S

JK, ME & DJ Meredith, Lydgate, Well Street, Malpas, Cheshire, SY14 8DE

798MMA	Leyland Leopard PSU3E/4R	Plaxton Supreme IV Express	B55F	1979	Clydeside, 1995
GEK13V	Leyland Atlantean AN68A/1R	East Lancashire	B45/31F	1980	Warrington, 1998
JED904	Ford R1114	Plaxton Supreme IV	C53F	1981	
ANA577Y	Leyland Atlantean AN68D/1R	Northern Counties	B43/32F	1982	Village, Bootle, 1998
884MMB	Volvo B10M-61	Plaxton Paramount 3200	C57F	1983	
122BLM	Volvo B10M-61	Plaxton Paramount 3200 II	C57F	1985	
2876WU	Leyland Tiger TRCTL11/3LZ	Wadham Stringer Vanguard	B71F	1985	Crown, Bristol, 1999
469KNP	Leyland Tiger TRCTL11/3LZ	Plaxton Derwent II	BC70F	1987	Crown, Bristol, 1999
SED253	Leyland Tiger TRCTL11/3LZ	Plaxton Derwent II	BC70F	1987	Crown, Bristol, 1999
OLG7	Volvo B10M-61	Plaxton Paramount 3500 III	C53F	1988	
JCM396	Volvo B10M-60	Plaxton Paramount 3200 III	C53F	1989	
F325MCA	Volvo B10M-61	Plaxton Paramount 3200 III	C57F	1989	Alexander's, Aberdeen, 1992
684DYX	Volvo B10M-62	Plaxton Premiére 320	C53F	1994	Dodsworth, Boroughbridge, 1998
LIL7810	Volvo B10M-62	Plaxton Premiére 320	C53F	1994	Britannia, Telford, 2000

Recent purchases by Meredith's have been Plaxton Premiére 320 coaches on either Volvo or Dennis chassis. Illustrating one of the Dennis products is HJI843. Meredith's also own two vintage Bedford coaches, the OB being the subject of a model. *Robert Edworthy*

Cheshire operator Meredith's coach fleet comprises only Plaxton-bodied products, though the buses carry more varied makes. Early examples of bus-seated coaches for school duties have been replaced with former military transport Leyland Tigers which are fitted with 3+2 seating. Shown at rest in Liverpool is JCM396 a Volvo B10M which carries Plaxton Paramount 3200 bodywork. *Ralph Stevens*

HJI843	Dennis Javelin 12SDA2131	Plaxton Premiére 320	C53F	1995
NAX511	Volvo B10M-62	Plaxton Premiére 320	C53F	1996
852RKN	Dennis Javelin GX	Plaxton Premiére 320	C53F	1997
510UMA	Dennis Javelin GX	Plaxton Premiére 320	C57F	1998
KSV408	Volvo B10M-62	Plaxton Premiére 320	C57F	1998

Special event vehicle:

| GUJ356 | Bedford OB | Duple Vista | C29F | 1950 | Mid Wales, Newtown, 1976 |
| NTU946C | Bedford SB3 | Duple Bella Vega | C41F | 1960 | |

Previous Registrations:

122BLM	From new	HJI843	M472ACA
469KNP	82KF39, D211JHY	JCM396	F238OFP
510UMA	-	JED904	WCA893W
684DYX	L738RUM	LIL7810	L734RUM
798MMA	-	NAX511	N514GTU
852RKN	P883RFM	NTU946C	884MMB
884MMB	From new	OLG7	E400BTU
2876WU	37KC26, B936YCT	SED253	87KF31, E669NOU
F325MCA	F102HSO, KSV408		

Livery: Beige, yellow and red

MERSEYLINE TRAVEL

Meadowhall Ltd, Unit 41 Garston Ind Est, Brunswick Street, Garston, Liverpool, L19 8JB

TWH703T	Leyland Fleetline FE30AGR	Northern Counties	B43/32F	1978	GMN, 1995
TWH704T	Leyland Fleetline FE30AGR	Northern Counties	B43/32F	1979	GMN, 1995
BCB617V	Leyland Fleetline FE30AGR	Northern Counties	B43/32F	1980	GMN, 1995
BCB618V	Leyland Fleetline FE30AGR	Northern Counties	B43/32F	1980	GMN, 1995
DWH685W	Leyland Fleetline FE30AGR	Northern Counties	B43/32F	1980	GMN, 1995
ORJ75W	MCW Metrobus DR102/21	MCW	B43/30F	1981	Stagecoach Manchester, 1997
KYV357X	Leyland Titan TNLXB/2RR	Leyland	B44/24D	1981	Aintree Coachline, 1998
KYV478X	Leyland Titan TNLXB/2RR	Leyland	B44/32F	1982	Aintree Coachline, 1998
SND123X	MCW Metrobus DR102/23	MCW	B43/30F	1982	Stagecoach South, 1997
ANA155Y	MCW Metrobus DR102/23	MCW	B43/30F	1982	Aintree Coachline, 1998
A862SUL	Leyland Titan TNLXB/2RR	Leyland	B44/26D	1983	London United, 1996
A865SUL	Leyland Titan TNLXB/2RR	Leyland	B44/26D	1983	London United, 1996
A903SYE	Leyland Titan TNLXB/2RR	Leyland	B44/32F	1983	Aintree Coachline, 1998
A904SYE	Leyland Titan TNLXB/2RR	Leyland	B44/26D	1983	Aintree Coachline, 1998
A910SYE	Leyland Titan TNLXB/2RR	Leyland	B44/26D	1983	London United, 1996
A934SYE	Leyland Titan TNLXB/2RR	Leyland	B44/26D	1984	London United, 1996
G803EKA	Leyland Lynx LX2R11C154ZR	Leyland Lynx	B51F	1990	Halton, 1999
H542FWM	Leyland Lynx LX2R11C154ZR	Leyland Lynx	B51F	1990	Halton, 1999
H543FWM	Leyland Lynx LX2R11C154ZR	Leyland Lynx 2	B51F	1990	Halton, 1999

Livery: White and blue

Three Metrobuses that were new to Greater Manchester have joined the otherwise Leyland-based Merseyline Travel fleet. Now in the blue and white livery, SND123X is seen heading for Kirkby. *R L Wilson*

MERSEYPRIDE TRAVEL

D A Hannell, 26 Skypark Industrial Estate, Speke Hall Avenue, Speke, Liverpool, L24 9H

JJT438N	Bristol VRT/SL2/6LX	Eastern Coach Works	B43/31F	1974	Merseypride (Peers), Speke, 1999
GMB652T	Leyland National 10351B/1R		B44F	1979	Merseypride (Peers), Speke, 1999
CTX394V	Bristol VRT/SL3/6LXB	Alexander AL	B44/31F	1981	Cardiff Bus, 1999
ARN888Y	Leyland National 2 NL116HLXB/1R		B52F	1983	Stagecoach Cumberland, 2000
A105HNC	Leyland Tiger TRCTL11/3R	Plaxton Paramount 3200	C47FT	1983	Allan Walton Travel, Speke, 1998
C67JTU	Leyland Tiger TRCTL11/3RH	Duple 340	C49FT	1985	Aintree Coachline, 1998

Livery: Various

One of two Bristol VR double-deck buses with Merseypride Travel is JJT438M a mark 2 version of this chassis supplied in large numbers to the National Bus Company fleets. The vehicle is seen outside Crewe rail station while undertaking rail replacement duties. *Cliff Beeton*

MOORLAND BUSES

S A Titterton, Weston Service Station, Weston Coyney, Stoke-on-Trent, ST3 6QB

D167NON	Freight Rover Sherpa	Carlyle	B16F	1987	Blue Buses, Bucknall, 1995
D62NOF	Freight Rover Sherpa	Carlyle	B16F	1987	Blue Buses, Bucknall, 1995
D39TKA	Freight Rover Sherpa	Dormobile	B16F	1987	Blue Buses, Bucknall, 1995
D754PTU	Freight Rover Sherpa	Dormobile	B16F	1986	non-pcv 1996
E135RAX	Freight Rover Sherpa	Carlyle Citybus 2	B20F	1987	Blakewater Coaches, Darwen, 1996
F889XOE	Freight Rover Sherpa	Carlyle Citybus 2	B20F	1988	Lionspeed, West Bromwich, 1997
F895XOE	Freight Rover Sherpa	Carlyle Citybus 2	B20F	1988	Lionspeed, West Bromwich, 1997
F202XBV	Freight Rover Sherpa	Carlyle Citybus 2	B20F	1989	Happy Days, Woodseaves, 1997
H713LOL	Freight Rover Sherpa	Carlyle Citybus 2	B20F	1990	Janeway, Wythenshaw, 2000

Livery: Blue and cream

Moorland Buses operate a fleet of Freight Rover Sherpa minibuses from the late 1980s in a smart blue and while livey. Shown here is E135RAX, which was new to National Welsh. *Cliff Beeton*

NIP-ON

K G Hatton, 26 Haywood Gardens, West Park, St Helens, WA10 4JU

Reg	Chassis	Body	Seating	Year	Owner
ROP835R	Leyland Leopard PSU3C/4R	Willowbrook Warrior (1990)	B62F	1977	County Bus, Seighford, 1998
AKZ4157	Leyland National 2 NL116L11/1R		B52F	1980	Arriva Cymru, 1999
ALZ8617	Leyland Tiger TRCTL11/2R	Duple Dominant IV Express	C49F	1982	South Lancs, St Helens, 1997
UJN634Y	Leyland Tiger TRCTL11/2R	Eastern Coach Works B51	BC49F	1982	County, 1997
HSB740Y	Volvo B10M-61	Duple Goldliner IV	C53F	1983	Victoria Travel, Earlestown, 1995
A150LFR	Leyland Tiger TRCTL11/2R	Duple Dominant IV Express	C53F	1983	Stagecoach Cumberland, 1996
PJI8366	DAF SB2300DHS585	Jonckheere Jubilee	C51FT	1984	Diamond Travel, Prescot, 1997
ORY640	DAF SB2305DHTD585	Plaxton Paramount 3200 III	C53F	1988	Stagecoach Cumberland, 1996
IIL2503	Dennis Javelin 12SDA1907	Duple 320	C52FT	1989	Merseybus, 1998
MIL1215	DAF MB230LB615	Plaxton Paramount 3500 III	C53F	1989	Ogden's, St Helens 2000
G590PKL	Mercedes-Benz 811D	Dormobile Routemaker	B25F	1989	Norbus, Kirkby, 1997
M89DEW	Dennis Dart 9.8SDL3054	Marshall C37	B40F	1994	Halton, 1999
P654HEG	Dennis Dart	Marshall C37	B40F	1996	
P655HEG	Dennis Dart	Marshall C37	B40F	1996	
R411XFL	Dennis Dart SLF	Marshall Capital	N43F	1998	Merseybus, 1998
R416XFL	Dennis Dart SLF	Marshall Capital	N36F	1998	
R417XFL	Dennis Dart SLF	Marshall Capital	N36F	1998	
T310MBU	Dennis Dart SLF	Marshall Capital	N28F	1999	
V660LWT	Dennis Dart SLF	Caetano Compass	N40F	1999	

Previous Registrations:

AKZ4157	LRB206W	ORY640	E986AHH
ALZ8617	CKC623X	PJI8366	B190AGK
HSB740Y	TSD149Y, WLT774	ROP835R	VCA995R, 2154K, WGD792R, UOI772
IIL2503	F33ALV	UJN634Y	WPH115Y, OIB3510
MIL1215	F215RJX		

Livery: Blue and red
Depots: Shaw Street, St Helens and Baxters Lane, Sutton, St Helens

Nip-On have expanded their fleet in St Helens corresponding with an increase in local bus services. While the latest arrivals are low floor Dennis Darts shown here, while heading for the town centre, Leyland National AKZ4157 is one of eighteen such examples new to Trent in 1980. *Richard Godfrey*

NORBUS

Norbus Travel Ltd, North Mersey Business Centre, Woodward Road, Liverpool, L33 7UZ

ALZ6420	Leyland National 2 NL106L11/1R		B44F	1980	Happy Al's, Birkenhead, 1998
CUL198V	Leyland Titan TNLXB/2RRSp	Park Royal	B44/26F	1980	Stagecoach East Kent (EKN), 2000
HWJ928W	Bristol VRT/SL3/501	Eastern Coach Works	B43/31F	1980	Happy Al's, Birkenhead, 1998
DCA534X	Bristol VRT/SL3/6LXB	Eastern Coach Works	B43/31F	1981	Arriva Cymru, 1998
HUF626X	Leyland National 2 NL116AL11/1R		B49F	1981	Stagecoach South (SxC), 2000
D602AFR	MCW MetroRider MF151/4	MCW	B23F	1987	Blackburn, 1999
D607AFR	MCW MetroRider MF151/4	MCW	B23F	1987	Blackburn, 1999
D608AFR	MCW MetroRider MF151/4	MCW	B23F	1987	Blackburn, 1999
D609AFR	MCW MetroRider MF151/4	MCW	B23F	1987	Blackburn, 1999
D632MDB	MCW MetroRider MF151/3	MCW	BC23F	1987	Stagecoach Manchester, 1997
D674NNE	MCW MetroRider MF151/3	MCW	BC23F	1987	Stagecoach Manchester, 1998
D676NNE	MCW MetroRider MF151/3	MCW	BC23F	1987	Stagecoach Manchester, 1997
J903OAY	Toyota Coaster HDB30R	Caetano Optimo II	C18F	1992	Ayres, Dalkeith, 1998
T468HNH	Dennis Dart SLF	Plaxton MPD	N29F	1999	
T469HNH	Dennis Dart SLF	Plaxton MPD	N29F	1999	
V899DNB	Dennis Dart SLF	Plaxton MPD	N29F	1999	

Previous Registrations

ALZ6420	DBV838W	HUF626X	RUF438X, 410DCD

Livery: Blue and grey

Norbus operate seven MetroRiders acquired from Blackburn and Stagecoach Manchester. One from the latter, D676NNE, is seen in St Helens on Merseytravel service 109. *Richard Godfrey*

OGDENS TRAVEL

J D Ogden, Baxter's Lane, Sutton, St Helens, Merseyside

OIJ2645	Leyland Leopard PSU3B/4R	Duple Dominant IV	C49F	1982	Mercer, Longridge, 1987
HIL6956	Leyland Tiger TLCTL11/2R	Plaxton Supreme V	C46F	1982	SUT, Sheffield, 1987
DOI9172	DAF SB2300DHS585	Plaxton Paramount 3200 II	C53F	1986	
HIL2381	DAF MB230LT615	Van Hool Alizée	C55FT	1987	Ardenvale, Knowle, 1991
E909EAY	DAF MB230DKFL615	Plaxton Paramount 3200 III	C57F	1987	Dennis's, Ashton-u-Lyne, 1994
JOI2949	DAF SB2305DHS585	Van Hool Alizée	C51FT	1988	Wood, Barnsley, 1995
470DOT	DAF MB230LB615	Plaxton Paramount 3500 III	C53F	1988	Smiths, Alcester, 1990
F660OHD	DAF SB2305DHTD585	Plaxton Paramount 3200 III	C53F	1988	Sweyne, Swinefleet, 1992
G228HCP	DAF MB230LT615	Plaxton Paramount 3500 III	C53F	1990	
K333DOT	DAF SB3000DKVF601	Van Hool Alizée	C51FT	1993	
L10GGY	Ford Transit VE6	Deansgate	M14	1993	
M252SRN	Ford Transit VE6	Ford	M8	1995	
W172CDN	DAF DE33WSSB3000	Van Hool T9 Alizée	C49FT	2000	

Previous Registrations:

470DOT	E641KCX	HIL2381	D618YCX	K333DOT	K540RJX
DOI9172	C631TUT, COI6771	HIL6956	NHL261X, JOI2949	OIJ2645	RHG911X
F660OHD	F660OHD, MIL2174	JOI2949	E644KCX	G228HCP	G228HCP, MIL2173

Livery: White, red and grey

The composition of Ogdens Travel fleet shows that DAF coaches have been the only intake of large vehicles for the coaching duties. Showing the SB3000 model with Van Hool Alizée bodywork is K333DOT in this view taken at Michael Wood services on the M5. *J C Walton*

PANDH TRAVEL

P A Harwood, Pandh House, Cashel Road Industrial Estate, Birkenhead, CH41 1DY

Reg	Chassis	Body	Seating	Year	History
ONF653R	Leyland Atlantean AN68A/1R	Northern Counties	B43/32F	1976	Aintree Coachline, 1998
WDA672T	Leyland Fleetline FE30AGR	Park Royal	B43/33F	1979	Helms, Bootle, 1999
FPR61V	Leyland National 11351A/1R		B49F	1979	Wilts & Dorset, 1999
VFV7V	Leyland Leopard PSU3E/4R	Duple Dominant II Express	C53F	1979	Castle Buses, Speke, 1998
WWM923W	Leyland Atlantean AN68B/1R	Willowbrook	B45/33F	1981	Castle Buses, Speke, 1997
TOS968X	Leyland Atlantean AN68A/1R	Alexander AL	B45/33F	1981	First Glasgow, 1999
ANA585Y	Leyland Atlantean AN68D/1R	Northern Counties	B43/32F	1982	Rossendale, 1999
A759NNA	Leyland Atlantean AN68D/1R	Northern Counties	B43/32F	1984	Aintree Coachline, 1997
B811YTC	Leyland Tiger TRCTL11/3LZ	Wadham Stringer Vanguard 2	BC68F	1985	MoD, 1999 ( )
B891YTC	Leyland Tiger TRCTL11/3LZ	Wadham Stringer Vanguard 2	BC68F	1985	MoD, 1999 ( )
170BHR	MCW MetroRider MF150/6	MCW	BC18F	1987	Rossendale, 1999
F54RFS	MCW MetroRider MF151/98	MCW	B25F	1988	Stagecoach Western Buses, 1997
P459EFL	Marshall Minibus	Marshall MM	N26F	1997	Glossopdale, Dukinfield, 2000
P461EFL	Marshall Minibus	Marshall MM	N26F	1997	Glossopdale, Dukinfield, 2000
V676FPO	Dennis Dart SLF	Caetano Compass	N38F	1999	
V677FPO	Dennis Dart SLF	Caetano Compass	N38F	1999	

Previous Registrations:

170BHR	D741ALR		
		TOS968X	CUS300X

Livery: Yellow and blue

Note: As we close for printing we are advised that this operation has now ceased.

Like at many operators in the area, former Greater Manchester Transport Atlanteans have found a home on school contracts. Pandh Travel now operate three of the type with A759NNA shown here. The operator's unusual name is quite simple P and H not the result of an obscure dialect. *Andrew Jarosz*

PROCTERS

F Procter & Son Ltd, Dewsbury Road, Fenton, Stoke-on-Trent, ST4 2TE

HRE128V	Leyland Leopard PSU3E/4R	Plaxton Supreme IV Express	C53F	1979	
HIL7622	Leyland Leopard PSU3E/4R	Plaxton Supreme IV Express	C53F	1979	
HIL7624	Leyland Leopard PSU3E/4R	Plaxton Supreme IV Express	C53F	1979	Antler, Rugeley, 1980
WCK128V	Leyland Leopard PSU3E/4R	Duple Dominant II Express	C53F	1979	Cumberland, 1988
HIL7621	Leyland Tiger TRCTL11/3R	Duple Dominant IV	C57F	1982	
HIL7623	Leyland Leopard PSU3E/4R	Plaxton Supreme VI Express	C53F	1982	
HIL2379	Leyland Tiger TRCTL11/3R	Duple Dominant IV	C57F	1982	
HIL2377	DAF SB2300DHS585	Duple 340	C57F	1986	Smiths, Alcester, 1987
HIL2375	DAF SB2300DHS585	Duple 340	C53F	1987	
HIL7620	Scania K112CRB	Van Hool Alizée	C49FT	1987	Stanley Gath, Dewsbury, 1992
NIL3943	DAF SB3000DKV601	Van Hool Alizée	C53F	1989	London Coaches, 1997
NIL3944	DAF SB3000DKV601	Van Hool Alizée	C53F	1989	London Coaches, 1997
H246MOE	Iveco Daily 49.10	Carlyle Dailybus 2	B25F	1990	Midland Fox, 1997
H247MOE	Iveco Daily 49.10	Carlyle Dailybus 2	B25F	1990	Midland Fox, 1997
HIL7386	DAF MB230LT615	Van Hool Alizée	C53F	1990	Smiths, Alcester, 1992
HIL7614	DAF DE33WSSB3000	Van Hool Alizée	C55FT	1997	C&H Coaches, Fleetwood, 1999
HIL7613	DAF DE33WSSB3000	Van Hool Alizée	C55FT	1998	Kavanagh, Farnham, 1999
HIL7615	Scania L94IB	Irizar Intercentury 12.32	C53F	1998	
HIL7616	Scania L94IB	Irizar Intercentury 12.32	C53F	1998	
HIL2376	Bova FHD12.370	Bova Futura	C36FT	2000	
HIL2378	Bova FHD12.370	Bova Futura	C48FT	2000	

Previous Registrations:

HIL2375	D294XCX	HIL7613	R68GNW	HIL7622	HRE129V
HIL2376	From new	HIL7614	P889PWW	HIL7623	WVT107X
HIL2377	C780MVH	HIL7615	R460SDT	HIL7624	JRE355V
HIL2378	From new	HIL7616	R461SDT	NIL3943	F259RJX
HIL2379	ARE508Y	HIL7620	E58VHL	NIL3944	F260RJX
HIL7386	G977KJX	HIL7621	WFA210X		

Livery: Blue and cream

Proctors are based in the Potteries town of Fenton and provide school services as well as general coaching activities. Illustrated here is HIL7624, a Leyland Leopard with Plaxton Supreme IV Express bodywork. This styling was popular in the late 1970s as the type quaified as a bus for grant purposes as the door was of the wider type and operated by the driver.
Cliff Beeton

SCRAGG'S

Scragg's - Blue Buses

Scragg's Coaches & Taxis, Bucknall Garage, Pennell Street, Stoke-on-Trent, ST2 9BD

9685VT	Bedford YNT (Cummins)	Duple 320	C53F	1987	Ashford Luxury Coaches, 1993
F741FDV	Mercedes-Benz 709D	Reeve Burgess Beaver	BC25F	1988	Stagecoach Devon, 1999
F762FDV	Mercedes-Benz 709D	Reeve Burgess Beaver	BC25F	1988	Stagecoach Devon, 1999
G678XVT	Mercedes-Benz 609D	Made-to-Measure	C25F	1990	
6879VT	Mercedes-Benz 609D	North West Coach Sales	C24F	1990	Graham's, Talke, 1993
4493VT	Mercedes-Benz 814D	Plaxton Beaver	BC33F	1993	Glen Coaches, Port Glasgow,1997
1672VT	Dennis Javelin GX 12SDA2125	Plaxton Premiére 350	C53F	1993	Perrett, Shipton Oliffe, 2000
JIL5227	Mercedes-Benz 709D	Reeve Burgess	BC25F	1988	?, 1999
1655VT	Mercedes-Benz 711D	Plaxton Beaver	BC25F	1995	Cosgroves, Preston, 2000
R722EEH	Mercedes-Benz 614D	Van Tech	BC24F	1997	
R755EEH	Mercedes-Benz Vario O814	Plaxton Beaver 2	BC33F	1998	

Previous Registrations:

1655VT	N990KUS	6879VT	G675BFA
1672VT	L352YNR	9685VT	D922GRU
4493VT	L355MKU	JIL5227	?

Livery: Blue (service buses), or cream, brown and yellow (coaches)

Scragg's Coaches latest arrival is a further Mercedes-Benz minibus and the first Vario for the fleet. Since 1997 Mercedes-Benz have been applying names to the Omnibus series as well as numbers. Their latest midibus, the Cito has been voted the Bus of the Year for 2000 though this is still only available in left-hand drive at the moment. Shown here is 4493VT, a Mercedes-Benz 814D with Plaxton Beaver bodywork. *Cliff Beeton*

SELWYNS

Selwyns Travel Ltd, Cavendish Farm Road, Weston, Runcorn, Halton, WA7 4LU

No.	Reg	Chassis	Body	Seating	Year	Notes
16	K3SEL	Mercedes-Benz 609D	Autobus Classique	C15F	1992	
20	P420ACT	Mercedes-Benz 814D	Autobus Classique Nouvelle	C29F	1996	
21	P621AJL	Mercedes-Benz 814D	Autobus Classique Nouvelle	C29F	1997	
22	F360MUT	Dennis Javelin 8.5SDL1903	Plaxton Paramount 3200 III	C26FT	1988	Davis, Minchinhampton, 1992
24	M390KVR	Dennis Javelin 8.5SDA2139	Berkhof Excellence 1000L	C33F	1994	Star Line, Knutsford, 1995
26	N627HDM	Mercedes-Benz 814D	Plaxton Beaver	BC33F	1996	
31	M799HPJ	Dennis Javelin 12SDA2134	Berkhof Excellence 1000	C49FT	1995	Dennis demonstrator, 1996
32	F724JTU	Volvo B10M-60	Plaxton Paramount 3500 III	C53F	1989	
33	SEL853	Volvo B10M-60	Plaxton Paramount 3500 III	C49FT	1989	
35	SEL36	Volvo B10M-60	Plaxton Paramount 3500 III	C37FT	1991	Dodsworth, Boroughbridge, 1994
38	M366AMA	Dennis Javelin 12SDA2125	Plaxton Premiére 350	C48FT	1995	
39	M602BCA	Dennis Javelin 12SDA2161	Plaxton Premiére 350	C49FT	1995	
54	SEL73	Neoplan N122/3	Neoplan Skyliner	C55/18CT	1988	Coach Europe, Ratby, 1990
59	SEL23	Volvo B10M-53	Van Hool Astral	C52/13CT	1988	Excelsior, 1995
60	M6SEL	Dennis Javelin 12SDA2131	Plaxton Expressliner 2	C46FT	1994	
61	M7SEL	Dennis Javelin 12SDA2131	Plaxton Expressliner 2	C46FT	1994	
67	M365AMA	Dennis Javelin 12SDA2125	Plaxton Expressliner 2	C46FT	1995	
70	P70SEL	Volvo B10M-62	Plaxton Premiére 350	C46FT	1996	
71	P522NMA	Volvo B10M-62	Plaxton Premiére 350	C44FT	1996	
	352STG	Volvo B10M-60	Van Hool Alizée	C49FT	1989	Coachlines, Warrington, 1997
	K701TTA	Neoplan N122/3	Neoplan Skyliner	C57/22CT	1992	Trathens, 2000
	K890UDB	Toyota Coaster HDB30R	Caetano Optimo II	C16F	1992	Arrowline, 1998
	SEL133	Dennis Javelin 10SDA2119	Berkhof Excellence 1000 Midi	C32FT	1993	Arrowline, 1998

Even though F399KTU has recently been withdrawn from the fleet, the Plaxton Paramount 3500 continues in use on three Volvo B10M. Selwyns provide vehicles for National Express duties on seven services (summer 2000 timetable) employing eight specially-liveried vehicles. *Phillip Stephenson*

During 2000 the Mercedes-Benz Vario O814 with Plaxton Cheetah bodywork has been increasing its arrival many coach fleets, Selwyns included. The coach, W929RET, is seen in the latest variant of Selwyns colours. Selwyns operate several smaller vehicles at Manchester International Airport and these form the company's airport division. *Andrew Jarosz*

SEL392	DAF SB3000DKV601	Van Hool Alizée	C51FT	1993	Arrowline, 1998
SEL702	DAF SB3000DKV601	Van Hool Alizée	C51FT	1993	Arrowline, 1998
K200SLT	Toyota Coaster HDB30R	Caetano Optimo II	C18F	1993	Arrowline, 1998
L3SLT	Toyota Coaster HZB50R	Caetano Optimo III	C21F	1994	Arrowline, 1998
L544EHD	DAF SB3000DKV601	Van Hool Alizée HE	C47FT	1994	Arrowline, 1998
M736VSC	Iveco TurboDaily 59.12	Mellor	B16F	1996	Royal Mail, 1997
P861PWW	DAF DE33WSSB3000	Van Hool Alizée HE	C44FT	1997	Arrowline, 1998
R71ECA	Volvo B10M-62	Plaxton Premiére 350	C46FT	1997	
R72ECA	Volvo B10M-62	Plaxton Premiére 350	C46FT	1997	
R73ECA	Volvo B10M-62	Plaxton Premiére 350	C46FT	1998	
R480GLG	Volvo B10M-62	Plaxton Excalibur	C49FT	1998	
R481GLG	Volvo B10M-62	Plaxton Excalibur	C49FT	1998	
T174AUA	DAF DE33WSSB3000	Van Hool T9 Alizée	C44FT	1999	
W929RET	Mercedes-Benz Vario O814	Plaxton Cheetah	C29F	2000	
W586YDM	Dennis Dart SLF	Plaxton MPD	N29F	2000	

Previous Registrations:

352STG	G100DTJ	SEL73	E483YWJ
K200SLT	K380NHU	SEL133	K100SLT
L3SLT	IIB847, L748EAY	SEL392	K523RJX
SEL23	E880RPR, XEL44, E902GHO	SEL702	K546RJX
SEL36	H723VWU, 352STG, H889CCA	SEL853	

Livery: White, green, orange and blue

SUPERTRAVEL

G Bolderson, STC House Speke Hall Road, Speke, Liverpool, L24 9HD

Reg	Chassis	Body	Code	Year	History
D135WCC	Freight Rover Sherpa	Carlyle	B18F	1987	Crosville Wales, 1992
D141WCC	Freight Rover Sherpa	Carlyle	BC20F	1987	Crosville Wales, 1993
F125JGS	Ford Transit VE6	Chassis Developments	M16	1988	Cannon Travel, Garston, 1996
G569BHP	Peugeot-Talbot Pullman	Talbot	BC22F	1990	JC Minis, Widnes, 1997
G639BHP	Peugeot-Talbot Pullman	Talbot	B22F	1990	Goosecroft, Stirling, 1996
H451AGB	Peugeot-Talbot Pullman	Talbot	BC22F	1991	JC Minis, Widnes, 1997
H562GDB	Peugeot-Talbot Pullman	Talbot	B22F	1991	Topline, Wavertree, 1994
H791UWA	Peugeot-Talbot Express	Crystals	M15	1991	
H271ACK	Fiat Ducato	Jubilee	M12	1991	?, 1994
H404BVR	Mercedes-Benz 814D	Carlyle	BC27F	1991	Arriva North West, 1998
H763GTJ	Iveco Daily 49.10	Mellor	M16L	1991	City of Liverpool, 1996
H173XYV	Ford Transit VE6	Dormobile	M8L	1991	private owner, 1997
L801LSX	Iveco Daily 49.10	Mellor	BC19F	1994	Mason, Bo'ness, 1995
M110TVH	Mercedes-Benz 814D	Plaxton Beaver	BC33F	1995	Courtesy, Werneth, 1997
M292XSF	Mercedes-Benz 814D	Plaxton Beaver	BC33F	1995	Doigs, Glasgow, 1998
P684HND	Mercedes-Benz 709D	Plaxton Beaver	B27F	1996	Courtesy, Werneth, 1997
P685HND	Mercedes-Benz 709D	Plaxton Beaver	B27F	1996	Courtesy, Werneth, 1997
P812LOK	LDV Convoy	LDV	M16	1997	private owner, 1998
P977ONC	LDV Convoy	LDV	M16	1997	private owner, 1998
P962SFR	Mercedes-Benz 814D	Plaxton Beaver	BC32F	1997	Lakeland, Hurst Green, 2000
R101VLX	Marshall Minibus	Marshall MM	N26F	1998	First Centrewest, 2000
R112VLX	Marshall Minibus	Marshall MM	N26F	1998	First Centrewest, 2000
R113VLX	Marshall Minibus	Marshall MM	N26F	1998	First Centrewest, 2000
R114VLX	Marshall Minibus	Marshall MM	N26F	1998	First Centrewest, 2000
S6STM	LDV Convoy	LDV	M16	1998	
S7STM	Mercedes-Benz O1120L	Ferqui Solera	C35F	1998	
S8STM	Mercedes-Benz Vario O814	Plaxton Beaver 2	B31F	1998	
S9STM	Mercedes-Benz Vario O814	Plaxton Beaver 2	B31F	1998	
S10STM	Mercedes-Benz Vario O814	Plaxton Beaver 2	B31F	1998	
T6STM	Dennis Dart SLF	Plaxton MPD	N29F	1999	
T7STM	Dennis Dart SLF	Plaxton MPD	N29F	1999	
V261BNV	Dennis Dart SLF	Plaxton MPD	N29F	1999	
V262BNV	Dennis Dart SLF	Plaxton MPD	N29F	1999	
V263BNV	Dennis Dart SLF	Plaxton MPD	N29F	1999	
V264BNV	Dennis Dart SLF	Plaxton MPD	N29F	1999	
V268BNV	Dennis Dart SLF	Plaxton MPD	N29F	1999	
X1STM	Dennis Dart SLF	Plaxton MPD	N29F	2000	
X11STM	Dennis Dart SLF	Plaxton MPD	N29F	2000	

Livery: White, mauve and green

The latest arrivals with Supertravel are seven Mini Pointer Darts. The first pair of the type carry Select index marks as illustarted by T6STM which was pictured arriving in Liverpool centre.
Cliff Beeton

SUTTON TRAVELWAYS

P Tranter, 32 Grappenhall Road, Great Sutton, South Wirral, CH65 7AT

MVK522R	Leyland Atlantean AN68A/2R	Alexander AL	B48/33F	1976	Kingsley, Birkley, 1998
OBN503R	Leyland Fleetline FE30AGR	Northern Counties	B43/32F	1977	Cook, Biggleswade, 1995
SCN251S	Leyland Atlantean AN68A/2R	Alexander AL	B48/33F	1978	Liverpool Motor Services, 2000
GHE739V	Leyland Leopard PSU5C/4R	Plaxton Supreme IV	C57F	1980	Britannia, Telford, 1999
KAD349V	Leyland Leopard PSU5C/4R	Plaxton Supreme IV	C57F	1980	Britannia, Telford, 1999
E760NHG	Peugeot-Talbot Pullman	Talbot	BC22F	1988	

Previous Registrations:
GHE739V   YHG189V, 170BHR, 942AYA

Livery: Brown and orange
Depot: Hooton Works, Hooton

From a base tucked away behind Hooton Works, Sutton Travelways operate three double-deck buses on school and works contracts while single-decks are employed in service as far south as Chester. Seen at the base is OBN503R which shows the destination area replaced with the operator's name.

TAXICO

G A Goldstrraw, D Brookhouse Industrial Estate, Cheadle, Stoke-on-Trent, ST10 2

	Reg	Chassis	Body	Seating	Year	History
	AUP650L	Bedford YRQ	Plaxton Panorama Elite III Exp	C45F	1973	Boydon, Winkhill, 1999
	PFN787M	AEC Reliance 6U3ZR	Duple Dominant	C51F	1974	Bowers, Chapel-en-le-Frith, 2000
	ODM193P	Leyland Leopard PSU3C/4R	Duple Dominant	C53F	1976	Bostocks, Congleton, 1999
	RVE651S	AEC Reliance 6U3ZR	Plaxton Supreme III Express	C49F	1977	Bowers, Chapel-en-le-Frith, 1999
	GAZ7117	Leyland Leopard PSU3E/4R	Willowbrook Warrior (1992)	B53F	1978	Countybus, Seighford, 1999
	ERC645T	Ford R1114	Duple Dominant II	C53F	1979	Alcock, Cheadle, 1997
	VFT187T	Leyland Atlantean AN68/2R	MCW	B49/37F	1979	Go-Ahead Northern, 2000
	LWU468V	Bristol VRT/SL3/6LXB	Eastern Coach Works	B43/31F	1981	Stagecoach Devon, 1998
	KAZ777	Bedford YMQ	Plaxton Supreme III	C45F	1980	Alcock, Cheadle, 1997
19	GAZ6666	Bedford YNT	Plaxton Paramount 3200	C53F	1984	?, , 2000
	GAZ7227	Bedford YNT	Plaxton Paramount 3200	C53F	1985	Kime, Folkingham, 2000
	BAZ7117	Bedford YNV Venturer	Plaxton Paramount 3200 II	C57F	1985	Timeline, Bolton, 1999
	D309UNT	Renault-Dodge S56	Alexander AM	B25F	1987	South Lancs Transport, St Helens, 1997
	D256NCS	Renault-Dodge S56	Alexander AM	B25F	1987	Buslink, Willenhall, 1997
	D414FEH	Freight Rover Sherpa	PMT Bursley	B20F	1987	Sherratt, Cold Meace, 1997
	D852KWR	Freight Rover Sherpa	Dormobile	B20F	1987	Alcock, Cheadle, 1997
	D198NON	Freight Rover Sherpa	Carlyle	B18F	1987	Breward, Smallthorne, 1994
	E49UKL	Mercedes-Benz 609D	Reeve Burgess	B20F	1987	Buchman, Congleton, 1999
	E856GFV	Mercedes-Benz 609D	Elme Orion	BC16F	1987	Handley, Denstone, 1998
16	TXI7007	Mercedes-Benz 811D	Robin Hood	B29F	1987	Stagecoach Ribble, 2000
	F874RJX	Ford Transit VE6	Mellor	B16FL	1988	Calderdale MBC, 2000
	F164XCS	Mercedes-Benz 609D	Scott	BC24F	1989	Stagecoach Bluebird, 1999
	H912XGA	Mercedes-Benz 814D	Reeve Burgess	BC31F	1990	Stagecoach Midland Red, 1999
	P104SUA	Ford Transit VE6	Ford	M8	1997	Althams, Burnley, 1999
	P106UVT	LDV Convoy	LDV	M16	1997	private owner, 1999
	R708EFA	LDV Pilot	LDV	M8	1998	private owner, 1999

Previous registrations

BAZ7117	C354FBO	GAZ7227	B193DVL, PAZ9319, B193DVL
D309UNT	D823RYS, KAZ1969	KAZ777	DBX547W
ERC645T	TSW8T	TXI7007	E86HRN
GAZ6666	A449HJF		
GAZ7117	XBF60S, PIJ660, XBF60S, YYJ995, VOV936S		

Livery: Blue and white

Representing the Taxico fleet is TXI7007, a Robin Hood-bodied Mercedes-Benz 811D. The vehicle was new to Burnley & Pendel before joining the Ribble fleet. It is seen carrying fleet number 16.
Cliff Beeton

WARRINGTON BOROUGH TRANSPORT

Warrington Borough Transport Ltd, Wilderspool Causeway, Warrington, WA4 6PT

1-18

1-18		Dennis Dart SLF		Marshall Capital		N40F	1999-2000		
1	T201AFM	5	T205AFM	9	V209JLG	13	V213JLG	16	V216JLG
2	T202AFM	6	T206AFM	10	V210JLG	14	V214JLG	17	V217JLG
3	T203AFM	7	T207AFM	11	V211JLG	15	V215JLG	18	V218JLG
4	T204AFM	8	T208AFM	12	V212JLG				

37	A207DTO	Leyland Olympian ONLXB/1R	East Lancashire	B45/29F	1984	Derby, 1987
38	A206DTO	Leyland Olympian ONLXB/1R	East Lancashire	B45/29F	1984	Derby, 1987
39	A209DTO	Leyland Olympian ONLXB/1R	East Lancashire	B45/29F	1984	Derby, 1987
40	A210DTO	Leyland Olympian ONLXB/1R	East Lancashire	B45/29F	1984	Derby, 1987
42	CLV42X	Dennis Dominator DDA156	East Lancashire	B51/37F	1982	
81	F121XEM	Dennis Dominator DDA1018	East Lancashire	B51/31F	1988	
82	F122XEM	Dennis Dominator DDA1018	East Lancashire	B51/31F	1988	
84	CLV84X	Leyland Olympian ONLXB/2R	East Lancashire	B51/37F	1982	
85	CLV85X	Leyland Olympian ONLXB/2R	East Lancashire	B51/37F	1982	
86	A486HKB	Leyland Olympian ONLXB/2R	East Lancashire	B51/37F	1984	
87	A487HKB	Leyland Olympian ONLXB/2R	East Lancashire	B51/37F	1984	
91	F101XEM	Dennis Dominator DDA1017	East Lancashire	B51/37F	1988	
92	F102XEM	Dennis Dominator DDA1017	East Lancashire	B51/37F	1988	
93	F103XEM	Dennis Dominator DDA1017	East Lancashire	B51/37F	1988	
94	F104XEM	Dennis Dominator DDA1017	East Lancashire	B51/37F	1988	

95-99

95-99		Dennis Dominator DDA1017		East Lancashire		B51/37F	1989		
95	F95STB	96	F96STB	97	F97STB	98	F98STB	99	F99STB

100	C100UBC	Dennis Dominator DDA1010	East Lancashire	B46/33F	1986	Leicester, 1989
101	C101UBC	Dennis Dominator DDA1010	East Lancashire	B46/33F	1986	Leicester, 1989
102	C102UBC	Dennis Dominator DDA1010	East Lancashire	B46/33F	1986	Leicester, 1989
103	C103UBC	Dennis Dominator DDA1010	East Lancashire	B46/33F	1986	Leicester, 1989

All of Warrington's double-deck fleet is bodied by East Lancashire Coachbuilders on a mixture of Leyland Olympian and Dennis Dominator chassis. Now one of the oldest buses in the operational fleet, 85, CLV85X, is seen in the town's bus station. This Olympian and 84 are licenced as Bristols.
Cliff Beeton

For a while Warrington painted its Dennis Darts in a blue and yellow livery similar to their Coachlines Warrington operation. The coach business has now closed while the buses have been repainted into standard colours. Shown working route 6 is 241, M241YCM, which carries a Marshall C36 body. The C36 signifies it is a Carlyle design acquired when that bodybuilder closed in the mid 1990s. *Paul Wigan*

112-123
Optare MetroRider MR35   Optare   B25F   1998-99

112	S112GUB	115	S115GUB	118	S118GUB	120	S120GUB	122	T322ELG
113	S113GUB	116	S116GUB	119	S119GUB	121	S121GUB	123	T323ELG
114	S114GUB	117	S117GUB						

207-219
Dennis Dart 9SDL3002   Carlyle Dartline   B35F*   1990-91   *212 is DP32F

207	H879LOX	210	H887LOX	213	H841NOC	216	H844NOC	218	H846NOC
208	H881LOX	211	H889LOX	214	H842NOC	217	H845NOC	219	H847NOC
209	H886LOX	212	H897LOX	215	H843NOC				

220	J10WBT	Dennis Dart 8.5SDL3003	Northern Counties Paladin	B31F	1991

221-225
Dennis Dart 9SDL3016   Northern Counties Paladin   B35F   1993

221	K221VTB	222	K222VTB	223	K223VTB	224	K224VTB	225	K225VTB

226-235
Dennis Dart 9SDL3034   Northern Counties Paladin   B35F   1993-94

226	L226SWM	228	L228SWM	230	L230SWM	232	L232SWM	234	L234SWM
227	L227SWM	229	L229SWM	231	L231SWM	233	L233SWM	235	L235SWM

236	M236YKD	Dennis Dart 9SDL3051	Plaxton Pointer	B35F	1995
237	M237YKD	Dennis Dart 9SDL3031	Plaxton Pointer	B35F	1995
238	M238YKD	Dennis Dart 9SDL3051	Plaxton Pointer	B35F	1995

239-243
Dennis Dart 9SDL3053   Marshall C36   B35F   1995

239	M239YCM	240	M240YCM	241	M241YCM	242	M242YCM	243	M243YCM

244	M593HKH	Dennis Dart 9.8SDL3040	Plaxton Pointer	B40F	1994	Plaxton demonstrator, 1995
245	M284HRH	Dennis Dart 9.8SDL3040	Plaxton Pointer	B40F	1994	Plaxton demonstrator, 1995
246	M246YWM	Dennis Dart 9.8SDL3054	Plaxton Pointer	B40F	1995	
247	M247YWM	Dennis Dart 9.8SDL3054	Marshall C37	B40F	1995	
248	M248YWM	Dennis Dart 9.8SDL3054	Marshall C37	B40F	1995	
318	MEK18W	Leyland Atlantean AN68B/1R	East Lancashire	B45/31F	1981	
319	MEK19W	Leyland Atlantean AN68B/1R	East Lancashire	B45/31F	1981	

Special event vehicle

148	BED729C	Leyland PD2/40 Sp	East Lancashire	B34/30F	1965

Livery: Red and ivory

Bodywork from Plaxton, Marshall, Northern Counties and Carlyle feature on the Dennis Darts purchased in the mid-1990s, at a time when the operator was competing with Arriva on local services. Illustrating the variations in styling 233, L233SWM which was built just a few kilometres north on the A49 by Northern Counties, is contrasted with 219, H847NOC, built by Carlyle.
Cliff Beeton/ Paul Wigan

WARRINGTON'S of ILAM

SM Warrington, The Cottage, Ilam, Ashbourne, DE6 2AZ

H153DJU	Dennis Javelin 11SDL1921	Plaxton Paramount 3200 III	C53F	1990	
J733KBC	Dennis Javelin 11SDL1921	Plaxton Paramount 3200 III	C53F	1991	
K4GWC	Mercedes-Benz 814D	Autobus Classique	C33F	1992	Parker, Nottingham, 1994
P369JSP	Mercedes-Benz 814D	Plaxton Beaver	BC33F	1997	Smith & Sons, Coupar Angus, 1999
R173HRF	Ford Transit VE6	Ford	M14	1998	
R246CVU	LDV Convoy	Concept Coachcraft	M16	1997	
T866JVR	LDV Convoy	Concept Coachcraft	M16	1999	
W636MKY	Dennis Javelin GX	Plaxton Premiére 350	C53F	2000	

Previous Registration
WJI7691   NFH529W

Livery: Red and cream

The latest arrival with Warrington's of Ilam is a third Dennis Javelin, this time with a Plaxton Premiére body. The vehicle is seen in the picturesque village, home to this small fleet.

WHITEGATE TRAVEL

K L Prince, 15 Beauty Bank, Whitegate, Northwich, Cheshire, CW8 2BP

D862OJA	Freight Rover Sherpa	Made-to-Measure	M16	1987	Castle, Weaverham, 1995
D403SGS	Freight Rover Sherpa	Carlyle	B20F	1987	Orion, Wemyss Bay, 1997
E333HJM	Mercedes-Benz 307D	Economy	M12	1988	Castle, Weaverham, 1995
F276CEY	Iveco Daily 49.10	Robin Hood City Nippy	B25F	1989	Midland, Cannock, 1998
G866BPD	Iveco Daily 49.10	Carlyle Dailybus 2	B25F	1989	Cardinal Coaches, Eythorne, 2000
G910KWF	Iveco Daily 49.10	Reeve Burgess Beaver	B25F	1989	Bunyan, Hemel Hempstead, 1999
K524EFL	Iveco Daily 49.10	Marshall C29	B25F	1993	Stagecoach Midland Red, 1999
CHR998	LDV 400	Concept	M16	1995	van, 1997
P419FDB	LDV Convoy	Concept	M16	1996	
P582JNE	LDV Convoy	Concept	M16	1997	
S990HUB	LDV Convoy	Concept	M16	1998	
V879RDN	LDV Convoy	Concept	M16	1999	
V818WUG	LDV Convoy	Concept	M16	1999	

Livery: Yellow & white

The Cheshire rural area around Northwich requires several minibus services to link the local centres of population. Whitegate Travel outstation minibuses to some of the villages, such as Beeston. Pictured in a lay-by on the A49 is K524EFL, an Iveco Daily with Marshall bodywork.

WINGATES TOURS

Coachmaster Ltd t/a Wingates Tours, Spencers Lane, Melling, Liverpool, L31 1HB

MIL8338	Volvo-Ailsa B55-10	Northern Counties	B45/32F	1982	Dunn-Line, Nottingham, 1999
OHV715Y	Leyland Titan TNLXB/2RR	Leyland	B44/26D	1983	Go-Ahead London, 2000
A895SYE	Leyland Titan TNLXB/2RR	Leyland	B44/26D	1984	Go-Ahead London, 1999
A906SYE	Leyland Titan TNLXB/2RR	Leyland	B44/26D	1984	Go-Ahead London, 2000
A909SYE	Leyland Titan TNLXB/2RR	Leyland	B44/26D	1984	Go-Ahead London, 2000
A923SYE	Leyland Titan TNLXB/2RR	Leyland	B44/26D	1984	Go-Ahead London, 1999
A924SYE	Leyland Titan TNLXB/2RR	Leyland	B44/26D	1984	Go-Ahead London, 2000
A929SYE	Leyland Titan TNLXB/2RR	Leyland	B44/26D	1984	Go-Ahead London, 2000
A937SYE	Leyland Titan TNLXB/2RR	Leyland	B44/26D	1984	Go-Ahead London, 1999
A940SYE	Leyland Titan TNLXB/2RR	Leyland	B44/26D	1984	Go-Ahead London, 2000
A957SYE	Leyland Titan TNLXB/2RR	Leyland	B44/26D	1984	Go-Ahead London, 2000
A959SYE	Leyland Titan TNLXB/2RR	Leyland	B44/26D	1984	Go-Ahead London, 1999
A972SYE	Leyland Titan TNLXB/2RR	Leyland	B44/26D	1984	Go-Ahead London, 2000
A977SYE	Leyland Titan TNLXB/2RR	Leyland	B44/26D	1984	Go-Ahead London, 2000
A609THV	Leyland Titan TNLXB/2RR	Leyland	B44/26D	1984	Go-Ahead London, 1999
A611THV	Leyland Titan TNLXB/2RR	Leyland	B44/26D	1984	Go-Ahead London, 2000
A615THV	Leyland Titan TNLXB/2RR	Leyland	B44/26D	1984	Go-Ahead London, 1999
A647THV	Leyland Titan TNLXB/2RR	Leyland	B44/26D	1984	Go-Ahead London, 2000
A653THV	Leyland Titan TNLXB/2RR	Leyland	B44/26D	1984	Go-Ahead London, 1999
B192PFA	Mercedes-Benz L608D	PMT Hanbridge	BC21F	1984	G&B, Crewe, 1998
B82WUV	Leyland Titan TNLXB/2RR	Leyland	B44/26D	1984	Go-Ahead London, 2000
B88WUV	Leyland Titan TNLXB/2RR	Leyland	B44/26D	1984	Go-Ahead London, 2000
D230NCS	Renault-Dodge S56	Alexander AM	B25F	1987	Evans, Tiverton Heath ??, 1999
D324UTU	Volvo B10M-61	Plaxton Paramount 3500	C51FT	1987	Skinner, Oxted, 1998
H407LVC	Volvo B10M-60	Ikarus Blue Danube 350	C51FT	1991	Flight's Birmingham, 1998
H130MRW	Volvo B10M-60	Ikarus Blue Danube 350	C51FT	1991	Flight's Birmingham, 1998
H131MRW	Volvo B10M-60	Ikarus Blue Danube 350	C49FT	1991	Flight's Birmingham, 1998
J844RAC	Volvo B10M-60	Ikarus Blue Danube 350	C49FT	1991	Flight's Birmingham, 1998
J845RAC	Volvo B10M-60	Ikarus Blue Danube 350	C49FT	1991	Flight's Birmingham, 1998
K59BAX	Volvo B10M-60	Jonckheere Deauville 45	C48FT	1993	Skinner, Oxted, 1998
L649ADS	Volvo B10M-60	Van Hool Alizée	C49FT	1993	Newline Coaches, Formby, 1998
L655ADS	Volvo B10M-60	Van Hool Alizée	C49FT	1993	Newline Coaches, Formby, 1998
L998CRY	Volvo B10M-62	Jonckheere Deauville 45	C51FT	1994	Newline Coaches, Formby, 1998
N377YNB	Mercedes-Benz 410D	Concept	M16	1995	Furlong, Kirkby, 1998
S315KNW	Optare MetroRider MR15	Optare MetroRider	B29F	1999	

Previous Registrations:

D324UTU	D289UDM, VLT288, 1260VT, VLT229, VLT177					
L649ADS	HSK647		L655ADS	HSK648	MIL8338	WRJ448X

Livery: White.

Recently withdrawn from Wingates fleet is Volvo B10M E838EUT which is seen carrying a Duple 340 body. The vehicle was new in 1987 and arrived into the fleet from Tain Coaches some eight years ago.

Vehicle Index

122BLM	Meredith's	3601RU	Bakers	A97HLV	Arriva NW
152ENM	Bostock's	4195PX	Boydons	A98HLV	Arriva NW
170BHR	Pandh Travel	4493VT	Scragg's	A99HLV	Arriva NW
240AJB	Liverpool MS	4614RU	Bakers	A100HLV	Arriva NW
284NHY	Matthews Travel	5457NF	Bennett's Travel	A104HLV	Arriva NW
352STG	Selwyns	556DHO	Boydons	A105HNC	Merseypride
367TYD	Matthews Travel	5621RU	Bakers	A105KRN	Chester
469KNP	Meredith's	5658RU	Bakers	A106KRN	Chester
470DOT	Ogden's	5946RU	Bakers	A110HLV	Arriva NW
479BOC	Liverpool MS	6280RU	Bakers	A110UCA	Chester
507EXA	First PMT	6577RU	Bakers	A111HLV	Arriva NW
510UMA	Meredith's	684DYX	Meredith's	A111UCA	Chester
765JTU	Bostock's	6879VT	Scragg's	A112HLV	Arriva NW
798MMA	Meredith's	7025RU	Bakers	A112UCA	Chester
852RKN	Meredith's	7092RU	Bakers	A113HLV	Arriva NW
882MMY	Arrowebrook	8150RU	Bakers	A114HLV	Arriva NW
884MMB	Meredith's	8399RU	Bakers	A115HLV	Arriva NW
917MMB	City Bus	8830RU	Bakers	A116ESA	Helms
951RMX	Maghull Coaches	9423RU	Bakers	A116HLV	Arriva NW
1497RU	Bakers	9530RU	Bakers	A118ESA	Helms
1513RU	Bakers	9685VT	Scragg's	A118HLV	Arriva NW
1655VT	Scragg's	9995RU	Bakers	A119HLV	Arriva NW
1672VT	Scragg's	A2BDO	A2B Travel	A120HLV	Arriva NW
1879RU	Bakers	A2BEO	A2B Travel	A121HLV	Arriva NW
2876WU	Meredith's	A2BTO	A2B Travel	A122HLV	Arriva NW
3093RU	Bakers	A2GFF	A2B Travel	A123HLV	Arriva NW
		A8GGT	Huggins	A125HLV	Arriva NW
		A9ALS	Happy Al's	A126HLV	Arriva NW
		A12ALS	Happy Al's	A128HLV	Arriva NW
		A13ALS	Happy Al's	A129HLV	Arriva NW
		A14ALS	Happy Al's	A130HLV	Arriva NW
		A16ALS	Happy Al's	A131HLV	Arriva NW
		A17ALS	Happy Al's	A132HLV	Arriva NW
		A18ALS	Happy Al's	A133FDC	Happy Al's
3102RU	Bakers	A19ALS	Happy Al's	A133HLV	Arriva NW
3275RU	Bakers	A20ALS	Happy Al's	A134HLV	Arriva NW
3353RU	Bakers	A53HRE	Helms	A136HLV	Arriva NW
3471RU	Bakers	A54KVM	Chester	A137HLV	Arriva NW
3563RU	Bakers	A96HLV	Arriva NW	A137SMA	First PMT
3566RU	Bakers				

A138HLV	Arriva NW
A139HLV	Arriva NW
A140HLV	Arriva NW
A140MRN	Arriva NW
A140SMA	Arriva NW
A141HLV	Arriva NW
A142HLV	Arriva NW
A142SMA	Arriva NW
A143SMA	First PMT
A144SMA	First PMT
A145HLV	Arriva NW
A146OFR	Arriva NW
A146UDM	First PMT
A147HLV	Arriva NW
A147OFR	Arriva NW
A148HLV	Arriva NW
A150LFR	Nip-On
A151UDM	Arriva NW
A153UDM	Arriva NW
A156UDM	First PMT
A157UDM	First PMT
A158UDM	First PMT
A159UDM	First PMT
A160UDM	First PMT
A161VDM	First PMT
A162VDM	First PMT
A163VDM	First PMT
A164VDM	First PMT
A165VDM	First PMT
A166VFM	First PMT
A167VFM	First PMT
A168VFM	First PMT
A169VFM	First PMT

Sutton Travelways operate two Leyland Leopards that letterly ran for the Telford operator Britannia Travel. GHE739V is shown during heavy rain at its base near Hooton rail station.

Huxley operate one Bova Europa coach, the predecessor of the Futura built in the Dutch town of Valkenswaard. Numbered YWO182, it is seen in Huxley Holidays colours. *Phillip Stephenson*

A170VFM	First PMT	A449VDW	Helms	A748GFY	Warrington	A941SYE	Liverpool MS
A171VFM	First PMT	A486HKB	Warrington	A754DUY	Bennett's Travel	A957SYE	Wingates Tours
A206DTO	Warrington	A487HKB	Warrington			A959SYE	Wingates Tours
A207DTO	Warrington	A499MHG	Jim Stones			A972SYE	Wingates Tours
A207OKJ	Liverpool MS	A503FSS	Dobson's			A976OST	Chester
A209DTO	Warrington	A518VKG	Happy Al's			A977SYE	Wingates Tours
A209EHN	Avon Coaches	A519VKG	Happy Al's			ACM721X	Arriva NW
A209OKJ	City Bus	A609THV	Wingates Tours			ACM725X	Arriva NW
A210DTO	Warrington	A611THV	Wingates Tours			ACM728X	Arriva NW
A288ANT	Anthony's Travel	A615THV	Wingates Tours			ACM730X	Arriva NW
		A647THV	Wingates Tours	A759NNA	Pandh Travel	ACM748X	Arriva NW
		A653THV	Wingates Tours	A762NNA	Liverpool MS	ACM750X	Arriva NW
		A658HNB	First PMT	A764NNA	Liverpool MS	ACM753X	Arriva NW
		A698HNB	Bettabus	A862SUL	Merseyline Travel	AED31B	Warrington
		A725THV	Huggins	A865SUL	Merseyline Travel	AFE805A	Local Motion
		A733GFA	First PMT	A879SUL	Arriva NW	AFH198T	Bennett's Travel
		A734GFA	First PMT	A884SUL	Gillmoss	AFY191X	Mark Perry
		A735GFA	First PMT	A887SYE	Avon Coaches	AHG948R	Local Motion
A309KDD	Bennett's Travel	A736GFA	First PMT	A895SYE	Wingates Tours	AHU514V	First PMT
A321GLV	Arriva NW	A737GFA	First PMT	A898SYE	Avon Coaches	AHW203V	First PMT
A322GLV	Arriva NW	A738GFA	First PMT	A903SYE	Merseyline Travel	AIA1120	A1A Travel
A323GLV	Arriva NW	A739GFA	First PMT	A904SYE	Merseyline Travel	AIA9000	A1A Travel
A324GLV	Arriva NW	A740GFA	First PMT	A906SYE	Wingates Tours	AJA118	Arriva NW
A325GLV	Arriva NW	A741GFA	First PMT	A909SYE	Wingates Tours	AJA142B	Arriva NW
A326GLV	Arriva NW	A742GFA	First PMT	A910SYE	Merseyline Travel	AKZ4157	Nip-On
A327GLV	Arriva NW	A743JRE	First PMT	A923SYE	Wingates Tours	ALS645V	Happy Al's
A328GLV	Arriva NW	A744JRE	First PMT	A924SYE	Wingates Tours	ALZ1221	Happy Al's
A332GLV	Arriva NW	A745JRE	First PMT	A929SYE	Wingates Tours	ALZ2928	Happy Al's
A333GLV	Arriva NW	A746JRE	First PMT	A934SYE	Merseyline Travel	ALZ3102	Happy Al's
A334GLV	Arriva NW	A747GFY	Warrington	A937SYE	Wingates Tours	ALZ3537	Happy Al's
A335GLV	Arriva NW	A747JRE	First PMT	A940SYE	Wingates Tours	ALZ3542	Happy Al's

Reg	Operator	Reg	Operator	Reg	Operator	Reg	Operator
ALZ3561	Happy Al's	B500MPY	Jim Stones	C376CAS	Arriva NW	D51RLG	D&G Bus Co
ALZ3566	Happy Al's	B532SAJ	Ladyline	C377CAS	Arriva NW	D62NOF	Moorland Buses
ALZ4162	Happy Al's	B551ATX	Liverpool MS	C378CAS	Chester	D81BCK	Mercury
ALZ4516	Happy Al's	B552ATX	Helms	C379CAS	Chester	D81UTF	Aintree Coachline
ALZ6244	Bostock's	B553ATX	Happy Al's	C380CAS	Chester	D89VCC	Arriva NW
ALZ6293	Happy Al's	B554ATX	Helms	C420VVN	D&G Bus Co	D108NDW	Arriva NW
ALZ6403	Happy Al's	B555ATX	Helms	C560GWO	Happy Al's	D110OWG	Huxley
ALZ6420	Norbus	B557ATX	Aintree Coachline	C561GWO	Happy Al's	D120WCC	Huxley
ALZ7211	Happy Al's	B558ATX	Aintree Coachline	C562GWO	Happy Al's	D131VRP	D&G Bus Co
ALZ8617	Nip-On	B576DRS	Local Motion	C563GWO	Happy Al's	D135WCC	Supertravel
ALZ9284	Happy Al's	B811YTC	Pandh Travel	C564GWO	Happy Al's	D139LTA	Mercury
ALZ9286	Happy Al's	B822GPT	Ladyline	C565GWO	Happy Al's	D141WCC	Supertravel
ALZ9328	Happy Al's	B891YTC	Pandh Travel	C567GWO	Happy Al's	D142RAK	D&G Bus Co
ANA116Y	Maghull Coaches	B926KWM	Arriva NW	C706JMB	First PMT	D148VRP	Bennett's Travel
ANA155Y	Merseyline Travel			C749OCN	Huggins	D155HML	Arriva NW
ANA215T	Dobson's			C750OCN	Avon Coaches	D157HML	Arriva NW
ANA553Y	Bettabus			C770OCN	Huggins	D167NON	Moorland Buses
ANA577Y	Meredith's			C770PUJ	First PMT	D182BEH	First PMT
ANA585Y	Pandh Travel			C772OCN	Huggins	D198NON	Taxico
ANA616Y	First PMT			C773OCN	Huggins	D223GLJ	Mercury
ANE2T	Aintree Coachline			C774OCN	Huggins	D226PPU	D&G Bus Co
ANT856T	Anthony's Travel			C776OCN	Avon Coaches	D230NCS	Wingates Tours
ARN888Y	Merseypride	B962WRN	Arriva NW	CBV124S	Local Motion	D256NCS	Taxico
AUP369W	Ladyline	B963WRN	Arriva NW	CBV305S	C M T	D302SDS	D&G Bus Co
AUP650L	Taxico	B965WRN	Arriva NW	CEO723W	Arriva NW	D309UNT	Taxico
AYR303T	C M T	B966WRN	Arriva NW	CFM87S	Chester	D317SDS	Mark Perry
B1BUS	Jim Stones	B967WRN	Arriva NW	CHR998	Whitegate	D324UTU	Wingates Tours
B1JYM	Jim Stones	B968WRN	Arriva NW	CKB165X	Arriva NW	D390SGS	City Bus
B10JYM	Jim Stones	B969WRN	Arriva NW	CKB166X	Arriva NW	D395KND	D&G Bus Co
B11JYM	Jim Stones	BAZ7117	Taxico	CKB167X	Arriva NW	D403SGS	Whitegate
B16TYG	Jim Stones	BCA126W	Bostock's	CKB169X	Gillmoss	D406SGS	Helms
B43UCK	Aintree Coachline	BCB613V	Chester	CLV42X	Warrington	D414FEH	Taxico
B82WUV	Wingates Tours	BCB617V	Merseyline Travel	CLV84X	Warrington	D431TCA	D&G Bus Co
B84SWX	Aintree Coachline	BCB618V	Merseyline Travel			D438TMB	Bostock's
B85SWX	Helms	BCW824V	Arriva NW			D451ERE	First PMT
B87CDS	Ladyline	BED729C	Warrington			D454ERE	First PMT
B88WUV	Wingates Tours	BFR303R	Maghull Coaches			D497NYS	First PMT
B107UFV	Chester	BNB242T	Bennett's Travel			D499NYS	First PMT
B108UFV	Chester	BOK3V	Aintree Coachline			D511RCK	D&G Bus Co
B111KPF	Helms	BRC681T	Bostock's			D513FAE	D&G Bus Co
B115NBF	First PMT	BTX206T	Avon Coaches			D525RCK	D&G Bus Co
B128VJX	A1A Travel	BUS1N	Jim Stones	CLV85X	Warrington	D602AFR	Norbus
B131SED	City Bus			CTX394V	Merseypride	D607AFR	Norbus
B151TRN	Arriva NW			CUL91V	Avon Coaches	D608AFR	Norbus
B153TRN	Arriva NW			CUL101V	Gillmoss	D609AFR	Norbus
B154TRN	Arriva NW			CUL109V	Gillmoss	D611AFR	Lancashire Rose
B154XUU	A2B Travel			CUL116V	Gillmoss	D632MDB	Norbus
B155TRN	Arriva NW			CUL121V	Arriva NW	D634BBV	Arriva NW
B179WYV	A2B Travel			CUL122V	Gillmoss	D636NOD	D&G Bus Co
B181BLG	First PMT	BUS1S	Jim Stones	CUL134V	Gillmoss	D639WNU	C M T
B182BLG	First PMT	BUS1T	Jim Stones	CUL147V	Gillmoss	D670SEM	Arrowebrook
B188BLG	First PMT	BVP782V	First PMT	CUL148V	Arriva NW	D672SEM	Arrowebrook
B192PFA	Wingates Tours	BYW430V	Arriva NW	CUL154V	Gillmoss	D674NNE	Norbus
B195BLG	First PMT	BYW432V	Arriva NW	CUL156V	Gillmoss	D676NNE	Norbus
B199DTU	First PMT	C67JTU	Merseypride	CUL159V	Gillmoss	D681SEM	Mark Perry
B200DTU	First PMT	C95CHM	Aintree Coachline	CUL177V	Gillmoss	D706YHK	Liverpool MS
B201DTU	First PMT	C100UBC	Warrington	CUL198V	Norbus	D710SKU	Clowes
B201EFM	Chester	C101UBC	Warrington	CUL211V	Gillmoss	D752DLO	First PMT
B202DTU	First PMT	C102UBC	Warrington	CUL220V	Arriva NW	D754PTU	Moorland Buses
B202EFM	Chester	C103UBC	Warrington	CUL73V	Arriva NW	D787NDV	D&G Bus Co
B203EFM	Chester	C108SFP	First PMT	CWM154C	Liverpool MS	D810NWW	First PMT
B204EFM	Chester	C120PNV	Bostock's	D29PVS	Mercury	D852KWR	Taxico
B224WEU	Bennett's Travel	C128VRE	First PMT	D32MWN	City Bus	D862OJA	Whitegate
B231RRU	Arrowebrook	C135VRE	D&G Bus Co	D32RWC	Liverpool MS	D865NVS	D&G Bus Co
B354WUL	Maghull Coaches			D39TKA	Moorland Buses	D875ELL	First PMT

D892NDS	A1A Travel	E56UKL	Arriva NW	E229WBG	Arriva NW	E972DNK	David Tanner
D893DSF	Lancashire Rose	E57UKL	Arriva NW	E230NFX	Maghull Coaches	E992DNK	David Tanner
D920MVU	Mercury	E63UKL	Arriva NW	E230WBG	Arriva NW	ECS889V	Bennett's Travel
D923PRJ	Arrowebrook	E64UKL	Arriva NW	E233DTV	David Tanner	EEC909W	Bowker
D941UDY	Bennett's Travel	E65XKE	Arriva NW	E233NFX	Maghull Coaches	EGB50T	First PMT
D959WJH	Clowes	E126LAD	Chester	E270BRG	Mercury	EKA224Y	Helms
DBV834W	Liverpool MS	E133SAT	Avon Coaches	E291TAX	Ladyline	ELZ2972	Clowes
DBV836W	Arriva NW	E134VOK	A1A Travel	E291TAX	Ladyline	EMB370S	City Bus
DBV840W	Arriva NW	E135RAX	Moorland Buses	E324SWY	C M T	EON830V	City Bus
DCA522X	Bostock's	E136SAT	Avon Coaches	E325SWY	C M T	ERC645T	Taxico
DCA534X	Norbus	E138SAT	Avon Coaches	E333HJM	Whitegate	ERF24Y	First PMT
DEM774Y	Arriva NW	E141RAX	Maghull Coaches	E337WYS	Huxley	ERP552T	C M T
DEM776Y	Arriva NW	E199XWG	Huxley	E342NFA	First PMT	ERP553T	C M T
DEM777Y	Arriva NW	E201WBG	Arriva NW	E371YRO	C M T		
DEM778Y	Arriva NW	E202EPB	David Tanner	E404EPE	Liverpool MS		
DEM779Y	Arriva NW	E202WBG	Arriva NW	E413DMA	Huggins		
DEM780Y	Arriva NW	E203WBG	Arriva NW	E417EPE	Huxley		
DEM781Y	Arriva NW	E204WBG	Arriva NW	E452SON	Arriva NW		
DEM782Y	Arriva NW	E205WBG	Arriva NW	E453SON	Arriva NW		
DEM783Y	Arriva NW	E206WBG	Arriva NW	E455SON	Arriva NW		
DEM784Y	Arriva NW	E207WBG	Arriva NW	E463ANC	Arrowebrook		
DEM785Y	Arriva NW	E208HRY	Clowes	E511PWR	Huggins	ESK807	Bostock's
DEM786Y	Arriva NW	E208WBG	Arriva NW	E564MAC	Huggins	ESK879	Huxley
DEM787Y	Arriva NW	E209WBG	Arriva NW	E571MAC	Huggins	EWY78Y	First PMT
DEM789Y	Arriva NW	E210WBG	Arriva NW	E577ANE	Ladyline	EWY79Y	First PMT
DEM790Y	Arriva NW	E212WBG	Arriva NW	E601HTF	Avon Coaches	EYE232V	Gillmoss
DEM791Y	Arriva NW	E213WBG	Arriva NW	E602HTF	Huxley	EYE234V	Gillmoss
DFM347H	Chester	E214WBG	Arriva NW	E607ARJ	Bennett's Warrington	EYE239V	Gillmoss
DLB790Y	Clowes	E215WBG	Arriva NW	E631BVK	Huxley	EYE247V	Gillmoss
DOC52V	Helms of Eastams	E216WBG	Arriva NW	E759HJF	Ogden's	F54RFS	Pandh Travel
DOI9172	Ogden's	E217WBG	Arriva NW	E760HBF	First PMT	F94JGE	D&G Bus Co
DUI4760	Bennett's Travel	E218WBG	Arriva NW	E760NHG	Sutton	F95STB	Warrington
DWH685W	Merseyline Travel	E219WBG	Arriva NW	E767HBF	First PMT	F96STB	Warrington
E25BTU	Chester	E220WBG	Arriva NW	E78DMA	Clowes	F97STB	Warrington
E38YFM	Chester	E221WBG	Arriva NW	E835EUT	A2B Travel	F98STB	Warrington
E41YMB	Chester	E222FLD	Huggins	E840EUT	C M T	F99STB	Warrington
E43SBO	Chester	E222WBG	Arriva NW	E848AAW	Matthews Travel	F100UEH	First PMT
E44UKL	Arriva NW	E223WBG	Arriva NW	E856GFV	Taxico	F101TML	Arriva NW
E47UKL	Arriva NW	E224WBG	Arriva NW	E909EAY	Ogden's	F101XEM	Warrington
E49UKL	Taxico	E225WBG	Arriva NW	E913KYR	Arriva NW	F102GRM	First PMT
E54UKL	Arriva NW	E226WBG	Arriva NW	E916KYR	Arriva NW	F102XEM	Warrington
E55UKL	Arriva NW	E227WBG	Arriva NW	E926KYR	Arriva NW	F103TML	Arriva NW
E56MMT	A2B Travel	E228WBG	Arriva NW	E928KYR	Arriva NW	F103XEM	Warrington

Since Cardiff Bus withdrew their batch of Alexander-bodied Bristol VRs the type has appeared with many interesting operators as the Welsh Bus Handbook shows. Now carrying the livery of Merseypride Travel is CTX394V.
Andrew Jarosz

F104TML	Arriva NW	F158XYG	First PMT	F247YTJ	Arriva NW	F354DVR	C M T
F104XEM	Warrington	F160XYG	First PMT	F248HDB	Dobson's	F358JVS	C M T
F105TML	Arriva NW	F162AWO	David Tanner	F248YTJ	Arriva NW	F359JVS	C M T
F106CWG	First PMT	F164XCS	Taxico	F249YTJ	Arriva NW	F360MUT	Selwyns
F106TML	Arriva NW	F166DNT	First PMT	F250YTJ	Arriva NW	F361YTJ	First PMT
F107CWG	First PMT	F202XBV	Moorland Buses	F251YTJ	Arriva NW	F362YTJ	First PMT
F107TML	Arriva NW	F203MBT	C M T	F252YTJ	Arriva NW	F363YTJ	First PMT
F108CWG	First PMT			F253YTJ	Arriva NW	F364YTJ	First PMT
F108TML	Arriva NW			F254YTJ	Arriva NW	F368CHE	Arrowebrook
F109CWG	First PMT			F255YTJ	Arriva NW	F388CKU	Mercury
F109TML	Arriva NW			F256YTJ	Arriva NW	F438AKB	Arriva NW
F110CWG	First PMT			F257YTJ	Arriva NW	F439AKB	Arriva NW
F110TML	Arriva NW			F258YTJ	Arriva NW	F440AKB	Arriva NW
F111YVP	Huxley			F259YTJ	Arriva NW	F441AKB	Arriva NW
F112TML	Arriva NW	F204MBT	C M T	F260YTJ	Arriva NW	F442AKB	Arriva NW
F113TML	Arriva NW	F205MBT	C M T	F261YTJ	Arriva NW	F452YHF	First PMT
F121XEM	Warrington	F206MBT	C M T	F262YTJ	Arriva NW	F455BKF	Arriva NW
F122XEM	Warrington	F207MBT	C M T	F263YTJ	Arriva NW	F456BKF	Arriva NW
F125JGS	Supertravel	F208AKG	Maghull Coaches	F264YTJ	Arriva NW	F457BKF	Arriva NW
F126JGS	Maghull Coaches	F208MBT	C M T	F265YTJ	Arriva NW	F458BKF	Arriva NW
F140MBC	First PMT	F209JMB	Chester	F266YTJ	Arriva NW	F459BKF	Arriva NW
F141MBC	First PMT	F210JMB	Chester	F267YTJ	Arriva NW	F465LTU	Maghull Coaches
F142MBC	First PMT	F212AKG	A1A Travel	F268YTJ	Arriva NW	F473MDN	David Tanner
		F215RJX	Ogden's	F269YTJ	Arriva NW	F474MDN	David Tanner
		F216AKG	Maghull Coaches	F270YTJ	Arriva NW	F477PAE	A2B Travel
		F217OFB	First PMT	F276CEY	Whitegate	F505CBO	Chester
		F226AWO	Maghull Coaches	F276LND	Greenbus	F523UVW	Bostock's
		F231YTJ	Arriva NW	F279AWW	C M T	F572UPB	Bostock's
		F232YTJ	Arriva NW	F296AWW	C M T	F608WBV	First PMT
		F233YTJ	Arriva NW	F296PTP	First PMT	F620HGO	Arrowebrook
		F234YTJ	Arriva NW	F298PTP	First PMT	F623UBV	Lancashire Rose
F145GVO	Ladyline	F235YTJ	Arriva NW	F303AWW	C M T	F630BKD	Arriva NW
		F236YTJ	Arriva NW	F310REH	First PMT	F631BKD	City Bus
		F237YTJ	Arriva NW	F311REH	First PMT	F632BKD	Arriva NW
		F238YTJ	Arriva NW	F312REH	First PMT	F633BKD	Arriva NW
		F239YTJ	Arriva NW	F313REH	First PMT	F634BKD	Arriva NW
		F240YTJ	Arriva NW	F314REH	First PMT	F635BKD	Arriva NW
		F241YTJ	Arriva NW	F315REH	First PMT	F660OHD	Ogden's
		F242YTJ	Arriva NW	F316REH	First PMT	F713OFH	First PMT
		F243YTJ	Arriva NW	F317REH	First PMT	F724JTU	Selwyns
F145MBC	First PMT	F244YTJ	Arriva NW	F325MCA	Meredith's	F731FDV	Matthews Travel
F147MBC	First PMT	F245YTJ	Arriva NW	F345VEF	David Tanner	F741FDV	Scragg's
F156XYG	First PMT	F246YTJ	Arriva NW	F349DMS	Maghull Coaches	F759FDV	Matthews Travel

Three Lynx now carry the blue and white livery of Merseyline, the Garston-based independent. Photographed in Walton is H542FWM which was new to Halton in 1990.
Richard Godfrey

F762FDV	Scragg's	G108TND	Arriva NW	G639BHP	Supertravel	GFV151W	C M T
F773GNA	Bostock's	G109TND	Arriva NW	G647EKA	Arriva NW	GGR406N	Arriva NW
F786ROO	Local Motion	G118TND	Arriva NW	G650EKA	Arriva NW	GHE739V	Sutton
F793TBC	Maghull Coaches	G119TND	Arriva NW	G651EKA	Arriva NW	GIL1909	Boydons
F801YLV	Arriva NW	G125RGT	Arriva NW	G652EKA	Arriva NW	GIL6343	Maghull Coaches
F802YLV	Arriva NW	G128RGT	Arriva NW	G653EKA	Arriva NW	GKA37N	Arriva NW
F803YLV	Arriva NW	G136YRY	First PMT	G655EVN	Arrowebrook		

F804YLV	Arriva NW	G202URO	C M T	G661DTJ	Arriva NW		
F805YLV	Arriva NW	G214AHP	Mercury	G678XVT	Scragg's		
F806YLV	Arriva NW	G227NCW	Arrowebrook	G689OHE	Bakers		
F807YLV	Arriva NW	G228HCP	Ogden's	G690OHE	Bakers		
F808YLV	Arriva NW	G267GKG	Maghull Coaches	G707VRY	Maghull Coaches		
F809YLV	Arriva NW	G302DPA	Arriva NW	G712VRY	Maghull Coaches		
F810YLV	Arriva NW	G303DPA	Arriva NW	G753XRE	First PMT	GKA449L	Arriva NW
F811YLV	Arriva NW	G304DPA	Arriva NW	G754XRE	First PMT	GKA524M	Arriva NW
F812YLV	Arriva NW	G305DPA	Arriva NW	G755XRE	First PMT	GMB652T	Merseypride
F813YLV	Arriva NW	G318YVT	First PMT			GRF701V	First PMT
F814YLV	Arriva NW	G330XRE	First PMT			GRF707V	First PMT
F815YLV	Arriva NW	G331XRE	First PMT			GRF708V	First PMT
F816YLV	Arriva NW	G332XRE	First PMT			GRF709V	First PMT
F817YLV	Arriva NW	G334XRE	First PMT			GSU7T	Boydons
F818YLV	Arriva NW	G335XRE	First PMT			GSU838T	First PMT
F819RJF	Maghull Coaches	G336XRE	First PMT			GSU845T	First PMT
F819YLV	Arriva NW	G338XRE	First PMT			GUJ356	Meredith's
F820YLV	Arriva NW	G339XRE	First PMT	G756XRE	First PMT	GUW441W	Huxley
F821YLV	Arriva NW	G340XRE	First PMT	G757XRE	First PMT	GUW489W	City Bus
F822YLV	Arriva NW	G341XRE	First PMT	G758XRE	First PMT	GYE255W	Gillmoss
F823YLV	Arriva NW	G342CBF	First PMT	G759XRE	First PMT	GYE256W	Gillmoss
F824YLV	Arriva NW	G343CBF	First PMT	G760XRE	First PMT	GYE257W	Gillmoss
F825YLV	Arriva NW	G344CBF	First PMT	G761XRE	First PMT	GYE259W	Gillmoss
F872TNH	Ladyline	G345CBF	First PMT	G762XRE	First PMT	GYE269W	Gillmoss
F872XOE	Maghull Coaches	G346CBF	First PMT	G769WFC	Chester	GYE276W	Gillmoss
F874RJX	Taxico			G770WFC	Chester	GYE278W	Gillmoss
				G771FJC	Mercury	H1JYM	Jim Stones
				G771WFC	Chester	H2HWD	Bostock's
				G772WFC	Chester	H35HBG	Halton
				G773WFC	Chester	H62WNN	A1A Travel
				G774FJC	Mercury	H78DVM	Arriva NW
				G774WFC	Chester	H85DVM	Arriva NW
		G381EKA	Arriva NW	G775WFC	Chester	H86DVM	Arriva NW
F882VSJ	Chester	G382EKA	Arriva NW	G776WFC	Chester	H87DVM	Arriva NW
F889XOE	Moorland Buses	G383EKA	Arriva NW	G802XLO	Helms	H87MOB	Arriva NW
F88CWG	First PMT	G384EKA	Arriva NW	G803EKA	Merseyline Travel	H91MOB	Arriva NW
F895XOE	Moorland Buses	G385EKA	Arriva NW	G805AAD	First PMT	H95MOB	Arriva NW
F945CUA	Maghull Coaches	G386EKA	Arriva NW	G866BPD	Whitegate	H96MOB	Arriva NW
F958HTO	Dobson's	G387EKA	Arriva NW	G879SKE	Dobson's	H101GEV	Arriva NW
F95CWG	First PMT	G388EKA	Arriva NW	G900CRW	Arrowebrook	H102GEV	Arriva NW
F999JGE	Anthony's Travel	G495FFA	First PMT	G909GOL	Huggins	H103GEV	Arriva NW
FAZ3525	Helms	G506SFT	Arriva NW	G910KWF	Whitegate	H104GEV	Arriva NW
FBX562W	Ladyline	G508SFT	Arriva NW	GAZ6666	Taxico	H105GEV	Arriva NW
FFR486S	Hollinshead Coaches	G509SFT	Arriva NW	GAZ7117	Taxico	H106GEV	Arriva NW
FGC309T	Bennett's Travel	G512SFT	Arriva NW	GAZ7227	Taxico	H107GEV	Arriva NW
FKK847Y	Bennett's Travel	G513SFT	Arriva NW	GBF78N	First PMT	H108GEV	Arriva NW
FPR61V	Pandh Travel	G521WJF	Arriva NW	GBW100V	Hollinshead Coaches	H109GEV	Arriva NW
FXI8653	First PMT	G522WJF	Arriva NW	GCS47V	Bennett's Travel	H110GEV	Arriva NW
G20ANT	Anthony's Travel	G523WJF	Arriva NW	GCS53V	Bennett's Travel	H112GEV	Arriva NW
G34UKP	Bennett's Warrington	G524WJF	Arriva NW	GEK13V	Meredith's	H113GEV	Arriva NW
G36HDW	Clowes	G525WJF	Arriva NW	GFM101X	First PMT	H114GEV	Arriva NW
G45VME	Arriva NW	G532CVT	First PMT	GFM102X	First PMT	H115GEV	Arriva NW
G67RND	First PMT	G549ERF	First PMT	GFM103X	First PMT	H130MRW	Wingates Tours
G82KUB	Lancashire Rose	G569BHP	Supertravel	GFM104X	First PMT	H131MRW	Wingates Tours
G100TND	Arriva NW	G574BHP	Huggins	GFM105X	First PMT	H132MOB	Arriva NW
G101EVT	First PMT	G590PKL	Nip-On	GFM106X	First PMT	H143MOB	Arriva NW
G107TND	Arriva NW	G602SJA	Dobson's	GFM108X	First PMT	H153DJU	Warrington's
				GFM109X	First PMT		

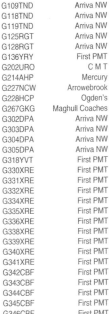

H160JRE	First PMT	H794HEM	A2B Travel	HIL7621	Procters	J431WFA	First PMT
H173XYV	Supertravel	H79DVM	Arriva NW	HIL7622	Procters	J444ABC	Greenbus
H189CNS	First PMT	H801GRE	First PMT	HIL7623	Procters	J484PVT	First PMT
H202JHP	First PMT	H802GRE	First PMT	HIL7624	Procters	J485PVT	First PMT
H203JHP	First PMT	H803GRE	First PMT	HIL8334	Matthews Travel	J486PVT	First PMT
H246MOE	Procters			HJI843	Meredith's	J626BWB	Bennett's Warrington
H247MOE	Procters			HKF151	Aintree Coachline	J628LHF	Halton
H271ACK	Supertravel			HMA104X	Chester	J629LHF	Halton
H352HRF	First PMT			HMA105X	Chester	J630LHF	Halton
H354HVT	First PMT			HMA106X	Chester	J733KBC	Warrington's
H355HVT	First PMT			HOI7544	Bostock's	J751AAW	First PMT
H356HVT	First PMT			HPV849	Happy Al's	J800ABC	C M T
H357HVT	First PMT			HRE128V	Procters	J844RAC	Wingates Tours
H358JRE	First PMT	H804GRE	First PMT	HSB740Y	Nip-On	J845RAC	Wingates Tours
H359JRE	First PMT	H805GRE	First PMT	HSC110T	C M T	J901SEH	First PMT
H361JRE	First PMT	H806GRE	First PMT	HSC113T	C M T	J902SEH	First PMT
H362JRE	First PMT	H807GRE	First PMT			J903OAY	Norbus
H363JRE	First PMT	H808GRE	First PMT			J903SEH	First PMT
H366LFA	First PMT	H809GRE	First PMT			J904SEH	First PMT
H367LFA	First PMT	H841NOC	Warrington			J905SEH	First PMT
H368LFA	First PMT	H842NOC	Warrington			J906SEH	First PMT
H369LFA	First PMT	H843NOC	Warrington			J907SEH	First PMT
H370LFA	First PMT	H844NOC	Warrington			J908SEH	First PMT
H371LFA	First PMT	H845NOC	Warrington			J909SEH	First PMT
H372MEH	First PMT	H846NOC	Warrington	HUF625X	Huxley	J910SEH	First PMT
H373MVT	First PMT	H847NOC	Warrington	HUF626X	Norbus	J911SEH	First PMT
H404BVR	Supertravel	H851GRE	First PMT	HWJ620W	Chester	J912SEH	First PMT
H407LVC	Wingates Tours	H852GRE	First PMT	HWJ928W	Norbus	J913SEH	First PMT
H434DVM	Arrowebrook	H853GRE	First PMT	IIJ145	Bowker	J914SEH	First PMT
H451AGB	Supertravel	H854GRE	First PMT	IIL6436	Bowker	J915HGD	Huggins
H458UGO	Arriva NW	H855GRE	First PMT	J3SLT	Arriva NW	J915SEH	First PMT
H460UGO	Arriva NW	H856GRE	First PMT	J5BUS	Jim Stones	J916SEH	First PMT
H461UGO	Arriva NW	H857GRE	First PMT	J6SLT	Arriva NW	J917SEH	First PMT
H463UGO	Arriva NW	H858GRE	First PMT	J7SLT	Arriva NW	J918LEM	Bennett's Warrington
H465UGO	Arriva NW	H859GRE	First PMT	J8SLT	Arriva NW	J918SEH	First PMT
H466UGO	Arriva NW	H860GRE	First PMT	J9SLT	Arriva NW	J921MKC	Halton
H467UGO	Arriva NW	H861GRE	First PMT	J10BUS	Hollinshead Coaches	J922MKC	Halton
H469UGO	Arriva NW	H879LOX	Warrington	J10SLT	Arriva NW	J923MKC	Halton
H483JRE	First PMT	H881LOX	Warrington	J10WBT	Warrington	J924MKC	Halton
H541EVM	Mercury	H886LOX	Warrington	J38VDW	Matthews Travel	J925MKC	Halton
H542FWM	Merseyline Travel	H887LOX	Warrington	J44ABC	C M T	J926MKC	Halton
H543FWM	Merseyline Travel	H889LOX	Warrington	J51EDM	Chester	J927MKC	Halton
H562GDB	Supertravel	H897LOX	Warrington	J52EDM	Chester	J928MKC	Halton
H588DVM	Arriva NW	H912XAG	Taxico	J53EDM	Chester	J929MKC	Halton
H660GPF	Arriva NW	H968LSF	Bennett's Warrington	J54EDM	Chester	JCK852W	Local Motion
H661GPF	Arriva NW	HDB124V	Chester	J55ABC	C M T	JCM396	Meredith's
		HFF234	Ogden's	J91JFR	Bostock's	JED904	Meredith's
		HFM186N	Arriva NW	J121LKO	A2B Travel	JIL4404	Helms
		HHJ374Y	First PMT	J136OBU	Ogden's	JIL5227	Scragg's
		HIL2375	Procters	J155EDM	Chester	JIL8627	Maghull Coaches
		HIL2376	Procters	J206KTT	Bakers		
		HIL2377	Procters	J220XKY	Bostock's		
		HIL2378	Procters	J249KWM	Halton		
		HIL2379	Procters	J250KWM	Halton		
		HIL2381	Ogden's	J251KWM	Halton		
H662GPF	Arriva NW	HIL3931	Huxley	J287NNC	Bostock's		
H665GPF	Arriva NW	HIL3934	Huxley	J288NNC	Bostock's		
H667GPF	Arriva NW	HIL3935	Huxley	J311WHJ	Arriva NW		
H679GPF	Arriva NW	HIL6956	Ogden's	J312WHJ	Arriva NW		
H713LOL	Moorland Buses	HIL7386	Procters	J313WHJ	Arriva NW		
H714LOL	Maghull Coaches	HIL7613	Procters	J314XVX	Arriva NW	JJT438N	Merseypride
H722CNC	First PMT	HIL7614	Procters	J315XVX	Arriva NW	JOI2949	Ogden's
H723CNC	First PMT	HIL7615	Procters	J332LVM	Dobson's	JSL282X	Chester
H744VHS	D&G Bus Co	HIL7616	Procters	J387PVR	Dobson's	JSL284X	Chester
H763GTJ	Supertravel	HIL7620	Procters	J430WFA	First PMT	JSV343	City Bus
H791UWA	Supertravel					JWM689P	Maghull Coaches
						K1SLT	Arriva NW

Reg	Operator	Reg	Operator	Reg	Operator	Reg	Operator
K2SLT	Arriva NW	K439XRF	First PMT	K882UDB	Arriva NW	KYN330X	Arriva NW
K3SEL	Selwyns	K440XRF	First PMT	K884UDB	Arriva NW	KYN332X	Gillmoss
K3SLT	Arriva NW	K441XRF	First PMT	K890UDB	Selwyns	KYN333X	Arriva NW
K3SUP	Hardings	K442XRF	First PMT	K911OEM	Arriva NW	KYN337X	Gillmoss
K4GWC	Warrington's	K444ANT	Anthony's Travel	K919XRF	First PMT	KYN338X	Arriva NW
K19AMB	Bennett's Warrington	K445XRF	First PMT	K920XRF	First PMT	KYN339X	Gillmoss
K20AMB	Express Travel	K446XRF	First PMT	K921XRF	First PMT	KYN344X	Arriva NW
K22ANT	Anthony's Travel	K448XRF	First PMT	K922XRF	First PMT	KYN347X	Gillmoss
K56LLG	Chester	K457EVC	Arriva NW	K923XRF	First PMT	KYN350X	Arriva NW
K57LLG	Chester	K487CVT	First PMT	K924XRF	First PMT	KYN351X	Gillmoss
K58LLG	Chester	K488CVT	First PMT	K925XRF	First PMT	KYN353X	Arriva NW
K59BAX	Wingates Tours	K489CVT	First PMT	K926XRF	First PMT	KYN354X	Arriva NW
K59LLG	Chester	K490CVT	First PMT	K927XRF	First PMT	KYN355X	Arriva NW
K73SRG	Arriva NW	K491CVT	First PMT	K928XRF	First PMT	KYN363X	Arriva NW
K74SRG	Arriva NW	K492CVT	First PMT	K929XRF	First PMT	KYN365X	Gillmoss
K75SRG	Arriva NW	K504WNR	Express Travel	K943EWG	Huggins	KYN374X	Arriva NW
K88ABC	Helms	K505WNR	Helms	K955PBG	Arriva NW	KYN376X	Arriva NW
K101OHF	Arriva NW	K506WNR	Express Travel	KAD349V	Sutton	KYN385X	Arriva NW
K102OHF	Arriva NW	K510RJX	Arriva NW	KAZ777	Taxico	KYN389X	Gillmoss
K103OHF	Arriva NW	K524EFL	Whitegate	KFM111Y	First PMT	KYN391X	Gillmoss
K104OHF	Arriva NW	K544XRF	First PMT	KFM112Y	First PMT	KYN400X	Arriva NW
K105OHF	Arriva NW	K555ANT	Anthony's Travel	KFM113Y	First PMT	KYN417X	Arriva NW
K106OHF	Arriva NW	K603OCA	Huggins	KFM115Y	First PMT	KYN424X	Arriva NW
K107OHF	Arriva NW	K701TTA	Selwyns	KFM189T	Helms	KYN430X	Gillmoss
K108OHF	Arriva NW	K756YFR	Hardings	KFM190T	Chester	KYN431X	Gillmoss
K130TCP	Arriva NW	K801NTJ	Arriva NW	KFM192T	Chester	KYN443X	Arriva NW
K131TCP	Arriva NW	K802NTJ	Arriva NW	KIB7027	Maghull Coaches	KYN449X	Arriva NW
K132TCP	Arriva NW	K803NTJ	Arriva NW	KLG106Y	Bostock's	KYN450X	Gillmoss
K133TCP	Arriva NW	K804NTJ	Arriva NW	KLG107Y	Chester	KYN463X	Gillmoss
K174EUX	First PMT	K805NTJ	Arriva NW	KLG108Y	Chester	KYN464X	Gillmoss
K200SLT	Selwyns	K806KWX	Hardings	KLG109Y	Chester	KYN468X	Arriva NW
K221VTB	Warrington	K807KWX	Hardings	KOI4484	Arrowebrook	KYN472X	Gillmoss
K222VTB	Warrington	K817NKH	Arriva NW	KRP564V	C M T	KYN483X	Arriva NW
K223VTB	Warrington	K852MTJ	Halton	KSD102W	Happy Al's	KYN489X	Gillmoss
K224VTB	Warrington	K853MTJ	Halton	KSV408	Meredith's	KYN491X	Arriva NW
K225VTB	Warrington	K877UDB	Arriva NW	KTB748F	Halton	KYN494X	Gillmoss
K333DOT	Ogden's			KWA23W	City Bus	KYN499X	Gillmoss
K374BRE	First PMT			KYN284X	Arriva NW	KYN509X	Gillmoss
K375BRE	First PMT			KYN293X	Gillmoss	KYN528X	Gillmoss
K400ABC	C M T			KYN301X	Gillmoss	KYV319X	City Bus
K434XRF	First PMT			KYN304X	Gillmoss	KYV343X	City Bus
K436XRF	First PMT			KYN315X	Gillmoss	KYV357X	Merseyline Travel
K437XRF	First PMT			KYN316X	Gillmoss	KYV478X	Merseyline Travel
K438XRF	First PMT						

ABC Travel of Ainsdale split during 1999 with the coach operation passing to Aintree Coachline while the Bus services are operated under CMT. ABC gathered a selection of ABC index marks including N600ABC. This vehicle is now 2019 in the CMT series and is a DAF SB220 with Northern Counties Paladin bodywork. It was in Southport when photographed.
Richard Godfrey

Reg	Operator	Reg	Operator	Reg	Operator	Reg	Operator
KYV482X	Avon Coaches	L213TKA	Arriva NW	L245TKA	Gillmoss	L496HRE	First PMT
L1SLT	Arriva NW	L214TKA	Arriva NW	L246TKA	Gillmoss	L497HRE	First PMT
L2SLT	Arriva NW	L215TKA	Arriva NW	L247TKA	Gillmoss	L498HRE	First PMT
L3SLT	Selwyns	L216TKA	Arriva NW	L248TKA	Gillmoss	L501TKA	Arriva NW
L5ABC	C M T	L217TKA	Arriva NW	L249TKA	Gillmoss	L502TKA	Arriva NW
L6ABC	C M T	L218TKA	Arriva NW	L250TKA	Gillmoss	L503TKA	Arriva NW
L6HWD	Bostock's	L219TKA	Arriva NW	L269GBU	First PMT	L504TKA	Arriva NW
L10GGY	Ogden's	L220TKA	Arriva NW	L301TEM	Arriva NW	L505TKA	Arriva NW
L11SLT	Arriva NW	L221TKA	Arriva NW	L302TEM	Arriva NW	L506TKA	Arriva NW
L20ABC	Helms	L222TKA	Arriva NW	L303TEM	Arriva NW	L507TKA	Arriva NW
L31ORC	A2B Travel	L223TKA	Arriva NW	L321HRE	First PMT	L508TKA	Arriva NW
L35AKP	A2B Travel	L224TKA	Arriva NW	L323NRF	First PMT	L509TKA	Arriva NW
L61PDM	Chester	L225TKA	Arriva NW	L331BFX	Maghull Coaches	L510TKA	Arriva NW
L62PDM	Chester	L226SWM	Warrington	L388YNV	Bostock's	L511TKA	Arriva NW
L63SFM	Chester	L226TKA	Arriva NW	L401LHE	Hardings	L512TKA	Arriva NW
L64SFM	Chester	L227SWM	Warrington	L402LHE	Hardings	L513TKA	Arriva NW
L111ANT	Anthony's Travel	L227TKA	Arriva NW	L402TKB	Arriva NW	L544EHD	Selwyns
L120YVK	Arriva NW	L228SWM	Warrington	L403LHE	Hardings	L553LVT	First PMT
L121YVK	Arriva NW	L228TKA	Arriva NW	L403TKB	Arriva NW	L554LVT	First PMT
L123YVK	Arriva NW	L229SWM	Warrington	L404TKB	Arriva NW	L556LVT	First PMT
L125YVK	Arriva NW	L229TKA	Arriva NW	L405TKB	Arriva NW	L557LVT	First PMT
L126YVK	Arriva NW	L230SWM	Warrington	L406LHE	Matthews Travel	L558LVT	First PMT
L150SBG	Arriva NW	L230TKA	Arriva NW	L406TKB	Arriva NW	L642DNA	Arriva NW
L151SBG	Arriva NW	L231NRE	First PMT	L407TKB	Arriva NW	L648DNA	Arriva NW
L151YVK	Arriva NW	L231SWM	Warrington	L408TKB	Arriva NW	L649ADS	Wingates Tours
L152SBG	Arriva NW	L231TKA	Arriva NW			L649DNA	Arriva NW
L153UKB	Arriva NW	L232SWM	Warrington			L655ADS	Wingates Tours
L154UKB	Arriva NW	L232TKA	Arriva NW			L700ABC	C M T
L155UKB	Arriva NW	L233SWM	Warrington			L705PHE	Express Travel
L156UKB	Arriva NW	L233TKA	Arriva NW			L706PHE	Express Travel
L160PDM	Chester	L234SWM	Warrington			L707PHE	Express Travel
L193DBC	Arriva NW	L234TKA	Arriva NW			L708PHE	Express Travel
L201TKA	Arriva NW	L235SWM	Warrington			L709PHE	Express Travel
L202TKA	Arriva NW	L235TKA	Arriva NW	L409TKB	Arriva NW	L710PHE	Express Travel
L203TKA	Arriva NW	L236TKA	Arriva NW	L410TKB	Arriva NW	L711PHE	Express Travel
L204TKA	Arriva NW	L237TKA	Arriva NW	L411UFY	Arriva NW	L712PHE	Express Travel
L205TKA	Arriva NW	L238TKA	Arriva NW	L412UFY	Arriva NW	L713PHE	Express Travel
L206TKA	Arriva NW	L239TKA	Arriva NW	L413TKB	Arriva NW	L714PHE	Express Travel
L208TKA	Arriva NW	L240TKA	Arriva NW	L455LVT	First PMT	L771RWW	Arriva NW
L209TKA	Arriva NW	L241TKA	Arriva NW	L483DOA	Dobson's	L772RWW	Arriva NW
L210TKA	Arriva NW	L242TKA	Arriva NW	L493HRE	First PMT	L775RWW	Arriva NW
L211TKA	Arriva NW	L243TKA	Arriva NW	L494HRE	First PMT	L776RWW	Arriva NW
L212TKA	Arriva NW	L244TKA	Arriva NW	L495HRE	First PMT	L778RWW	Arriva NW

First PMT operate several buses in Linxx livery for the Flintshire tendered services based on Holywell. Seen in Upper Northgate Street in Chester is 58, T158BBF which carries the livery for this scheme.
Richard Godfrey

Reg	Operator	Reg	Operator	Reg	Operator	Reg	Operator
L779RWW	Arriva NW	M71AKA	Halton	M196YKA	Arriva NW	M292XSF	Supertravel
L801LSX	Supertravel	M73AKA	Halton	M197YKA	Arriva NW	M301YBG	Gillmoss
L806TFY	Arriva NW	M74AKA	Halton	M198YKA	Arriva NW	M302YBG	Gillmoss
L862HFA	First PMT	M77ABC	C M T	M199YKA	Arriva NW	M303YBG	Gillmoss
L931HFA	First PMT	M89DEW	Nip-On	M201YKA	Arriva NW	M322AKB	Arriva NW
L932HFA	First PMT	M109XKC	Arriva NW	M202YKA	Arriva NW	M333ANT	Anthony's Travel
L933HFA	First PMT	M110TVH	Supertravel			M335KRY	Bostock's
L934HFA	First PMT	M110XKC	Arriva NW			M363KVR	Arriva NW
L935HFA	First PMT	M112XKC	Arriva NW			M364KVR	Arriva NW
L936HFA	First PMT	M113XKC	Arriva NW			M365AMA	Selwyns
L937LRF	First PMT	M120YCM	Arriva NW			M365KVR	Arriva NW
L938LRF	First PMT	M121YCM	Arriva NW			M366AMA	Selwyns
L939LRF	First PMT	M122YCM	Arriva NW			M366KVR	Arriva NW
L940LRF	First PMT	M123YCM	Arriva NW			M367KVR	Arriva NW
L941LRF	First PMT	M124YCM	Arriva NW	M203YKA	Arriva NW	M368KVR	Arriva NW
L942LRF	First PMT	M125YCM	Arriva NW	M204YKA	Arriva NW	M369KVR	Arriva NW
L9810TFY	Gillmoss	M126YCM	Arriva NW	M205YKA	Arriva NW	M370KVR	Arriva NW
L998CRY	Wingates Tours	M128YCM	Arriva NW	M206YKA	Arriva NW	M371KVR	Arriva NW
		M129UWM	Aintree Coachline	M207YKA	Arriva NW	M372KVR	Arriva NW
		M156LNC	Arriva NW	M208PAN	Hardings	M377SRE	First PMT
		M157LNC	Arriva NW	M208YKA	Arriva NW	M378SRE	First PMT
		M157WKA	Arriva NW	M209YKA	Arriva NW	M379SRE	First PMT
		M158WKA	Arriva NW	M210YKA	Arriva NW	M380SRE	First PMT
		M159WKA	Arriva NW	M211YKD	Arriva NW	M381SRE	First PMT
		M160WKA	Arriva NW	M212YKD	Arriva NW	M382SRE	First PMT
		M160WTJ	Arriva NW	M213YKD	Arriva NW	M383SRE	First PMT
LAG188V	Chester	M161WKA	Arriva NW	M214YKD	Arriva NW	M390KVR	Selwyns
LCA183Y	Bostock's	M162WKA	Arriva NW	M215YKD	Arriva NW	M397ACK	Hardings
LCW731W	City Bus	M163WKA	Arriva NW	M216YKD	Arriva NW	M514WHF	Arriva NW
LED72P	Warrington	M164WKA	Arriva NW	M217AKB	Arriva NW	M515WHF	Arriva NW
LHA452V	Bennett's Travel	M165WKA	Arriva NW	M218AKB	Arriva NW	M516WHF	Arriva NW
LHE254W	Bostock's	M165XMA	Chester	M219AKB	Arriva NW	M517WHF	Arriva NW
LIB6438	Bostock's	M166LNC	Arriva NW	M220AKB	Arriva NW	M518WHF	Arriva NW
LIB6440	Bostock's	M166WKA	Arriva NW	M221AKB	Arriva NW	M519WHF	Arriva NW
LIL7810	Meredith's	M166XMA	Chester	M223AKB	Arriva NW	M520WHF	Arriva NW
LPB222P	C M T	M167LNC	Arriva NW	M224AKB	Arriva NW	M521WHF	Arriva NW
LWU468V	Taxico	M167WKA	Arriva NW	M225AKB	Arriva NW	M522WHF	Arriva NW
LWU470V	Liverpool MS	M168WKA	Arriva NW	M226AKB	Arriva NW	M523WHF	Arriva NW
M1BUS	Jim Stones	M169WKA	Arriva NW	M227AKB	Arriva NW	M524WHF	Arriva NW
M2SLT	Arriva NW	M170WKA	Arriva NW	M228AKB	Arriva NW	M525WHF	Arriva NW
M5SLT	Arriva NW	M171YKA	Arriva NW	M229AKB	Arriva NW	M526WHF	Arriva NW
M6SEL	Selwyns	M172YKA	Arriva NW	M230AKB	Arriva NW	M527WHF	Arriva NW
M7ABC	C M T	M173YKA	Arriva NW	M231AKB	Arriva NW	M528WHF	Arriva NW
M7SEL	Selwyns	M174YKA	Arriva NW	M232AKB	Arriva NW	M529WHF	Arriva NW
M13BUS	A1A Travel	M175YKA	Arriva NW	M236YKD	Warrington	M530WHF	Arriva NW
M20GGY	Arriva NW	M176YKA	Arriva NW	M237YKD	Warrington	M531WHF	Arriva NW
M25YRE	First PMT	M177YKA	Arriva NW	M238YKD	Warrington	M532WHF	Arriva NW
M26YRE	First PMT	M178YKA	Arriva NW	M239YCM	Warrington	M533WHF	Arriva NW
M27YRE	First PMT	M179YKA	Arriva NW	M240YCM	Warrington	M534WHF	Arriva NW
M28YRE	First PMT	M180YKA	Arriva NW			M535WHF	Arriva NW
M30GGY	Arriva NW	M181YKA	Arriva NW			M536WHF	Arriva NW
M31KAX	Bostock's	M182YKA	Arriva NW			M537WHF	Arriva NW
M43HSU	Bostock's	M183YKA	Arriva NW			M538WHF	Arriva NW
M59WKA	Arriva NW	M184YKA	Arriva NW			M540WHF	Arriva NW
M61WKA	Arriva NW	M185YKA	Arriva NW			M541WHF	Arriva NW
M64WKA	Arriva NW	M186YKA	Arriva NW			M542WHF	Arriva NW
		M187YKA	Arriva NW			M543WHF	Arriva NW
		M188YKA	Arriva NW	M241YCM	Warrington	M544WTJ	Arriva NW
		M189YKA	Arriva NW	M242YCM	Warrington	M545WTJ	Arriva NW
		M190YKA	Arriva NW	M243YCM	Warrington	M546WTJ	Arriva NW
		M191YKA	Arriva NW	M246YWM	Warrington	M547WTJ	Arriva NW
		M192YKA	Arriva NW	M247YWM	Warrington	M548WTJ	Arriva NW
		M193YKA	Arriva NW	M248YWM	Warrington	M549WTJ	Arriva NW
		M194YKA	Arriva NW	M252SRN	Ogden's	M550WTJ	Arriva NW
M65WKA	Arriva NW	M195YKA	Arriva NW	M284HRH	Warrington	M551WTJ	Arriva NW

T469HNH is one of three Dennis Darts that are operating in Norbus livery. Seen passing through Bootle while on route 143, the vehicle is of the shorter Mini Pointer Dart model. *Richard Godfrey*

M552WTJ	Arriva NW	M572SRE	First PMT	M932EYS	Arriva NW	M970XVT	First PMT
M553WTJ	Arriva NW	M572YEM	Arriva NW	M933EYS	Arriva NW	M971XVT	First PMT
M554WTJ	Arriva NW	M573SRE	First PMT	M934EYS	Arriva NW	M972XVT	First PMT
M556WTJ	Arriva NW	M573YEM	Arriva NW	M935EYS	Arriva NW	MAB181X	Bennett's Travel
M557WTJ	Arriva NW	M574YEM	Arriva NW	M936EYS	Arriva NW	MCN548W	Maghull Coaches
M558WTJ	Arriva NW	M575YEM	Arriva NW	M943SRE	First PMT	MDT238W	First PMT
M559SRE	First PMT	M579WLV	Halton	M944SRE	First PMT	MEF825W	City Bus
M559WTJ	Arriva NW	M580WLV	Halton	M945SRE	First PMT	MEK18W	Warrington
M561SRE	First PMT	M581WLV	Halton	M946SRE	First PMT	MEK19W	Warrington
M561WTJ	Arriva NW	M582WLV	Halton	M947SRE	First PMT	MFA723V	First PMT
M562SRE	First PMT	M583WLV	Halton	M948SRE	First PMT	MFE504	Huxley
M562TJL	Bennett's Travel	M584WLV	Halton	M949SRE	First PMT	MIB104	Copeland Tours
M562WTJ	Arriva NW	M593HKH	Warrington	M951SRE	First PMT	MIB116	Copeland Tours
M563SRE	First PMT	M602BCA	Selwyns	M952SRE	First PMT		
M563WTJ	Arriva NW	M647YLV	C M T	M953XVT	First PMT		
M564SRE	First PMT	M648YLV	C M T	M954XVT	First PMT		
M564YEM	Arriva NW	M649YLV	C M T	M955XVT	First PMT		
M565SRE	First PMT	M650YLV	C M T	M956XVT	First PMT		
M565YEM	Arriva NW	M660SRE	First PMT	M957XVT	First PMT		
M566SRE	First PMT	M736VSC	Selwyns	M958XVT	First PMT		
M566YEM	Arriva NW	M777ABC	C M T	M959XVT	First PMT		
M567SRE	First PMT	M799HPJ	Selwyns	M960XVT	First PMT	MIB268	Copeland Tours
M567YEM	Arriva NW	M841RCP	Arriva NW	M961XVT	First PMT	MIB279	Copeland Tours
M568SRE	First PMT	M842RCP	Arriva NW	M962XVT	First PMT	MIB302	Copeland Tours
M568YEM	Arriva NW	M843RCP	Arriva NW	M963XVT	First PMT	MIB346	Copeland Tours
M569SRE	First PMT	M848LTX	Bostock's	M964XVT	First PMT	MIB520	Copeland Tours
M569YEM	Arriva NW	M886SKU	Bennett's Warrington	M965XVT	First PMT	MIB537	Copeland Tours
M570SRE	First PMT	M927EYS	Arriva NW	M966XVT	First PMT	MIB542	Copeland Tours
M570YEM	Arriva NW	M928EYS	Arriva NW	M967XVT	First PMT	MIB614	Copeland Tours
M571SRE	First PMT	M929EYS	Arriva NW	M968XVT	First PMT	MIB615	Copeland Tours
M571YEM	Arriva NW	M931EYS	Arriva NW	M969XVT	First PMT	MIB746	Copeland Tours

CMT have increased their presence in Liverpool since the last edition of this book when the fleet mostly comprised Leyland Nationals. Pictured near Lime Street station is Volvo 2040, S451KCW which illustrates the many vinyl graphics applied to the side of the vehicles reminding the potential passenger of the features of the modern bus. *R L Wilson*

MIB761	Copeland Tours	N104YVU	Arriva NW	N175DWM	Arriva NW	N255CKA	Arriva NW
MIB783	Copeland Tours	N105YVU	Arriva NW	N176DWM	Arriva NW	N256CKA	Arriva NW
MIB864	Copeland Tours	N106DWM	Arriva NW	N177DWM	Arriva NW	N257CKA	Arriva NW
MIB4964	Boydons	N107DWM	Arriva NW	N178DWM	Arriva NW	N258CKA	Arriva NW
MIL1215	Nip-On	N108DWM	Arriva NW	N179DWM	Arriva NW	N259CKA	Arriva NW
MIL2267	Hardings	N109DWM	Arriva NW	N205VRX	Hardings	N260CKA	Arriva NW
MIL2654	Bennett's Warrington	N110DWM	Arriva NW	N206VRX	Hardings	N261CKA	Arriva NW
MIL8338	Wingates Tours	N112DWM	Arriva NW	N211DWM	Arriva NW	N262CKA	Arriva NW
MIL9765	Happy Al's	N113DWM	Arriva NW	N233CKA	Arriva NW	N263CKA	Arriva NW
MNC519W	Mark Perry	N114DWM	Arriva NW	N234CKA	Arriva NW	N263FMA	Dobson's
MNH571V	C M T	N115DWM	Arriva NW	N235CKA	Arriva NW	N264CKA	Arriva NW
MNH576V	C M T	N116DWM	Arriva NW	N236CKA	Arriva NW	N271CKB	Arriva NW
MNS48Y	Happy Al's	N117DWM	Arriva NW	N237CKA	Arriva NW	N272CKB	Arriva NW
MNS51Y	Happy Al's	N118DWM	Arriva NW	N238CKA	Arriva NW	N273CKB	Arriva NW
MPY908P	Bowker	N119DWM	Arriva NW	N239CKA	Arriva NW	N274CKB	Arriva NW
MRY7W	Ladyline	N120DWM	Arriva NW	N240CKA	Arriva NW	N275CKB	Arriva NW
MTU120Y	First PMT	N121DWM	Arriva NW	N241CKA	Arriva NW	N276CKB	Arriva NW
MTU122Y	First PMT	N122DWM	Arriva NW	N242CKA	Arriva NW	N277CKB	Arriva NW
MTU123Y	First PMT	N123DWM	Arriva NW	N243CKA	Arriva NW	N278CKB	Arriva NW
MTU124Y	First PMT	N124DWM	Arriva NW	N244CKA	Arriva NW	N279CKB	Arriva NW
MUP713T	Arriva NW	N125DWM	Arriva NW	N245CKA	Arriva NW	N281CKB	Arriva NW
MVK522R	Sutton	N126DWM	Arriva NW	N246CKA	Arriva NW	N282CKB	Arriva NW
N8ABC	C M T	N127DWM	Arriva NW	N247CKA	Arriva NW	N283CKB	Arriva NW
N9ABC	C M T	N128DWM	Arriva NW	N248CKA	Arriva NW	N284CKB	Arriva NW
N17ALS	Happy Al's	N129DWM	Arriva NW	N249CKA	Arriva NW	N285CKB	Arriva NW
N18ALS	Happy Al's	N130DWM	Arriva NW	N250CKA	Arriva NW	N286CKB	Arriva NW
N66ABC	C M T	N131DWM	Arriva NW	N251CKA	Arriva NW	N287CKB	Arriva NW
N100ALS	Happy Al's	N132DWM	Arriva NW	N252CKA	Arriva NW	N288CKB	Arriva NW
N101YVU	Arriva NW	N133DWM	Arriva NW	N253CKA	Arriva NW	N289CKB	Arriva NW
N103YVU	Arriva NW	N134DWM	Arriva NW	N254CKA	Arriva NW	N290CKB	Arriva NW

MTL chose the Marshall Capital body for their large order of Dennis Darts. Photographed while on Muihead Avenue, 7602, T602JBA, is the first of the normal length Darts and one of the type placed at Gillmoss for the disposal of that garage. As we go to press the vehicles for sale with the depot had been identified and placed in a separate listing and shown as Gillmoss in the vehicle index. *Richard Godfrey*

N291CKB	Arriva NW	N574CEH	First PMT	N590CEH	First PMT	N615CKA	Arriva NW
N292CKB	Arriva NW	N575CEH	First PMT	N590CKA	Arriva NW	N616CKA	Arriva NW
N293CKB	Arriva NW	N576CEH	First PMT	N591CEH	First PMT	N617CKA	Arriva NW
N294CKB	Arriva NW	N576CKA	Arriva NW	N591CKA	Arriva NW	N618CKA	Arriva NW
N295CKB	Arriva NW	N577CEH	First PMT	N592CEH	First PMT		
N295DWE	Bennett's Travel	N577CKA	Arriva NW	N592CKA	Arriva NW		
N296CKB	Arriva NW	N578CEH	First PMT	N593CEH	First PMT		
N297CKB	Arriva NW	N578CKA	Arriva NW	N593CKA	Arriva NW		
N298CKB	Arriva NW	N579CEH	First PMT	N594CEH	First PMT		
N299CKB	Arriva NW	N579CKA	Arriva NW	N594CKA	Arriva NW		
N301CKB	Arriva NW	N580CEH	First PMT	N595CKA	Arriva NW		
N302CKB	Arriva NW	N580CKA	Arriva NW	N596CKA	Arriva NW		
N303CKB	Arriva NW	N581CEH	First PMT	N597CKA	Arriva NW	N619CKA	Arriva NW
N304CKB	Arriva NW	N581CKA	Arriva NW	N598CKA	Arriva NW	N620CKA	Arriva NW
N305CKB	Arriva NW	N582CEH	First PMT	N599CKA	Arriva NW	N621CKA	Arriva NW
N306CKB	Arriva NW	N582CKA	Arriva NW	N600ABC	C M T	N622CKA	Arriva NW
N307CKB	Arriva NW	N583CEH	First PMT	N601CKA	Arriva NW	N623CKA	Arriva NW
N308CKB	Arriva NW	N583CKA	Arriva NW	N602CKA	Arriva NW	N627HDM	Selwyns
N377YNB	Wingates Tours	N584CEH	First PMT	N603CKA	Arriva NW	N652CHF	C M T
N405HVT	First PMT	N584CKA	Arriva NW	N604CKA	Arriva NW	N653CHF	C M T
N406HVT	First PMT	N585CEH	First PMT	N605CKA	Arriva NW	N654CHF	C M T
N407HVT	First PMT	N585CKA	Arriva NW	N606CKA	Arriva NW	N655CHF	C M T
N408HVT	First PMT	N586CEH	First PMT	N607CKA	Arriva NW	N656CHF	C M T
N409HVT	First PMT	N586CKA	Arriva NW	N608CKA	Arriva NW	N657CHF	C M T
N410HVT	First PMT	N587CEH	First PMT	N609CKA	Arriva NW	N658CHF	C M T
N411HVT	First PMT	N587CKA	Arriva NW	N610CKA	Arriva NW	N659EKD	C M T
N412HVT	First PMT	N588CEH	First PMT	N611CKA	Arriva NW	N660EKD	C M T
N459EEY	Chester	N588CKA	Arriva NW	N612CKA	Arriva NW	N671CLV	Halton
N531DWN	Arriva NW	N589CEH	First PMT	N613CKA	Arriva NW	N672CLV	Halton
N532DWN	Arriva NW	N589CKA	Arriva NW	N614CKA	Arriva NW	N673CLV	Halton

Reg	Operator	Reg	Operator	Reg	Operator	Reg	Operator
N780EUA	Arriva NW	OHV741Y	Arriva NW	P303HEM	Arriva NW	P459EFL	Pandh Travel
N784ORY	Bostock's	OHV746Y	Gillmoss	P304HEM	Arriva NW		
N811CKA	Gillmoss	OHV753Y	Gillmoss	P305HEM	Arriva NW		
N863CEH	First PMT	OHV754Y	Gillmoss	P306HEM	Arriva NW		
N864CEH	First PMT	OHV807Y	Arriva NW	P307HEM	Arriva NW		
N865CEH	First PMT	OIJ2645	Ogden's	P308HEM	Arriva NW		
N866CEH	First PMT	OJD55R	Ladyline	P309HEM	Arriva NW		
N867CEH	First PMT	OLG7	Meredith's	P310HEM	Arriva NW		
N897KFA	Bostock's	OLV551M	Arriva NW	P311HEM	Arriva NW		
N898KFA	Bostock's	ONF653R	Pandh Travel	P312HEM	Arriva NW	P460DCW	Express Travel
N900ALS	Happy Al's	OOP958X	Maghull Coaches	P313HEM	Arriva NW	P461DCW	Express Travel
N910DWJ	Bostock's	ORJ75W	Merseyline Travel	P314HEM	Arriva NW	P461EFL	Pandh Travel
NAX511	Meredith's	ORY640	Nip-On	P315HEM	Arriva NW	P522NMA	Selwyns
NEH728W	First PMT	OSR197R	Liverpool MS	P316HEM	Arriva NW	P524UGA	Arriva NW
NEH729W	First PMT	P3SLT	Arriva NW	P317HEM	Arriva NW	P525UGA	Arriva NW
NEH731W	First PMT			P318HEM	Arriva NW	P533MBU	Arriva NW
NIB3264	Bennett's Travel			P319HEM	Arriva NW	P534MBU	Arriva NW
				P320HEM	Arriva NW	P535MBU	Arriva NW
				P331VWR	Aintree Coachline	P536MBU	Arriva NW
				P333ABC	C M T	P537MBU	Arriva NW
		P5ACL	Aintree Coachline	P341OEW	Halton	P538MBU	Arriva NW
		P30ANT	Anthony's Travel	P342OEW	Halton	P539MBU	Arriva NW
NIB8317	Hollinshead Coaches	P41MVU	Arriva NW	P343OEW	Halton	P540MBU	Arriva NW
NIB8318	Hollinshead Coaches	P42MVU	Arriva NW	P344OEW	Halton	P541MBU	Arriva NW
NIL2994	Hardings	P43MVU	Arriva NW	P345OEW	Halton	P542MBU	Arriva NW
NIL3943	Procters	P45MVU	Arriva NW	P369JSP	Warrington's	P543MBU	Arriva NW
NIL3944	Procters	P46MVU	Arriva NW	P384MEH	First PMT	P544MBU	Arriva NW
NIL5675	Bostock's	P49MVU	Arriva NW	P385MEH	First PMT	P545MBU	Arriva NW
NIL7716	Boydons	P52MVU	Arriva NW	P386MEH	First PMT	P582JNE	Whitegate
NIL7948	Huggins	P53MVU	Arriva NW	P387MEH	First PMT	P654HEG	Nip-On
NIL8905	Boydons	P56MVU	Arriva NW	P388MEH	First PMT	P655HEG	Nip-On
NKU197X	Liverpool MS	P58MVU	Arriva NW	P389MEH	First PMT	P684HND	Supertravel
NLS987W	Huxley	P61MVU	Arriva NW	P390MEH	First PMT	P685HND	Supertravel
NMY655E	Liverpool MS	P70SEL	Selwyns	P402KAV	Avon Coaches	P746HND	David Tanner
NNN476W	Dobson's	P104SUA	Taxico	P404KAV	Avon Coaches	P812LOK	Supertravel
NPK249R	C M T	P106UVT	Taxico	P409KAV	Avon Coaches	P842WUG	Express Travel
NTU946C	Meredith's	P135GND	Arriva NW	P413NFA	First PMT	P861PWW	Selwyns
NUW561Y	Gillmoss	P136GND	Arriva NW	P414NFA	First PMT	P868MBF	First PMT
NUW570Y	Arriva NW	P137GND	Arriva NW	P415NFA	First PMT	P869MBF	First PMT
NUW599Y	Gillmoss	P138GND	Arriva NW	P416NFA	First PMT	P870MBF	First PMT
NUW612Y	Gillmoss	P139GND	Arriva NW	P417NFA	First PMT	P909YCW	C M T
NUW628Y	Gillmoss	P140GND	Arriva NW	P418NFA	First PMT	P910YCW	C M T
NUW638Y	Gillmoss	P149LMA	Chester	P419FDB	Whitegate	P911YCW	C M T
NUW655Y	Gillmoss	P150LMA	Chester	P419NFA	First PMT	P912YCW	C M T
NUW656Y	Gillmoss	P178FNF	Arriva NW	P420ACT	Selwyns	P913YCW	C M T
OBN503R	Sutton	P179FNF	Arriva NW	P420MEH	First PMT	P914YCW	C M T
OCS34X	Chester	P180FNF	Arriva NW	P421ACT	Selwyns	P915YCW	C M T
OCU820R	Dobson's	P180GND	Arriva NW	P421MEH	First PMT	P916YCW	C M T
ODM193P	Taxico	P181FNF	Arriva NW	P422MEH	First PMT	P917YCW	C M T
OHF858S	Aintree Coachline	P181GND	Arriva NW	P423MEH	First PMT	P918YCW	C M T
OHV682Y	Gillmoss	P182FNF	Arriva NW	P424MEH	First PMT	P919YCW	C M T
OHV690Y	Arriva NW	P182GND	Arriva NW	P425MEH	First PMT	P920YCW	C M T
OHV692Y	Gillmoss	P183FNF	Arriva NW	P426MEH	First PMT	P962SFR	Supertravel
OHV695Y	Arriva NW	P183GND	Arriva NW	P427MEH	First PMT	P973MBF	First PMT
OHV698Y	Gillmoss	P184GND	Arriva NW	P428MEH	First PMT	P974MBF	First PMT
OHV703Y	Gillmoss	P222ABC	C M T	P429MEH	First PMT	P975MBF	First PMT
OHV715Y	Wingates Tours	P223YGG	Hollinshead Coaches	P445SWX	City Bus	P976MBF	First PMT
OHV726Y	Gillmoss	P244NBA	Arriva NW	P450SWX	A1A Travel	P977ONC	Supertravel
OHV727Y	Arriva NW	P250NBA	Arriva NW	P451SWX	A1A Travel	PDZ6265	Local Motion
OHV730Y	Gillmoss	P260NBA	Arriva NW	P454DCW	Express Travel	PDZ6269	Copeland Tours
OHV733Y	Gillmoss	P301HEM	Arriva NW	P455DCW	Express Travel	PEV695R	C M T
		P302HEM	Arriva NW	P456DCW	Express Travel	PFC513W	Happy Al's
				P457DCW	Express Travel	PFM126Y	Arriva NW
				P458DCW	Express Travel	PFM129Y	Arriva NW
				P459DCW	Express Travel	PFN787M	Taxico

PJI8366	Nip-On	R152GNW	Arriva NW	R307CVU	Arriva NW	R416XFL	Nip-On
PJT272R	C M T	R153GNW	Arriva NW	R308CVU	Arriva NW	R417XFL	Nip-On
PTT79R	C M T	R173HRF	Warrington's	R309CVU	Arriva NW	R438ALS	First PMT
PTX466Y	Arrowebrook	R232ERE	First PMT	R309WVR	Gillmoss	R439ALS	First PMT
PXI6348	Maghull Coaches	R233ERE	First PMT	R310CVU	Arriva NW	R440ALS	First PMT
R7BOS	Bostock's	R234ERE	First PMT	R310WVR	Gillmoss	R441ALS	First PMT
R11ABC	C M T	R235ERE	First PMT	R311CVU	Arriva NW	R442ALS	First PMT
R14ALS	Happy Al's	R236ERE	First PMT	R311WVR	Gillmoss	R480GLG	Selwyns
R15ALS	Happy Al's	R237ERE	First PMT	R312CVU	Arriva NW	R481GLG	Selwyns
R40ANT	Anthony's Travel	R238ERE	First PMT	R312WVR	Gillmoss	R546ABA	Arriva NW
R47XVM	Arriva NW	R239ERE	First PMT	R313CVU	Arriva NW	R547ABA	Arriva NW
R48XVM	Arriva NW	R240ERE	First PMT	R313WVR	Gillmoss	R548ABA	Arriva NW
R51XVM	Arriva NW	R241ERE	First PMT	R314WVR	Gillmoss	R549ABA	Arriva NW
		R242ERE	First PMT	R315WVR	Gillmoss	R550ABA	Arriva NW
		R243ERE	First PMT	R317WVR	Gillmoss	R551ABA	Arriva NW
		R244ERE	First PMT	R319WVR	Gillmoss	R552ABA	Arriva NW
		R245ERE	First PMT	R321WVR	Gillmoss	R553ABA	Arriva NW
		R246ERE	First PMT	R322WVR	Gillmoss	R554ABA	Arriva NW
		R247ERE	First PMT	R324WVR	Gillmoss	R556ABA	Arriva NW
		R248ERE	First PMT	R326WVR	Gillmoss	R557ABA	Arriva NW
		R249ERE	First PMT	R327WVR	Gillmoss	R558ABA	Arriva NW
R54OCK	Avon Coaches	R250ERE	First PMT	R329WVR	Gillmoss	R559ABA	Arriva NW
R54XVM	Arriva NW	R251ERE	First PMT	R330WVR	Gillmoss	R560ABA	Arriva NW
R55ACL	Aintree Coachline	R252ERE	First PMT	R331WVR	Gillmoss	R561ABA	Arriva NW
R57XVM	Arriva NW	R253ERE	First PMT	R332WVR	Gillmoss	R562ABA	Arriva NW
R59XVM	Arriva NW	R254ERE	First PMT	R334WVR	Gillmoss	R563ABA	Arriva NW
R71ECA	Selwyns	R255ERE	First PMT	R335WVR	Gillmoss	R564ABA	Arriva NW
R72ECA	Selwyns	R255WRJ	Arriva NW	R336WVR	Gillmoss	R565ABA	Arriva NW
R73ECA	Selwyns	R256ERE	First PMT	R337WVR	Gillmoss	R566ABA	Arriva NW
R81EMB	Chester	R257ERE	First PMT	R391ERE	First PMT	R567ABA	Arriva NW
R82EMB	Chester	R258ERE	First PMT	R392ERE	First PMT	R568ABA	Arriva NW
R83EMB	Chester	R301PCW	Arriva NW	R393ERE	First PMT	R569ABA	Arriva NW
R84EMB	Chester	R302CVU	Arriva NW	R394ERE	First PMT	R570ABA	Arriva NW
R85EMB	Chester	R303CVU	Arriva NW	R395ERE	First PMT	R571ABA	Arriva NW
R101VLX	Supertravel	R304CVU	Arriva NW	R396ERE	First PMT	R578GDS	Bakers
R102HUA	City Bus	R305CVU	Arriva NW	R401XFL	Halton	R606FBU	Arriva NW
R104VLX	Avon Coaches			R402XFL	Halton	R708EFA	Taxico
R112VLX	Supertravel			R403XFL	Halton	R712MEW	Halton
R113VLX	Supertravel			R407XFL	Halton	R713MEW	Halton
R114DNV	Bakers			R408XFL	Halton	R714MEW	Halton
R114VLX	Supertravel			R409XFL	Halton	R722EEH	Scragg's
R115DNV	Bakers			R410XFL	Halton	R755EEH	Scragg's
R151GNW	Arriva NW			R411XFL	Nip-On	R810NVT	First PMT

In 1996 Chester took delivery of two integral Marshall Mini-buses. This model was introduced the previous Autumn at the Bus & Coach show, though the type has seen few sales outside London. Number 250, P150LMA, carries the livery of Chesters city rail link. *R L Wilson*

Travel with Happy Al's and you may get a chance to ride on N17ALS, a DAF SB220 with Ikarus Citibus bodywork. The model was introduced into the UK to provide an alternative to the Optare Delta, which uses the same chassis. *Aiden Proctor*

R811NVT	First PMT	R878ERE	First PMT	RIB3524	Clowes	S7STM	Supertravel
R812NVT	First PMT	R879HRF	First PMT	RIB5092	Arrowebrook	S8BOS	Bostock's
R845FWW	A1A Travel	R880HRF	First PMT	RIB8034	Boydons	S8STM	Supertravel
		R880SDT	Hardings	RIB8636	Clowes	S9BOS	Bostock's
		R881HRF	First PMT	RIB8747	Bostock's	S9STM	Supertravel
		R890SDT	Hardings	RIL1015	Hollinshead Coaches	S10STM	Supertravel
		R954JYS	A1A Travel	RIL1016	Hollinshead Coaches	S22ABC	C M T
		R970MGB	A1A Travel	RIL1017	Hollinshead Coaches	S33ABC	C M T
		R977NVT	First PMT	RIL1023	Hollinshead Coaches	S41FWY	A1A Travel
		R978NVT	First PMT	RIL7382	Boydons	S42FWY	A1A Travel
		R979NVT	First PMT	RIL9157	Huggins	S44ABC	C M T
R846FWW	A1A Travel	R980NVT	First PMT	RIL9158	Huggins	S70ANT	Anthony's Travel
R866LHG	C M T	R981NVT	First PMT	RIL9160	Huggins	S80ANT	Anthony's Travel
R867LHG	C M T	RAW32R	Clowes	RIL9161	Huggins	S111ABC	C M T
R868LHG	C M T	RBZ4209	D&G Bus Co	RIL9162	Huggins	S112GUB	Warrington
R869LHG	C M T	RDZ1701	Arriva NW	RIL9163	Huggins	S113GUB	Warrington
R86EMB	Chester	RDZ1702	Arriva NW	RIL9164	Huggins	S114GUB	Warrington
R870LHG	C M T	RDZ1703	Arriva NW	RJR247Y	Bennett's Travel	S115GUB	Warrington
R871ERE	First PMT	RDZ1704	Arriva NW	ROP835R	Nip-On	S116GUB	Warrington
R871LHG	C M T	RDZ1705	Arriva NW			S117GUB	Warrington
R872ERE	First PMT	RDZ1706	Arriva NW			S118GUB	Warrington
R872LHG	C M T	RDZ1707	Arriva NW			S119GUB	Warrington
R873ERE	First PMT	RDZ1708	Arriva NW			S120GUB	Warrington
R873LHG	C M T	RDZ1709	Arriva NW			S121GUB	Warrington
R874ERE	First PMT	RDZ1710	Arriva NW			S194FFM	Halton
R874LHG	C M T	RDZ1711	Arriva NW			S195FFM	Halton
R875ERE	First PMT	RDZ1712	Arriva NW			S196FFM	Halton
R875LHG	C M T	RDZ1713	Arriva NW	RUT131W	Maghull Coaches	S197FFM	Halton
R876ERE	First PMT	RDZ1714	Arriva NW	RVE651S	Taxico	S248UVR	Arriva NW
R877ERE	First PMT	RFM267L	Maghull Coaches	S6STM	Supertravel	S249UVR	Arriva NW

PMT is one of the operators who chose to use excess workshop capacity to produce its own bodywork, later going on to sell the minibus and midibus products to others. The Knype is the name given to the model built on the Leyland Swift. While some have now become driver-trainers, 318, G318YUT is now part of the Flexi fleet, an operation that started as a dial-a-ride service. *Cliff Beeton*

S250UVR	Arriva NW	S447KCW	C M T	S760RNE	Arrowebrook	SED253	Meredith's
S251AFA	First PMT	S448KCW	C M T	S813AEH	First PMT	SEL23	Selwyns
S251UVR	Arriva NW	S449KCW	C M T	S814AEH	First PMT	SEL36	Selwyns
S252AFA	First PMT	S450KCW	C M T	S815AEH	First PMT	SEL73	Selwyns
		S451KCW	C M T	S816AEH	First PMT	SEL133	Selwyns
		S452KCW	C M T	S817AEH	First PMT	SEL392	Selwyns
		S453KCW	C M T	S818AEH	First PMT	SEL702	Selwyns
		S454KCW	C M T	S819AEH	First PMT	SEL853	Selwyns
		S455KCW	C M T	S820AEH	First PMT	SIB3053	Boydons
		S456KCW	C M T	S821AEH	First PMT	SIB6710	Local Motion
		S509NFR	Express Travel	S872SNB	Arriva NW	SIB6715	Local Motion
				S873SNB	Arriva NW	SIB7882	Boydons
S253AFA	First PMT			S874SNB	Arriva NW	SJI5066	Local Motion
S254AFA	First PMT			S875SNB	Arriva NW	SMB601V	Bostock's
S255AFA	First PMT			S876SNB	Arriva NW		
S256AFA	First PMT			S877SNB	Arriva NW		
S259SFA	First PMT			S878SNB	Arriva NW		
S260SFA	First PMT			S879SNB	Arriva NW		
S261SFA	First PMT			S990HUB	Whitegate		
S262SFA	First PMT	S511KFL	City Bus	SCN251S	Sutton		
S263SFA	First PMT	S512KFL	City Bus	SCN254S	Helms		
S264SFA	First PMT	S54NCW	Avon Coaches	SCN266S	Helms		
S265SFA	First PMT	S620KUT	Arrowebrook	SCN276S	Helms	SND123X	Merseyline Travel
S266SFA	First PMT			SDC146H	Liverpool MS	SND290X	Bennett's Warrington
S267SFA	First PMT			SDM94V	Chester	SND437X	A2B Travel
S268SFA	First PMT			SDM95V	Chester	SND440X	A2B Travel
S269SFA	First PMT			SDM96V	Chester	SPC266R	C M T
S270SFA	First PMT			SDM97V	Chester	SPC267R	C M T
S315KNW	Wingates Tours			SDM98V	Chester	SPC278R	C M T
S443BSG	First PMT			SDZ6287	Bennett's Travel	SPC284R	C M T

SPC286R	C M T	T134ARE	First PMT	T316PNB	Arriva NW	T822SFS	First PMT
SPC291R	C M T	T135ARE	First PMT	T317PNB	Arriva NW	T823SFS	First PMT
SVL174W	City Bus	T136ARE	First PMT	T318PNB	Arriva NW	T824SFS	First PMT
T1KET	Jim Stones	T157BBF	First PMT	T319PNB	Arriva NW	T825SFS	First PMT
		T158BBF	First PMT	T320PNB	Arriva NW	T826SFS	First PMT
		T159BBF	First PMT	T322ELG	Warrington	T827SFS	First PMT
		T160BBF	First PMT	T322PNB	Arriva NW	T828SFS	First PMT
		T161BBF	First PMT	T323ELG	Warrington	T829SFS	First PMT

				T323PNB	Arriva NW	T840CCK	Express Travel
				T324PNB	Arriva NW	T841CCK	Express Travel
T6STM	Supertravel			T468HNH	Norbus	T982LBF	First PMT
T7STM	Supertravel			T469HNH	Norbus	T983LBF	First PMT
				T552ADN	C M T	T984LBF	First PMT
				T601JBA	Gillmoss	T985LBF	First PMT
				T602JBA	Gillmoss	T986LBF	First PMT

		T162BBF	First PMT	T603JBA	Gillmoss	T987LBF	First PMT
		T163BBF	First PMT	T604JBA	Gillmoss	TCK821	C M T
		T164BBF	First PMT	T605JBA	Gillmoss	TCK847	Liverpool MS
		T165BBF	First PMT	T606JBA	Gillmoss	TIB2865	Boydons
		T166BBF	First PMT	T607JBA	Gillmoss	TJI4828	First PMT
		T167BBF	First PMT	T608JBA	Gillmoss	TJI8791	Ladyline
T36CCK	Greenbus	T168BBF	First PMT	T609JBA	Gillmoss	TOI6161	Boydons
T37CCK	Greenbus	T174AUA	Selwyns	T610JBA	Gillmoss	TOS799X	Bowker
T48JBA	Bennett's Travel	T201AFM	Warrington	T611JBA	Gillmoss	TOS968X	Pandh Travel
T62JBA	Arriva NW	T202AFM	Warrington	T612PNC	Arriva NW	TSU604	Anthony's Travel
T63JBA	Arriva NW	T203AFM	Warrington	T613PNC	Arriva NW	TWH694T	Chester
T64JBA	Arriva NW	T204AFM	Warrington	T614PNC	Arriva NW	TWH703T	Merseyline Travel
T65JBA	Arriva NW	T205AFM	Warrington	T615PNC	Arriva NW	TWH704T	Merseyline Travel
T111JBA	A1A Travel	T206AFM	Warrington	T616PNC	Arriva NW	TXI7007	Taxico
		T207AFM	Warrington	T617PNC	Arriva NW	TXI8757	Bennett's Warrington
		T208AFM	Warrington	T618PNC	Arriva NW	UEM36V	Arriva NW
		T294ROF	Jim Stones	T619PNC	Arriva NW	UJN634Y	Nip-On
		T310MBU	Nip-On	T620PNC	Arriva NW	ULO441R	Liverpool MS
		T314PNB	Arriva NW	T621PNC	Arriva NW	UMB338R	Local Motion
		T315PNB	Arriva NW	T622PNC	Arriva NW	UPB308S	C M T

				T623PNC	Arriva NW	UPB309S	C M T
				T741JHE	Hardings	UPB317S	C M T
T129XVT	Bakers			T742JHE	Hardings	UUY600V	Bennett's Travel
T131ARE	First PMT			T757LFM	Halton	UWW1X	Chester
T132ARE	First PMT			T758LFM	Halton	UWW2X	Chester
T133ARE	First PMT			T759LFM	Halton	V69GEH	First PMT
				T760LFM	Halton	V71GEH	First PMT
				T821PNB	Arriva NW	V117DLH	First PMT

Former London Buses Leyland Titans are to be found with several of the operators in this book, and carrying a varity of colour schemes. Seen working route 86 is KYV319X which carries th colours of City Coaches.
Dave Heath

If you are reading this book you must be interested in public transport.
So why not join the premier transport society?

The enthusiasts with the professional touch -

- regular depot visits
- meetings & slide shows
- extensive library & archive
- nationwide associations

- day & weekend tours
- top speakers
- national magazine
- monthly local bulletin

Can you afford not to be a member?
For more details, a free bulletin and magazine, write to

**The Secretary, North Western & Yorkshire Branch,
10 Bradley Close, Timperley, Altrincham WAl 5 65H**

THERE ARE MANY BUS SOCIETIES
BUT ONLY ONE OMNIBUS SOCIETY

Merseytravel livery is carried by Dennis Dart 1315, T315PNB, seen passing Roe Street in Liverpool on route1. The batch carry Plaxton Pointer 2 bodies. *Tony Wilson*

V209JLG	Warrington	V412ENC	Arriva NW	V648DVU	Arriva NW	V670DVU	Arriva NW
V210JLG	Warrington	V413ENC	Arriva NW	V649DVU	Arriva NW	V671DVU	Arriva NW
V211JLG	Warrington	V414ENC	Arriva NW	V650DVU	Arriva NW	V672DVU	Arriva NW
V212JLG	Warrington	V415ENC	Arriva NW	V651DVU	Arriva NW	V673DVU	Arriva NW
V213JLG	Warrington	V470GBF	First PMT	V652DVU	Arriva NW	V674DVU	Arriva NW
V214JLG	Warrington	V472GBF	First PMT	V653DVU	Arriva NW	V675DVU	Arriva NW
V215JLG	Warrington	V624DBN	Arriva NW	V654DVU	Arriva NW	V676DVU	Arriva NW
V216JLG	Warrington	V625DVU	Arriva NW	V655DVU	Arriva NW	V676FPO	Pandh Travel
V217JLG	Warrington	V626DVU	Arriva NW	V656DVU	Arriva NW	V677FPO	Pandh Travel
V218JLG	Warrington	V627DVU	Arriva NW	V657DVU	Arriva NW	V818WUG	Whitegate
V261BNV	Supertravel	V628DVU	Arriva NW	V658DVU	Arriva NW	V830GBF	First PMT
V262BNV	Supertravel	V629DVU	Arriva NW	V659DVU	Arriva NW	V831GBF	First PMT
V263BNV	Supertravel	V630DVU	Arriva NW	V660DVU	Arriva NW	V832GBF	First PMT
V264BNV	Supertravel	V631DVU	Arriva NW	V660LWT	Nip-On	V879RDN	Whitegate
V268BNV	Supertravel	V632DVU	Arriva NW	V661DVU	Arriva NW	V899DNB	Norbus
V368KLG	Chester	V633DVU	Arriva NW	V662DVU	Arriva NW	V988GBF	First PMT
V369KLG	Chester	V634DVU	Arriva NW	V663DVU	Arriva NW	V989GBF	First PMT
V370KLG	Chester	V635DVU	Arriva NW	V664DVU	Arriva NW	V993LLG	Halton
V371KLG	Chester	V636DVU	Arriva NW	V665DVU	Arriva NW	V994LLG	Halton
V372KLG	Chester	V637DVU	Arriva NW	V667DVU	Arriva NW	V995LLG	Halton
V373KLG	Chester	V638DVU	Arriva NW	V668DVU	Arriva NW	VBG101V	Arriva NW
V374KLG	Chester	V639DVU	Arriva NW	V669DVU	Arriva NW	VBG102V	Arriva NW
V404ENC	Arriva NW	V640DVU	Arriva NW			VBG104V	Arriva NW
V405ENC	Arriva NW	V641DVU	Arriva NW			VBG106V	Arriva NW
V406ENC	Arriva NW	V642DVU	Arriva NW			VBG110V	Arriva NW
V407ENC	Arriva NW	V643DVU	Arriva NW			VBG111V	Arriva NW
V408ENC	Arriva NW	V644DVU	Arriva NW			VBG116V	Arriva NW
V409ENC	Arriva NW	V645DVU	Arriva NW			VBG121V	Arriva NW
V410ENC	Arriva NW	V646DVU	Arriva NW			VBG129V	Arriva NW
V411ENC	Arriva NW	V647DVU	Arriva NW			VCA452W	First PMT

Walton is the location of this view of Merseyline KYV357X, a Leyland Titan new to London Buses. As seen from the vehicle index, the transfer to the provinces is quickening with the provision of many new buses in to the capital by all the major players who either sell or move mid-life buses where they become gainfully employed on school contracts. *Richard Godfrey*

Reg	Operator	Reg	Operator	Reg	Operator	Reg	Operator
VCA464W	First PMT	W476SVT	First PMT	WRA688Y	Bowker	X1STM	Supertravel
VDB916	Arriva NW	W477SVT	First PMT	WSU442S	Arriva NW	X11STM	Supertravel
VEE66V	Boydons	W478SVT	First PMT	WSU450S	Arriva NW	X201ANC	Arriva NW
VFV7V	Pandh Travel	W586YDM	Selwyns	WTU465W	First PMT	X202ANC	Arriva NW
VFV8V	Clowes	W636MKY	Warrington's	WTU472W	First PMT	X203ANC	Arriva NW
VIB6165	Boydons	W781NFG	Chester			X204ANC	Arriva NW
VRA124Y	Chester	W782NFG	Chester			X207ANC	Arriva NW
VRA125Y	Chester	W783NFG	Chester			X208ANC	Arriva NW
VRY1X	Clowes	W784NFG	Chester			X209ANC	Arriva NW
W5ACL	Aintree Coachline	W785NFG	Chester			X211ANC	Arriva NW
W10ANT	Anthony's Travel	W929RET	Selwyns			X212ANC	Arriva NW
W465CRN	C M T	W985XMA	Halton			X213ANC	Arriva NW
W466CRN	C M T	W986XMA	Halton			X214ANC	Arriva NW
W467CRN	C M T	W987XMA	Halton	WTU483W	First PMT	X215ANC	Arriva NW
W468CRN	C M T	W991XDM	City Bus	WTU496W	Local Motion	X216ANC	Arriva NW
W471VMA	Halton	WAV122X	Maghull Coaches	WTX37T	Helms	X217ANC	Arriva NW
W473SVT	First PMT	WCK128V	Procters	WWM908W	Arriva NW	X218ANC	Arriva NW
W474SVT	First PMT	WDA672T	Pandh Travel	WWM912W	Arriva NW	X219ANC	Arriva NW
W475SVT	First PMT	WDM347R	Local Motion	WWM914W	Arriva NW	X221ANC	Arriva NW
		WDZ6951	A1A Travel	WWM920W	Mark Perry	X223ANC	Arriva NW
		WDZ6962	A1A Travel	WWM923W	Pandh Travel	X224ANC	Arriva NW
		WJI3499	Local Motion	WYV44T	Gillmoss	X226ANC	Arriva NW
		WJI3507	Local Motion	WYV45T	Gillmoss	X227ANC	Arriva NW
		WJI3508	Local Motion	WYV46T	Gillmoss	X228ANC	Arriva NW
		WJI5239	First PMT	WYV65T	Gillmoss	X229ANC	Arriva NW
		WJI7691	Warrington's	WYV70T	Gillmoss	X231ANC	Arriva NW

X232ANC	Arriva NW	X431AJA	Arriva NW	X967ULG	Halton	XLV156W	Arriva NW
X233ANC	Arriva NW	X432AJA	Arriva NW	X968ULG	Halton	XLV157W	Arriva NW
X234ANC	Arriva NW	X433AJA	Arriva NW	X991FFA	First PMT	XLV158W	Arriva NW
X235ANC	Arriva NW	X434AJA	Arriva NW			XLV159W	Arriva NW
X236ANC	Arriva NW	X435AJA	Arriva NW			XLV160W	Arriva NW

X237ANC	Arriva NW	X436AJA	Arriva NW				
X238ANC	Arriva NW	X437AJA	Arriva NW				
X239ANC	Arriva NW	X438AJA	Arriva NW				
X241ANC	Arriva NW	X801AJA	Arriva NW				
X242ANC	Arriva NW	X802AJA	Arriva NW				
X243HJA	Arriva NW	X803AJA	Arriva NW				

X244HJA	Arriva NW	X804AJA	Arriva NW	X992FFA	First PMT		
X246HJA	Arriva NW	X805AJA	Arriva NW	X993FFA	First PMT		
X247HJA	Arriva NW	X806AJA	Arriva NW	X994FFA	First PMT	XLV161W	Arriva NW
X248HJA	Arriva NW	X807AJA	Arriva NW	X995FFA	First PMT	XOV750T	Local Motion
X249HJA	Arriva NW	X808AJA	Arriva NW	XAD835	Happy Al's	XRF1X	First PMT
X251HJA	Arriva NW	X809AJA	Arriva NW	XAK457T	Local Motion	XRF2X	First PMT
X252HJA	Arriva NW	X811AJA	Arriva NW	XAZ1361	Happy Al's	XWX182S	Bowker
X253HJA	Arriva NW	X812AJA	Arriva NW	XAZ1362	Happy Al's	YAJ155Y	Dobson's
X254HJA	Arriva NW	X813AJA	Arriva NW	XAZ1363	Happy Al's	YBN630V	Huxley
X256HJA	Arriva NW	X814AJA	Arriva NW	XAZ1364	Happy Al's	YBN632V	Huxley
X257HJA	Arriva NW	X815AJA	Arriva NW	XAZ1370	Happy Al's	YBW489V	First PMT
X258HJA	Arriva NW	X816AJA	Arriva NW	XAZ1371	Happy Al's	YFB971V	Ladyline
X259HJA	Arriva NW	X817AJA	Arriva NW	XAZ1372	Happy Al's	YLW895X	Dobson's
X261OBN	Arriva NW	X818AJA	Arriva NW	XAZ1373	Happy Al's	YMA99W	Chester
X262OBN	Arriva NW	X819AJA	Arriva NW	XAZ1865	Happy Al's	YMA100W	Chester
X416AJA	Arriva NW	X821AJA	Arriva NW	XEM881W	Arriva NW	YMA101W	Chester
X417AJA	Arriva NW	X822AJA	Arriva NW	XEM903W	Arriva NW	YMA102W	Chester
X418AJA	Arriva NW	X924AEN	A2B Travel	XEM904W	Arriva NW	YMA103W	Chester
X419AJA	Arriva NW	X926AEN	A2B Travel	XEM905W	Arriva NW	YOI7373	Clowes
X421AJA	Arriva NW	X927AEN	A2B Travel	XEM906W	Arriva NW	YPD108Y	Bennett's Travel
X422AJA	Arriva NW	X928AEN	A2B Travel	XEM909W	Arriva NW	YTE587V	Aintree Coachline
X423AJA	Arriva NW	X929AEN	A2B Travel	XEM910W	Arriva NW	YWO182	Huxley
X424AJA	Arriva NW	X945AEN	A2B Travel	XFM211	Chester	YXI6366	Clowes
X426AJA	Arriva NW	X946AEN	A2B Travel	XJG812V	Bennett's Travel	YXI6367	Clowes
X427AJA	Arriva NW	X947AEN	A2B Travel	XLV140W	Arriva NW		
X428AJA	Arriva NW	X965ULG	Halton	XLV151W	Arriva NW		
X429AJA	Arriva NW	X966ULG	Halton	XLV153W	Arriva NW		

ISBN 1 897990 46 4
© Published by *British Bus Publishing Ltd* , November 2000
The Vyne, 16 St Margarets Drive, Wellington, Telford, TF1 3PH
Telephone: 01952 255669 - Facsimile: 01952 222397
www.britishbuspublishing.co.uk - E-mail editorial@britishbuspublishing.co.uk